THE SCOPE OF GRACE

Pencil sketch of
Joseph Sittler
by Siegfried Reinhardt

For Dr. Sittler
Gratefully
Siegfried Reinhardt

THE SCOPE OF GRACE

essays on NATURE AND GRACE
in honor of JOSEPH SITTLER

BR
50
H46

edited by PHILIP J. HEFNER

FORTRESS PRESS PHILADELPHIA

PRESENTATION TO JOSEPH SITTLER

"Honor" and "tribute" are words that crop up persistently in prefaces to volumes such as this. Similarly, the essays in this volume, presented to Joseph Sittler on his sixtieth birthday, certainly mean to honor the man and pay tribute to the scope of his work and influence. The word affection, however, more aptly defines the spirit that engendered this volume, as the word conversation more aptly states its purpose. For we dedicate our efforts to a man who in full vigor is even now exploring new fields of thought, giving new formulation to theological questions. This collection of essays is no parting salute; it celebrates a continuing dialogue. The conversations which have been so ineradicably a part of Joseph Sittler's career—conversations with colleagues and all of culture—are carried forward in this volume, now with Sittler himself, for once, on the quiet receiving end. But not for long! Even as this volume leaves the press, we await the publication of his Gray Lectures delivered at Duke University, and the new momentum they will add to the conversation. It may be that this book will be unique in the sense that the thoughts expressed here will leave reverberations as those chapters take final shape. We are bold enough to hope so; therefore the contributors have directed their own thinking to the theme of the Gray Lectures: Nature and Grace.

The title of this volume is taken from one of Professor Sittler's earlier essays on Christian ethics:

> The thrust of the redemptive action of God is into the structures of mankind, society, the family, economic orders. The scope of that redemptive activity, restoration to God in faith and active in love, can clearly be no more restricted than its originating action.[1]

[1] Joseph Sittler, *The Structure of Christian Ethics* (Baton Rouge: Louisiana State University Press, 1958).

In selecting this concept as its theme, however, this volume points beyond the current conversation to a persisting Sittlerian concern. Without engaging in the tedium of analysis, one may be permitted to point to a note sounded again and again in Sittler's work: that God's sovereignty includes his freedom to work boundlessly and irrepressibly within his own creation to testify of himself and to set in motion his recreative action. In *The Doctrine of the Word* (1948), Sittler insisted that a proper appreciation of God's freedom in his Word would set off a "theological chain reaction" that would charge through traditional Protestant doctrinal patterns. His essay on "The Structure of Christian Ethics" a decade later set this same concern within an ethical context; he concluded that, just as all of creation is "malleable to the perverse purposes of evil," so also it is "invested with the promise and potency of grace"—a grace that is unrestricted both in its divine origin and in its scope of realization.

This conviction concerning the freedom and sovereignty of God's work in his world stands at the root of later assertions that whereas architecture, for example, can enflesh the divine testimony, whereas men's legal codes can celebrate God's grace, no *definitive* concrete forms of enfleshment or celebration can be erected—in architecture, law, or any other "natural" activity of man. We have here not simply a negative assertion that the finite cannot imprison or domesticate the divine, but also the positive statement that God's gracious power is free to course where it will through the concrete stuff of its own creation. This essentially positive emphasis has given a full-orbed character to Sittler's thought so far. His later work, in particular, indicates that he is fully as attentive to the natural milieu which God does recreate as he is to the divine power in and of itself.

This singular attention he pays to the natural milieu of grace, an inspired complement to the conviction as to God's sovereignty, informs his attempt to sketch a "Theology of Earth," to call for an intensified "Care of the Earth." His decisive address at New Delhi in 1961, which called for "a doctrine of the cosmos, the theatre of man's selfhood under God, in corporation with his neighbor, and in caring-relationship with nature, his sister," obviously carries the implications of the unrestricted scope of grace to their farthest conclusions. Where does one go from here? Little wonder that we stand on tiptoe as we await the final form of the Gray Lectures to elaborate more fully Joseph Sittler's New Delhi theme.

PHILIP J. HEFNER

The Festival of the Reformation
October 31, 1963

ACKNOWLEDGMENTS

Thanks are due to many who assisted in one way or another with this volume, especially Mrs. Margaret Ermarth, for her counsel; the Rev. Earl Knaus, Jr., for assistance in preparing the bibliography; and Mrs. Shirley Tranquill, for secretarial assistance. Several men who had hoped to contribute essays were kept from doing so by ill health or inescapable commitments.

P. J. H.

Acknowledgment is made to the following for permission to quote from works for which they hold copyright: A. R. Mowbray & Company, Ltd.; Bollingen Foundation; Doubleday & Company, Inc.; E. J. Brill; Faber and Faber, Ltd.; George Allen & Unwin, Ltd.; Harcourt, Brace & World, Inc.; Harper & Row; Herder and Herder New York; Holt, Rinehart and Winston, Inc.; John Knox Press; Louisiana State University Press; The Macmillan Company; Methuen & Company, Ltd.; National Christian Student Federation; Random House, Inc.; Routledge & Kegan Paul, Ltd.; Student Christian Movement Press; Sheed & Ward, Inc.

CONTENTS

THE SCOPE OF GRACE

THE CONTRIBUTORS

Conrad Bergendoff — President-Emeritus, Augustana College, Rock Island, Illinois

Jerald C. Brauer — Dean, The Divinity School, The University of Chicago

H. Grady Davis — Professor of Functional Theology, Lutheran School of Theology at Chicago

Joseph Haroutunian — Professor of Christian Theology, The Divinity School, The University of Chicago

Philip J. Hefner — Professor of Systematic Theology, Lutheran Theological Seminary, Gettysburg, Pennsylvania

Karl H. Hertz — Professor of Sociology, Wittenberg University

Johannes Knudsen — Dean of Graduate Studies, Lutheran School of Theology at Chicago

Bernard Eugene Meland — Professor of Constructive Theology, The Divinity School, The University of Chicago

Jaroslav Pelikan — Titus Street Professor of Ecclesiastical History, The Divinity School, Yale University

Siegfried Reinhardt — artist, designer and executor of stained glass windows, Instructor of Painting, Washington University

Nathan A. Scott, Jr. — Professor of Theology and Literature, The Divinity School, The University of Chicago

Franklin Sherman — Tutor and Dean of Lutheran Students, Mansfield College, Oxford University

Arthur Vööbus — Professor of New Testament Interpretation, Lutheran School of Theology at Chicago

MIMESIS AND TIME
IN MODERN LITERATURE

Nathan A. Scott, Jr.

MIMESIS AND TIME
IN MODERN LITERATURE*

Human life is drenched in time, in its restless rhythm and dynamic periodicity. Indeed, in the most primary sense in which any predication of it can be made, the reality of human existence is a temporal reality, for time is both the milieu and the medium of the human enterprise: in every dimension of man's life his most vital and immediate horizon is the horizon of time. And this, undoubtedly, is why it is that time is also inevitably the medium of the arts of story, of all those forms of literature which have it as their function to present a narrative account of the human adventure in the concrete terms of action and plot and character. It is in fact precisely in literature's way of taking time into itself that we have a central index of drift or tendency in the realm of the imagination. And this is certainly an angle from which the literature of the modern period does most insistently ask to be considered, as Wyndham Lewis reminded us in his crankily brilliant book of 1928, *Time and Western Man.* For with most of the characteristic writers of our period—with Proust, Joyce, Mann, Virginia Woolf, Eliot, Hermann Broch, Ezra Pound, and Faulkner, to mention only a few—time is an abiding problem. Ours is a literature obsessed with time, with time lost and time recaptured, with time as duration and time as disintegration: and most of the major texts in our poetry and fiction and drama prove, on examination, to be various kinds of metaphors on the nature of time.

The special sensibility that lies behind this fascination has perhaps its most immediate root in the sheer crowdedness of the time that has been experienced by people living in the Western world during the last hundred years. Since Wendell Willkie

*©1964 by Nathan A. Scott, Jr.

3

first taught us, on the outbreak of World War II, to think of
the human community today as forming "one world," we have
grown accustomed to the use of the phrase in purely political
discussions that emphasize the impossibility of conducting politics
any longer on the assumption that the nation-state retains its
traditional autonomy. But fearsomely as this lesson has been
proved by the events of the past quarter-century, there is a
deeper, spiritual sense in which ours is "one world," though here
too the meaning is by no means unconnected with the techno-
logical advance that has created many of our political dilemmas.
For the same marvelous techniques of modern communication
that bring Washington and London and Paris and Moscow into
such close proximity not only set the terms within which our
statesmen have to work but also contribute very largely to the
formation of the whole evanescent atmosphere in which the men
and women of our time experience what the psychologists have
come to call "human identity." And what is at issue here is
simply the fact that an event today can, as it were, be instantly
recorded by our newspapers and radio and television networks:
we live in an age in which no longer is there any real interim
between the happening of a significant occurrence and its being
learned about all across the globe: and thus, through the immediate ripples of reaction that are set up and through the waves
of counterreaction that follow, indeed through large complex
chains of reaction, our various reportorial agencies can and
actually do initiate what Erich Kahler speaks of as a "mass production of events."[1] "The result of all this," says Professor
Kahler, "is a crowding of events in the domain of our vision and
consciousness, an oppressive closeness and overwhelming shiftiness of events, an excess of details and complexities in every
single event—in short, what I would call an overpopulation of
the surfaces."[2] To leaf through the pages of so characteristic a
phenomenon of our culture as *Life* magazine is—as one looks at
bathing beauties in Atlantic City and Negro civil rights demon-

[1]Erich Kahler, *The Tower and the Abyss* (New York: George
Braziller, 1957), p. 95.   [2]*Ibid.*, pp. 95-96.

strators on the streets of Birmingham and the bier of Pope John in the Vatican and a fancy house party in Connecticut and a Buddhist priest burning himself to death on a thoroughfare in Saigon—to feel that one is being flicked at by something like an antique movie. And the whole of contemporary life is very much like an early cinema show: the sensation that is everywhere felt is that of being flicked at: the surfaces are overpopulated because of the sheer mass-production of events, and time has a crowdedness unexperienced by men in earlier periods of history.

It is this enormous density of what may be called "modern time" that gives rise to our characteristic vertigo, to the sense that "all time is eternally present,"[3] that all the fragments of all possible experience are somehow simultaneously coexistent in the present. For the present has taken on a kind of kaleidoscopic boundlessness—and, as a consequence, it seems no longer possible for the mind to distinguish between and define its own fundamental categories: everything appears to be whirling into everything else, to be flowing into the heterogeneous and unstable present. Indeed, the very principle of temporality seems no longer possible of assumption, for not only is time spatialized in the simultaneity of the kaleidoscopic present but the violence of international politics has given the spaces of modern life a new kind of temporal character, so that space itself is no longer a fact of nature but rather a fact of culture, an issue of contention between statesmen, which has entered into the continuum of historical time.

Whereas life once appeared to be a pilgrimage and like a journey, it now seems to be very much more like Grand Central Station (on a busy holiday weekend). And thus Arnold Hauser speaks of ours as "the film age,"[4] for it is the cinema which is not only the invention of the modern age but which has come

[3]T. S. Eliot, "Burnt Norton," *Four Quartets* (New York: Harcourt, Brace and World, Inc.; London: Faber and Faber Ltd., 1943), p. 3. Lines from *Four Quarters* are used by permission.

[4]*Vide* Arnold Hauser, *The Social History of Art* (New York: Vintage Books, 1958), Vol. IV, Chap. viii.

to be the artistic medium that, through its commingling of space and time, most perfectly symbolizes our sense of the fluidity of experience. In the temporal medium of a film, says Dr. Hauser, "time . . . loses, on the one hand, its uninterrupted continuity, on the other, its irreversible direction. It can be brought to a standstill: in close-ups; reversed: in flash-backs; repeated: in recollections; and skipped across: in visions of the future. Concurrent, simultaneous events can be shown successively, and temporally distinct events simultaneously—by double exposure and alternation; the earlier can appear later, the later before its time."[5] And it is just this irregularity of cinematic time that forms so large a part of the distinctively modern experience.

So, since the tempo of human existence in this late stage of modern history leads men to experience time as scattered, as amorphous and fluid, inevitably there arises the anxious surmise that there may be nothing any longer that can be counted on to hold time together, to order it and stabilize it and give it firm anchorage. Which is to say that Eternity is felt to be in eclipse, and all is in doubt: for time has lost all coherence: one instant is indistinguishable from another or is merely engulfed by another, and all moments have fallen into a strange kind of impoverishment and mediocrity in which they know neither any design nor any repose. All is turmoil, dishevelment, muddle. And, as a consequence, the drama of life in time is felt to have the form of tragedy: for time itself is sheer anguish: it is servitude and captivity, it is hopelessness and homesickness, and abandonment. T. S. Eliot summarizes the modern sense of time in this wise: he says that, in this "drifting wreckage," it appears that

. . . the way up is the way down, the way forward is the way back.
You cannot face it steadily, but this thing is sure,
That time is no healer. . . .[6]

The attitude of the modern imagination towards time does, in other words, begin very nearly to approach a kind of stifled panic. "Time surely would scatter all," reflects Joyce in *Ulysses*,

[5]*Ibid.*, p. 241.
[6]T. S. Eliot, "The Dry Salvages," *op. cit.*, p. 25.

and Stephen Dedalus says: "History is a nightmare from which I am trying to awake." And this young Dublin aesthete thus brings to a nice point the baffled anguish that is everywhere so much a part of the sensibility that is expressed in the most representative literature of the past fifty or seventy-five years, when it confronts the mystery of time.

"We must get rid of our superstition of chronology," said Simone Weil, "in order to find eternity."[7] And it is just such a desire to negate time and to achieve a timeless eternity that is often expressed in much of the literature of our period which tends generally to place itself most insistently *sub specie aeternitatis.* And its rebellion against time may be regarded as having two principal philosophic guides and patron saints, the one being the eighteenth-century Neapolitan Giovanni Battista Vico and the other being Henri Bergson.

The *Scienza Nuova* (1725)— the modern discovery of which was the accomplishment of the French historian Jules Michelet, in the 1820's—was the product of a loyal Roman Catholic intelligence, but Vico so consistently interpreted the providential element in history in terms of a *lumen naturale* operative in human decision that any genuinely transcendent dimension was well-nigh completely obscured. Though he derived the basic direction of history from its ultimate source in God, the actualization of this nisus was so much an affair of the inner necessities arising out of the dynamism of the human drama itself that he ended in a virtually secular historicism. But Vico's significance in the history of thought is largely a result of his having elaborated this prevenient Hegelianism in the terms of a cyclical theory of time. For since he envisaged no likelihood of any direct or drastic ingression of the divine into the natural order, he conceived the movement of history to be a cyclical rhythm of *corso* and *ricorso,* of course and recurrence. His version of "the eternal return" does not, however, entail such a brutal fatalism as would destroy the possibility of any kind of significant novelty in history, for the

[7] Quoted by William F. Lynch, S.J., in *Christ and Apollo* (New York: Sheed and Ward, 1960), p. 34.

cycles of *corso* and *ricorso*, in his view, are not endlessly identical. Yet the cyclical motion of time is itself sufficiently rigorous to preclude the possibility of the temporal process ever reaching any definitive fulfillment.

Now there are, of course, numerous figures in modern intellectual tradition—from Nietzsche to Toynbee—in whom the cyclical interpretation of history has won various kinds of restatement. But it is this remarkably independent Italian thinker on the threshold of the Enlightenment who makes perhaps the best claim to be regarded as the presiding genius behind the very considerable renascence of the cyclical imagination in our time: and that he should have been a direct and primary influence on James Joyce, one of the major exemplars of cyclical thinking in the modern novel, is perhaps the sufficient proof that there is no historical whimiscality at all involved in discerning it to be his shadow that falls across a large phase of twentieth-century literature.

It is the historian of religion, Mircea Eliade, who has given us perhaps the best insight that recent scholarship affords into the essential meaning of "the myth of the eternal return." In the remarkably brilliant book of his that bears this title, Professor Eliade is not, of course, immediately concerned with any particular aspect of modern spirituality: his theme instead bears on the world of archaic man and how he renders that world imaginatively tolerable. But, in his analysis of archaic ideologies of archetypes and repetition, he has notably illumined a form of thought which man has perennially employed in interpreting his experience and whose inner logic is disclosed with especial clarity in pre-modern or "traditional" cultures. These are the cultures that "include both the world usually known as 'primitive' and the ancient cultures of Asia, Europe, and America."[8] And Professor Eliade finds ontological speculation in all these various systems of life to reveal an exceedingly low tolerance of history and a profound desire to apprehend structures of reality that

[8] Mircea Eliade, *The Myth of the Eternal Return*, trans. Willard R. Trask (London: Routledge & Kegan Paul, 1955), p. 3.

may offer man some defense against the virulence of time. Indeed, archaic man feels so threatened by concrete, historical time that his aim is to abolish it: this is partly achieved by regarding every reality in the phenomenal world as modeled on an extraterrestrial archetype and by regarding all the significant patterns of human action (which are, of course, ritual actions) as imitations or repetitions of archetypal gestures primordially performed by the gods: and in this way "profane time and duration are suspended."[9] But, even more decisively, time is abolished by its continuous regeneration through New Year festivals and through periodic purification rites that expel demons and disease and sin. And nowhere is the regeneration of time more fully proved for the primitive than in lunar rhythms, for the phases of the moon not only provide a convenient method of measuring profane time but also reveal the "eternal return," reveal "an ontology uncontaminated by time and becoming" which,

> . . . by conferring a cyclic direction upon time, annuls its irreversibility. Everything begins over again at its commencement every instant. The past is but a prefiguration of the future. No event is irreversible and no transformation is final. In a certain sense, it is even possible to say that nothing new happens in the world, for everything is but the repetition of the same primordial archetypes; this repetition, by actualizing the mythical moment when the archetypal gesture was revealed, constantly maintains the world in the same auroral instant of the beginnings. Time but makes possible the appearance and existence of things. It has no final influence upon their existence since it is itself constantly regenerated.[10]

So, for archaic man, it is as Hegel declared, that there is "nothing new under the sun": for him things repeat themselves for ever and ever: but this is not an altogether unprofitable repetition, for it accomplishes the suspension, as it were, of time, and permits him therefore to refuse history and to rescue himself from the meaninglessness of profane time.

Now it is the powerful reassertion of just such a vision of the

[9]*Ibid.*, p. 35.
[10]*Ibid.*, pp. 89-90.

world in terms of cyclical periodicity that is noticeable in much of the literature of this century—and most especially so in its tendency to mythicize experience. For the myth is that form in which the imagination undertakes to grasp the eternal present, the Time which is above and outside of time, the Great Time, in which all the concrete times and seasons of life eternally return to the same. It is T. S. Eliot who was perhaps the first to suggest the essential clue to what is at stake here when, in November of 1923, in his review of James Joyce's *Ulysses* in the *Dial*, he remarked Joyce's derivation of his narrative order from Homer's *Odyssey* and suggested that, "in using the myth, in manipulating a continuous parallel between contemporaneity and antiquity, Mr. Joyce is pursuing a method which others must pursue after him."[11] This, said Mr. Eliot, is Joyce's way of "making the modern world possible for art." One suspects, of course, that at this point, as on so many other occasions in his criticism, he may really have been talking also about the affairs that are closest to his heart—namely, the affairs of poetry, and even of his own poetry: for this was precisely the way in which he had himself just attempted in *The Waste Land* to make the modern world possible for art, by manipulating mythical parallels between contemporaneity and antiquity. And this is the stratagem that many of his contemporaries in poetry (Yeats, for example, or, in another way, the Greek poet Constantine Cavafy or, in still another way, the Frenchman St-John Perse) were also employing. Nor can the force of his observation, simply as it stands, be questioned, for Joyce's *Ulysses* furnishes one of the richest examples in modern literature of the mythical imagination at work on the recalcitrant stuff of twentieth-century life: indeed—as we follow Leopold Bloom through all the adventures and misadventures of a day in his life in Dublin, and as we contemplate all the cunning parallels with the career of Homer's Odysseus, from Bloom's encounter with his Telemachus in young

[11]T. S. Eliot, *"Ulysses,* Order, and Myth"* (most readily accessible) in *Critiques and Essays on Modern Fiction*, ed. John W. Aldridge (New York: Ronald Press, 1952), p. 426.

Stephen Dedalus to his return to his disingenuous Penelope in the person of Molly Bloom—we feel that here is Vico all over again.

But Joyce (in *Ulysses* and *Finnegans Wake*) provides only one of many other significant examples that our fiction presents of the modern artist making his art possible by way of the mythical method. Just two years after the appearance of *Ulysses*, Thomas Mann was already realizing in *The Magic Mountain* that, since the motion of time is circular, it "might almost equally well be described as rest, as cessation of movement—for the there repeats itself constantly in the here, the past in the present."[12] At least as early as 1924, in other words, Schopenhauer's *nunc stans*—the Eternal Now, which is at the heart of all the illusory flux of time—had prepared Mann for the direction which he was to begin to pursue a few years later in the *Joseph* saga, whose major premise is that, since "it *is*, always *is*, however much we may say It was," the "timeless schema" of the myth is therefore the aptest instrument for story-telling, for it is the myth that plunges us down through the deep well of the past to the essential timelessness that engulfs the human story. And Joyce and Mann provide only the most distinguished examples of a tendency exhibited by many other writers of our period, in both fiction and drama (the Lawrence of *The Plumed Serpent*, the Gide of *Oedipe* and *Thésée*, the Giraudoux of *La Guerre de Troie*, the Sartre of *Les Mouches*), to find the enabling principle of their art in the primordial world of myth.

Now Professor Eliade has prepared us to discern what lies behind this whole style of imagination, for the mythical manipulation of parallels between contemporaneity and antiquity is a way of moving beyond or of getting on top of this uncongenial present. The attempt to recover, through the myth, what is timelessly archetypal in the complex history of man surely represents in part a reinstatement of the traditional vision of "the eternal return," and, as such, it is at one with that most ancient

[12] Thomas Mann, *The Magic Mountain*, trans. H. T. Lowe-Porter (New York: Alfred A. Knopf, 1944), p. 344.

metaphysic—the real *philosophia perennis*—whose purpose, as Professor Eliade has taught us to understand, is not only to defend us against time but also effectively to abolish time, in the interests of a timeless eternity. The dying Hotspur, in the final act of *Henry IV*, Part I, says to Harry Monmouth:

> But thought's the slave of life, and life's time's fool,
> And time, that takes survey of all the world,
> Must have a stop.

And it is Hotspur's third clause—"time . . . must have a stop"—which summarizes, with a beautiful concision, a major part of the testimony of modern literature.

This, then, is the one way in which the modern rebellion against time proceeds—the way of Vico. And the other way is the way of Bergson, whose theory of time is perhaps the more widely advertised and the one (popularly) most likely to be thought of as representing distinctively modern sensibility, for the author of the *Essai sur les données immédiates de la conscience* (1889) and of *Matière et mémoire* (1896) is generally considered to be the philosopher of time *par excellence* in the modern period.

Bergson's initial preoccupation would seem to have been with the question as to what kind of unity constitutes the essential ground of selfhood. That is to say, man is beckoned toward the world by a thousand different interests and is engaged in innumerable transactions with his environment—all of which leave their residue in the mind in the form of the myriad impressions that furnish the self with a basis for the conduct of the daily business of life. But surely man is more than merely the bundle of discontinuous states of consciousness of which Hume spoke, and that this is so is indicated, Bergson felt, by the recurrent experiences that we do in fact have of the unity of our personal existence. These are experiences of which the catalyst is memory, for it is through the creative act of memory, he argued, that human interiority becomes something more than merely an aggregate of discontinuous impressions and achieves the unity of selfhood. The self constitutes itself, in other words, through a process of

> ... deep introspection, which leads us to grasp our inner states as living things, constantly becoming, as states not amenable to measure, which permeate one another and of which the succession in duration has nothing in common with juxtaposition in homogeneous space. But the moments at which we thus grasp ourselves are rare, and that is just why we are rarely free. The greater part of the time we live outside ourselves, hardly perceiving anything of ourselves but our own ghost, a colorless shadow which pure duration projects into homogenous space. Hence our life unfolds in space rather than in time; we live for the external world rather than for ourselves; we speak rather than think; we "are acted" rather than act ourselves. To act freely is to recover possession of oneself, and to get back into pure duration.[13]

So, in order to enter deeply into its personal identity, the self must cultivate a profound attentiveness to its own inner history, the kind of attentiveness that so integrates experiences of the past with those of the present that they cease to be a heterogeneous continuum and begin to flow into one another, to reenter the stream of pure duration.

Simultanéité des états d'âmes is, then, the hallmark of the Bergsonian *durée*. And the preeminence that Bergson is generally felt to have in modern reflection on the meaning of time is doubtless in part a result of the recognition that it is the actual experience of "simultaneity" that does in fact largely define the special situation of the men and women of our age. We fly from one continent to another in a few hours: a transatlantic telephone can take a New York merchant into the office of an associate in Antwerp in virtually a matter of seconds: the miracles of television now bring into a living room in Indianapolis events that transpired only a few hours earlier in South Viet Nam: and the enormous growth of historical consciousness gives to the average educated man of our time a knowledge of the past unimaginable a century ago, and this not only of one segment of the past but of the total experience of the race. And it is just this boundless-

[13]Henri Bergson, *Time and Free Will,* trans. Pogson (London: George Allen, 1912), p. 23 ff.

ness of the modern horizon that induces the feeling that everything is happening at once, that everything is dovetailing into everything else, and that the whole of reality is engulfed by the stream of interrelation.

"Simultaneity" is, therefore, the name of the time that men are given by modern civilization: so it is not surprising that modern literature should, in one of its aspects, express a sense of time that so closely resembles the *simultanéité* of Bergsonian *durée*. For what might be called Newtonian time is no longer a part of the time-sense of the age, and—to paraphrase a remark of Gertrude Stein—the composition in which we live makes for an art in which time takes on a new kind of imprecision and ambiguousness.[14] This is why it is that so many of the great storytellers of this century—Virginia Woolf and William Faulkner and André Malraux and Malcolm Lowry—do not any longer, as it were, begin at one end and end at another. Instead, they are concerned to express the shiftiness and the dynamism of time, and this often entails a kind of reorchestration of empirical time that, in form, has a very striking affinity with the cinematic technique of montage. Indeed, much of twentieth-century fiction—Gide's *Les Faux-Monnayeurs*, Joyce's *Ulysses*, Dos Passos' *U. S. A.* trilogy, Faulkner's *The Sound and the Fury*, Malraux's *L'Espoir*—does make us feel that perhaps it has more in common with the art of the cinema than with any other contemporary art-form.

The art of the cinema was very largely the invention of the American director David Wark Griffith, in the years between 1908 and 1916 (which culminated in his great films *The Birth of a Nation* and *Intolerance*). But it is to the Germans and the Russians that we are chiefly indebted for the formal elaboration of film aesthetic, and this was a development of the twenties, when German and Russian studios were producing such early masterpieces as Robert Wiene's *The Cabinet of Dr. Caligari* and Eisenstein's *Potemkin* and providing centers for the most creative film work being done anywhere. The basic theoretical work was

[14]*Vide* Gertrude Stein, *Picasso* (New York: Charles Scribner's Sons, 1946), p. 11.

mainly the accomplishment of three men—the Russian directors
Vsevolod I. Pudovkin[15] and Sergei Eisenstein,[16] and the German
Rudolf Arnheim.[17] And by the thirties, when theorists in the
English-speaking world like John Grierson and Raymond Spottis-
woode and John Howard Lawson began to take hold of the new
medium, what Pudovkin and Eisenstein had helped to make clear
was that a film aesthetic is very largely an aesthetic of montage.
The full meaning of the French term eludes transmission through
any English rendering of it, but Eisenstein at least offers us a
fairly simple working definition, when he says that by montage
he means simply this, that *"representation A and representation
B must be so selected from all the possible features within the
theme that is being developed . . . that their juxtaposition . . .
shall evoke in the perception and feelings of the spectator the
most complete image of the theme itself."*[18] And here the implication is clear: that the creation of a film is a process of editing
whereby the director, when finally faced with the great mass of
celluloid rushes, so puts together or *mounts* a series of visual
images as to build a coherent work of dramatic art. But the special kind of montage that Eisenstein was experimenting with in
films like *Potemkin* and *Ten Days That Shook the World* tended
to alter somewhat the primary meaning of the term, for "as first
Potemkin, then *Ten Days* swept through the Western world
taking film makers and critics by storm, the word montage came
to identify not cutting in general, but specifically the rapid,
shock cutting that Eisenstein employed in his films."[19] And it is
this secondary meaning of the term that we often have in mind

[15]*Vide* V. I. Pudovkin, *Film Technique* (London: Gollancz, 1929).

[16]*Vide* Sergei M. Eisenstein, *The Film Sense*, trans. Jay Leyda (London: Faber and Faber Ltd., 1943); also Eisenstein's *Film Form*, trans.
Jay Leyda (New York: Harcourt, Brace and Co., 1949).

[17]*Vide* Rudolf Arnheim, *Film* (London: Faber and Faber Ltd.,
1933.)

[18]Sergei M. Eisenstein, *The Film Sense*, p. 19.

[19]Arthur Knight, *The Liveliest Art* (New York: The New American Library, 1959), p. 80.

today and that makes us think most immediately of the conven-
tion (deriving from Eisenstein's early experiments) of those sequences of blurred double exposures in which a large span of
clock-time is drastically condensed in such a way as to make the
elements of a process—say, the hero's journey by plane from one
city to another—simultaneously present.[20]

Now it is precisely the kind of synchronization involved in
cinematic montage that has become a staple of modern narrative
art, giving it a remarkable adeptness in breaking up concrete,
empirical time, so that different periods of time may coalesce and
flow into one another to form a time that has been decontami-
nated of concrete temporality. And, in thus presenting us with
snapshots of long, complicated sequences of action, the modern
novel has tended to spatialize time: indeed, its form—in Joyce's
Ulysses, in Virginia Woolf's *To the Lighthouse*, in Dos Passos'
The 42nd Parallel, in Djuna Barnes's *Nightwood*, in Philip Toynbee's *Tea With Mrs. Goodman*—can be said often to have been
a "spatial form," insofar as it has tended to make temporal passage an instantaneous thing that could be directly gazed upon in
its entirety, as though it were in front of us—in space.[21] Faulkner's
The Sound and the Fury, for example, presents a typical case,
where the actual time covered by the narrative is only four days
but where these four days in fact hurtle us through the entire
tragic history of the Compson family which is itself the history
of the whole South, in microcosm. The first major part of the
book is dated April the 7th, 1928, and the perspective is that of
the idiot Benjy. The section which follows is dated eighteen
years earlier and is devoted to the day of Quentin's suicide in
June of 1910. Then, in the third section, on the 6th of April,
1910, things are seen from the point of view of Jason Compson.
And the day which dawns "bleak and chill" in the final section
is the 8th of April, 1928, on which Dilsey, having " 'seed de

[20]*Vide ibid.*

[21]This issue has been most profoundly studied in Joseph Frank's brilliant and now classic essay, "Spatial Form in Modern Literature,"
The Sewanee Review, Vol. LIII (Spring, Summer, Autumn; 1945).

beginnin, . . . now . . . sees de endin.'" The novel's refusal to accommodate itself to the sequences of empirical time finds its major symbolic image in Quentin Compson, who despises the "round stupid assertion of the clock" and who, in a rage against the bulging obscenity of time, rips the hands off his father's watch: he suspects that "Christ was not crucified . . . [but] was worn away by a minute clicking of little wheels," and he tells himself that time is his "misfortune." So the menacing emptiness of time, as it were, persuades the novel to annihilate it by montage, in pure "duration," as it is annihilated in much of the representative literature of the modern period.

Though the techniques for the spatialization of time in the novel have grown more radical since the period of Proust, it is he who presents what is still the most truly classic case, and the one which offers perhaps the clearest clue to the final intent of the whole tradition in modern literature whose philosophic master is Bergson.[22] Superficially viewed, *A la recherche du temps perdu* may, of course, seem to exist outside that ambiance designated by the term "spatial form," for it is bent not so much on immobilizing the flow of time as on recovering "all the hours of days gone by": but the essential thing is its invocation of *simultanéité des états d'âmes*, and, in this, it joins in quite the same kind of effort at the abolition of time that is undertaken more radically, say, in Faulkner's *The Sound and the Fury*.

The drama that is at the heart of Proust's fiction is the drama of what Jacques Maritain (in his discussions of Descartes[23]) has called "angelism," the refusal of the creature to submit to or to

[22]It is, of course, in a way ironical that it is in the literature of "spatial form" that we should find the Bergsonian *durée*, since the achievement of the pure time of "duration" was, for Bergson, precisely contingent on our reaching *beneath* the spatialized self of discontinuous impressions and "homogenous time"—the self that conducts the banal, mundane business of everyday—to that more fundamental core of selfhood which is the seat of "pure duration."

[23]*Vide* Jacques Maritain, *Three Reformers* (New York: Charles Scribner's Sons, 1937; and *The Dream of Descartes*, trans. Mabelle L. Andison (New York: Philosophical Library 1944).

be ruled by any of the exigencies of the created natural order. The angel is angelic precisely because, despite its creatureliness, it undertakes the ambitious program of finding a habitation outside the natural order: it will not accept any commitment to the natural world, for its goal is a realm of pure spirit, where all the scattered leaves of life are into one Volume bound, where substance and accidents, and their various modes, are all fused together into one blazing flame: this is the object of the angelic quest. And it is just toward such a goal that all the motions of Proust's long novel are launched. For he too viewed the spectacle of man's life in history as one of sheer futility and indigence, since it is dominated by Time, which allows permanence to nothing under the sun, which, "like an ever-rolling stream,/ Bears all its sons away." So, he reasoned, man's dignity requires that he get outside of time, and the sixteen volumes of *A la recherche du temps perdu* comprise his account of how this may be done.

The vehicle of the Proustian transcendence of time is memory, involuntary memory, which is, he says, "the better part of our memory," the part that "exists outside ourselves, in a patter of rain, in the smell of an unaired room or of the crackling brushwood fire in a cold grate, wherever, in short, we happen upon what our minds, having no use for it, had rejected, the lost treasure that the past has in store, the richest, that which when all our flow of tears seems to have dried at the source can make us weep again." That is to say, the tinkle of a bell, the taste of a crumb of cake dipped in tea, the sudden rising of an odor, the sound of rain pounding on the roof of one's room in the middle of the night, the sight of the rays of the afternoon sun slanting across a garden, and a thousand other accidents of experience have the power instantly to bring flooding back, after the lapse of many years, large segments of the past that had been forgotten. In such moments, Proust believed, it is possible "to seize, isolate, immobilize for the duration of a lightning flash" a fragment of "pure time," of a time that is altogether outside the scope of the ordinary fractures and discontinuities of historical time. And this is a time which, when it is rescued from the well of the past, is discovered never really to have been lost at all but to have been incorporated, to have been "incarnate," all along in the deepest part of the mind, indeed in the very body itself.

So it was in the phenomenon of involuntary memory that Proust found the formative idea for the great project of his career—namely, that of dramatizing a voyage in quest of *"temps perdu,"* of lost time.

At the end of his novel, his narrator, after having spent many years in a sanatorium, away from the aristocratic circles of high fashion in which he had formerly moved, comes out of his retirement one afternoon to pay his respects at the modish salon of the Princesse de Guermantes. There he meets again a host of old friends and former associates, but people who have been so transformed by the ravages of time as at first to be virtually unidentifiable. And he is dizzied a little by the contradictory images that flood his mind, of this person and that as they used to be and as they now are. But gradually he begins to realize that it is just through such disparate images as these that time may be transcended, for to have vividly present in one's mind two pictures of some significant reality, two pictures that record a previous stage of its history as well as its present formation—to have two such images present in one's mind is, he realizes, no longer to be submerged in the flux of time: it is to have risen above it and to be able to grasp the past and the present in the simultaneity of "pure time." So the narrator decides to write a novel whose controlling idea will be this newly won insight. But, of course, such a novel as this is precisely the novel that is now drawing to a close. And what we begin to realize at this late stage of things is that, through the discarding of the "superstition of chronology," through the swift juxtaposition of incidents separated by large spans of time and through various subtle and complicated techniques of montage, Proust has been inducing in us the same experience that his narrator had that afternoon at the reception of the Princesse de Guermantes. The reading of *A la recherche du temps perdu* is, in other words, itself intended to be for us a practice-exercise in the negation of time and the quest of eternity.

The essentially duplicitous position of modern literature with respect to the matter of time takes, then, a dual form: one of two ways may be chosen, the way of Vico or the way of Bergson: but, whether through the "eternal return" of the myth or through the simultaneity of montage and "spatial form," the intent is to perform an act of assassination, to abolish the structures of concrete historical time with such effectiveness that the impurity of their finitude may be utterly escaped and access may be won to a timeless Eternity, to a Great Time, which is beyond anything resembling empirical temporality.

Now it is one of the interesting ironies of contemporary intellectual life that, in a period when a profound nostalgia for a vanished Eternity is leading the literary imagination to regard time as a great embarrassment and inconvenience, as the Great Enemy, the Christian theological community is, on the other hand, steadily moving towards a position that refuses to envisage the relation between time and eternity as one of radical antinomy. Forty years ago Karl Barth, for example, was, to be sure, declaring that, "if I have a system, it is limited to what Kierkegaard called the 'infinite qualitative distinction' between time and eternity."[24] But, in more recent years, he has been eager to declare that "God [Himself] does not live without time. He is supremely temporal. For His eternity is authentic temporality, and therefore the source of all time."[25] And, as he says, "God would not be my God if He were only eternal in Himself, if He had no time for me."[26] Dr. Barth represents, of course, one of the extremest types of eschatological rigorism in Christian theology of the modern period, and that he should be moving now toward a

[24]Karl Barth, Preface to the Second Edition (included in the Sixth Edition), *The Epistle to the Romans*, trans. Edwyn C. Hoskyns (London: Oxford University Press, 1933), p. 10.

[25]Karl Barth, *Church Dogmatics*, Vol. III, Part II ("The Doctrine of Creation"), trans. Harold Knight *et al.* (Edinburgh: T. & T. Clark, 1960), p. 437.

[26]*Ibid.*, p. 522.

refusal of any absolute disjunction between time and eternity is
something that, against the background of much recent theological ferment, appears to be a significant indication of basic realign-
ment.

It is indeed a kind of revolution in Christian sensibility that
recent theology is by way of achieving in the whole area of
reflection on the relationship between time and eternity. In his
Gifford Lectures, back in the early thirties, the late William
Temple was already resisting the whole concept of time as a
moving image of the static changelessness of eternity, as a realm
ontologically inferior (by reason of its secondariness) to the
absolute sufficiency of eternity—for, said he, "if there were no
History, or if History were other than in fact it is, the Eternal
would not be what the Eternal is. . . . The historical is . . . a
necessary self-expression of a Being whose essential activity is at
once self-communication and self-discovery in that to which He
communicates Himself."[27] The residual Hegelianism in Temple's
thought does, of course, today give to his idiom a certain air
of remoteness; but the general direction in which he was driving
is apparent, and it is now made much more fully manifest by
two such thinkers as divergent from each other and as distant
from Temple as Rudolf Bultmann and Emil Brunner. In an essay
written a few years prior to Temple's Gifford Lectures but now
given a fresh importance by his *Entmythologisierung* phase, Dr.
Bultmann, for example, declares:

> Belief in God is no more a mysticism rising superior to the world
> and imagining it will find God in timelessness, than it is a
> *Weltanschauung*, interpreting everything in the world on the
> basis of one principle. God is the mysterious, enigmatic power that
> meets us *in* the world and *in* time. . . . Belief implies an awareness
> that the human soul is not a special something in which man can
> free himself from involvement in the affairs of the world in
> order to fling himself into the arms of eternity. . . . It implies
> that what man has *done* and *does*—his decisions—constitute him

[27]William Temple, *Nature, Man and God* (London: Macmillan
Co., 1934), pp. 447-48.

in his true nature, that he is *essentially* a temporal being, and
that wishing to escape from the temporal simply means wishing
to escape from his own reality, and therefore from God, who is
to be found by him no where else but in this temporal reality.[28]

And just a few years ago, in quite a similar tone, Emil Brunner
was declaring that, from the perspective of the Christian faith,
eternity must be seen to be not merely a

> ... negation of temporality but its fulfillment. Since God Himself
> has come into time, He has united time with His own Eternity.
> God has, so to speak, pledged Himself to time inasmuch as He
> has pledged Himself to temporal man. The Incarnation of the
> eternal Son of God means also His *Intemporation*. . . . When we
> say that Eternity is the end or the goal, that is not a negation of
> time, but merely the negation of its negations. Eternal life is not
> Platonic timelessness, but fulfilled time.[29]

Now the general movement in contemporary Christian thought
represented by these and numerous other writers who could also
be cited is one which involves, at bottom, a profound discomfort
with the kind of radical distinction between time and eternity
that has persistently figured in theological tradition. And this is
a discomfort that is consequent upon a repossession in our period
of "the strange new world within the Bible"—to which we have
begun to see how utterly alien is the essentially Hellenic way in
which Christian theology has traditionally approached "the
problem of time." Indeed, Dr. Brunner, in the passage that has
just been quoted, still reveals a remnant of this mode of thought
when he speaks of the Incarnation as having involved Eternity
coming "*into*" time. For it is just the conception of eternity as
irrupting *into* time, with the prior conception of a fundamental
difference *in kind* between time and eternity—it is just this that
has been persistently determinative of Christian theism, from the

[28]Rudolf Bultmann, "The Crisis in Belief" (1931), in *Essays, Philosophical and Theological*, trans. James C. G. Grieg (New York:
Macmillan Co.; London: SCM Press, 1955), p. 9.

[29]Emil Brunner, "The Christian Understanding of Time," *Scottish
Journal of Theology*, IV, 8.

patristic period on into the quite recent past. But what now begins to be discovered is that the whole notion of time and eternity as radically disjunctive descends not from the distinctively
biblical sources of Christian tradition but rather from the Hellenic (and, more specifically, Platonist) background of patristic
thought. For the New Testament consistently proposes that that
lambent point at which the meaning of human existence is most
fully disclosed is located not outside time but within the historical continuum, and it is not untrue to say therefore that, for the
biblical community, time is not so much to be understood *sub
specie aeternitatis* as eternity is to be understood *sub specie tempo-
ralitatis*. Karl Barth even goes so far as to define God's eternity
as his "readiness for time." For, as he says, "in Jesus Christ it
comes about that God . . . is present for us in the form of our
own existence and our own world, not simply embracing our
time and ruling it, but submitting Himself to it, and permitting
created time to become and be the form of His eternity."[30] Eternity as a divine attribute means, for Dr. Barth, that "the defects
of our time, its fleetingness and its separations, are alien to [God]
and disappear, and in Him all beginning, continuation and ending
form a unique Now, steadfast yet moving, moving yet steadfast.
He is temporal in that our time with its defects is not so alien
to Him that He cannot take it to Himself in His grace, mercy
and patience, Himself rectifying and healing it and lifting it up
to the time of eternal life."[31] And he asserts that, unless God's
eternity does in fact have such temporality as this, the Christian
message is nothing more than a pious myth. "For the content of
this message depends on the fact that God was and is and is to
be, that our existence stands under the sign of a divine past,
present, and future, that in its differentiation this sign does not
point away into space, to a God who, in fact, is neither past,
present nor future. Without God's complete temporality the

[30]Karl Barth, *Church Dogmatics*, Vol. II, Part I ("The Doctrine of
God"), trans. T. H. L. Parker *et al.* (Edinburgh: T: T: Clark, 1957),
p. 616.

[31]*Ibid.*, pp. 617-18.

content of the Christian message has no shape. Its proclamation is only an inarticulate mumbling. Therefore everything depends on whether God's temporality is the simple truth which cannot be attacked from any quarter because it has its basis in God Himself. . . ."[32]

The witness of the biblical literature on this whole issue is being actively canvassed todya by many scholars,[33] but perhaps by none with such radicalism as characterizes the brilliantly controversial work of the Professor of New Testament Studies at Basel, Oscar Cullmann's *Christ and Time*. And what is most emphatically distinctive about Professor Cullmann's argument is that it flatly asserts that, for primitive Christianity, there is no difference at all between time and eternity, that eternity, far from being viewed as any kind of static timelessness, is simply time without limit—"or, to put it better, what we call 'time' is nothing but a part, defined and delimited by God, of this same unending duration of God's time."[34]

In Professor Cullmann's rendering of things, time proceeds, in the biblical view, along a constantly rectilinear line, "which is unlimited in both the backward and the forward direction. . . ."[35] And this line has a threefold division—into (1) the age before

---

[32]*Ibid.*, p. 620.

[33]*Vide* John Marsh, *The Fulness of Time* (London: Nisbet & Co., Ltd., 1952); Paul S. Minear, *Eyes of Faith. A Study in the Biblical Point of View* (Philadelphia: Westminster Press, 1946), especially Chaps. vi and xvi, and also Professor Minear's article "The Time of Hope in the New Testament," *Scottish Journal of Theology*, Vol. VI, No. 4 (December, 1953), pp. 337-61; Thorlief Boman, *Hebrew Thought Compared with Greek* (London: SCM Press, 1960), Chap. iii; J. A. T. Robinson, *In the End, God* . . . (Naperville, Ill.: Alec Allenson, 1950); James Barr, *Biblical Words for Time*, No. 33 of "Studies in Biblical Theology" (London: SCM Press, 1962); and James Muilenberg, "The Biblical View of Time," *The Harvard Theological Review*, Vol. LIV, No. 4 (October, 1961), pp. 226-52.

[34]Oscar Cullmann, *Christ and Time,* trans. Floyd V. Filson (London: SCM Press, 1951), p. 62.

[35]*Ibid.*, p. 48.

the Creation, (2) the present age which lies between the Creation and the End, and (3) the age to come in which the eschatological drama will be enacted: for this whole pageant the time framework is one that moves continuously forward, and it involves no dualism of any kind between time and a timeless eternity. Instead of the characteristically Hellenic preoccupation with time (whose movement is cyclical rather than linear) and a supra-temporal eternity, the polarity that is basic to Hebraic thought involves a contrast between this age *(aion)* and the *aion* to come, and both are conceived temporally. And, insofar as the New Testament approaches any concept of eternity at all, it is not a dimension of life that can ever be hellenized into something qualitatively incommensurable with concrete historical time: on the contrary, the New Testament understanding of eternity embraces nothing more than "the endless succession of the ages *(aiōnes)*."[36]

Nor does the advent of Christ entail the emergence of a fundamentally new kind of time: the new thing that Christ brought to the biblical community, Professor Cullmann suggests, was redemption from a purely futurist orientation to time. For Jewish Messianism had conceived of time in terms of a twofold division, into the present age and the coming age which would be the messianic time of salvation: for Israel the center of history lay in the future, in the expected coming of the Messiah, and it was this great miracle that was counted on to establish a decisive midpoint between the ages. But the advent of Christ brought that mid-point out of the future and into the "present" age, for in him the primitive Christian community found the meaning of all time to be revealed: the center of history is no longer the Parousia but the Cross and Resurrection of Christ: in these events "the age to come" does in fact already supervene upon this "present" age, and the joy of D-Day brings with it the assurance of the ultimate triumph of V-Day. It is, in short, says Cullmann, in the story of Jesus that the earliest Christians find the absolute norm that gives the full clue to the meaning of all time, for He is the One who is believed to have been appointed of God to

[36]*Ibid.*, p. 62.

represent the whole of creation, and through him all times and
all seasons are reconciled with God: "making peace by the blood
of his cross" (Col. 1:20), all things through him, "whether they
be things in earth, or things in heaven," are brought into soli-
darity with God. In Jesus Christ God establishes his Lordship
over time, and through him the days of our years are set in order.

Professor Cullmann insists, however, that, for primitive Christianity, time (that is, time as redemptive time) does not come
to a standstill with Jesus Christ. And this is why he feels that
Kierkegaard's notion of "contemporaneity" is in error, insofar
as it implies that the present cannot be the scene of *Heilsgeschichte*. Kierkegaard believed that the Christian man, by the
power of his faith, is translated into the time of the Incarnation
and made contemporaneous with the original witnesses; but, as
Professor Cullmann argues, to see things in this way is to suppose
that the history of redemption came to a stop with Jesus Christ
and that, in order to enter the realm of salvation, we must somehow escape out of our own moment in time back into an earlier
period. It is indeed to deny that in "the post-Easter present" the
redemptive process continues, and it is insufficiently to estimate
the eschatological urgency of the mission of the church in the
time between the Resurrection and the Parousia, as this is under-
lined in the injunction of our Lord in Matthew 28: "Go . . . and
make disciples of all nations . . . and lo, I am with you always,
to the close of the age." The present age, so far as the history of
redemption is concerned, is not, in other words, a time of impoverishment, as the Kierkegaardian doctrine of "contemporaneity" would seem to imply: it is, on the contrary, *the final
time before the end*, and it is filled with the dialectical tension
that results from its being poised between the decisive deed of
God in Jesus Christ and the *aion* that is to come. But the dialectic here is not a "dialectic between this world and the Beyond
. . . not that between time and eternity; it is rather *the dialectic
of present and future*,"[37] the future when every knee shall bow in
acknowledgment of the reign of God and when "the glory . . .

[37]*Ibid.*, p. 146.

shall be revealed in us" (Rom. 8:18 A.V.). This coming age "has in the so-called eschatological drama its beginning and so a limit; but in the forward direction it is unlimited, unending, and only in this sense is it eternal."[38] For biblical religion, in short, "salvation is bound to a *continuous time process* which embraces past, present, and future,"[39] and every event in the entire drama of redemption is understood by the people of the New Testament in terms of its relation to the *one historical fact* at the mid-point. Nor is the event of Jesus Christ which constitutes this mid-point understood as an *invasion* of time by eternity. "We must rather say that in Christ time has reached its mid-point, and that at the same time the moment has thereby come in which this is preached to men, so that with the establishment of the new division of time they are able to believe in it and in this faith to understand time 'in a Christian way,' that is, by taking Christ as the center."[40] Nowhere does the New Testament know anything that genuinely approximates the Greek contrast between time and eternity: it "knows only the linear time concept of Today, Yesterday, and Tomorrow; [and] all philosophical reinterpretation and dissolution into timeless metaphysics is foreign to it."[41]

Now this entire thesis has, of course, in many of its details, been submitted to the most drastic criticism, and most notably perhaps by Principal Marsh of Mansfield College, Oxford,[42] and Professor Barr of Princeton Seminary.[43] But what is primarily significant in this context is not the particular valuation that is to be placed upon this or that aspect of Professor Cullmann's total

[38]*Ibid.*, p. 48.

[39]*Ibid.*, p. 32.

[40]*Ibid.*, p. 93.

[41]*Ibid.*, p. 53.

[42]*Vide* John Marsh, *op. cit.*, "Appendix: Professor Cullmann's *Christ and Time*," pp. 174-81.

[43]*Vide* James Barr, *op. cit.*, Chap. iii. In a note on page 80 of this work Professor Barr lists a number of the major critiques of Cullmann's work.

argument but rather the whole style of thought in recent theology of which it is so brusque an expression. For, however the
lexical method and the scriptural exegesis and the systematic
theological orientation of *Christ and Time* may be assessed in all
their particulars, its vigorous denial that "other-worldliness" is
an organic part of New Testament faith is in essential harmony
with a general testimony that is being made today with increasing
force. Indeed, many of the most important Christian thinkers of
our period, as a result both of reexamination of the biblical material and of systematic theological reconstruction, are by various
routes reaching the conclusion that Christian theology, far from
being any kind of metaphysic, is (as it was put by the late Théo
Preiss) "essentially a *commentary*, a reminder, an interpretation
and declaration of a series of events, of an *oikonomia*, an *ordo
salutis*."[44] Or, if the theologian's denial of any metaphysical pre-
tension is unacceptable, then, it is being said, he must at least be
understood to write metaphysics only in the sense in which the
Bible writes it, "as though metaphysics were history."[45] For time
and history are not only the medium in which the revelatory
events occurred to which the Bible witnesses: they are also, and
inevitably, the single medium in which all of man's transactions
with reality take place and by which those transactions are quali-
fied at every point. To contemplate the ultimate meaning of
human existence is, therefore, to face a historical question, for
history is the medium in which man has whatever is real for him.
And, as a consequence, Christian faith is not metaphysical, not
ontological, but radically historical and eschatological, for its
message is addressed to questions about the meaning of existence
arising out of the restlessly disruptive motions of history. But
not only do the *questions* to which it is an answer *arise* out of
history: it is also the case—and this is really the major premise

[44]Théo Preiss, *Life in Christ*, trans. Harold Knight, No. 13 of "Studies in Biblical Theology" (London: SCM Press, 1954), p. 66.

[45]J. V. Langmead Casserley, *The Christian in Philosophy* (London:
Faber and Faber Ltd., 1949), p. 66: "The Bible writes metaphysics as
though metaphysics were history."

of a thinker like Cullmann—that the only absolute norm which the Christian faith knows how to invoke for the settling of these questions is a norm that is discovered in time, in history: it is not any sort of transcendent datum lying beyond all time. "The Primitive Christian norm . . . consists not only in a single historical fact, but in a temporally connected historical series of a special kind, namely, the Biblical history."[46]

It is indeed something like this that constitutes a newly emerging consensus in the theological conversation of the present time. It is the impulse to accord a new dignity in the Christian dispensation to time, it is the determination to discover anew the profound truth enunciated by Schleiermacher when he said that "religion begins and ends with history"[47]—it is this that one feels to lie behind the thought of such Europeans as the late Dietrich Bonhoeffer, the later Karl Barth, Rudolf Bultmann, Friedrich Gogarten, Ernst Fuchs, and Gerhard Ebeling; and it is also most noticeably a chief motive in the recent work of such thinkers in the English-speaking world as Professor Richard Niebuhr of Harvard, Profesor Carl Michalson of Drew, and Dr. J. A. T. Robinson, the Bishop of Woolwich in England. In fact, wherever one turns today on the map of current theological thought, the general tendency, it seems, is toward something like "an historical critique of the theological reason."[48]

So we are confronting, then, as a major phenomenon of contemporary cultural life, a sharply reversive movement: for, whereas the literary imagination often wants very much to escape from time altogether and to find a timeless eternity, the theological imagination, on the other hand—to the perplexed astonishment, one imagines, of an old-fashioned secularism, relying on its conventional critiques of "other-worldliness"—begins

[46]Oscar Cullmann, *op. cit.*, p. 21.

[47]Friedrich Schleiermacher, *On Religion: Speeches to Its Cultured Despisers*, trans. John Oman (New York: Harper & Row, 1958), p. 80.

[48]The phrase, with its allusive echo of Wilhelm Dilthey, is Carl Michalson's and forms the sub-title of his recent book *The Rationality of Faith* (New York: Charles Scribner's Sons, 1963).

to regard the eternity of the traditional Christian vision as largely misconceived, if not chimerical. "The Christian faith," says Professor Michalson, "is an essentially historical reality embracing acts of faith as historical response to God's self-manifestation in history."[49] And this is the testimony of virtually every major theologian of our period.

Now if it is true, as I believe it to be, that man steps into maturity and comes of age when he consents to accept his temporality as a permanent and undisposable part of the human state as such, then—given the profound mistrust of time that is expressed in modern literature—the question must inevitably arise as to what may be the Christian mission to the literary imagination of our age and as to how the theological community may assist the artist in learning something of the same lesson in his sphere that it has already learned in its own. Is there, in other words, any possibility of dispelling the wistfulness in modern literature for an eternity which may have had to disappear before a tough and authentic historical maturity could be achieved?

Of course, to raise any question at all about how, in the realm of belief and fundamental outlook, the literary imagination may be moved from one point to another may be to risk seeming to take a bullying kind of position. And if bullying it really be, it is surely bound to be the most fruitless kind of intimidatory effort, for only the stupidest sort of henchman of Agit-Prop could suppose that the life of high art can be tricked into permitting itself to be managed in any way at all. The notion of l'art engagé attempts in fact to give a heavy dignity to what is, after all, fundamentally dishonest, the sort of dishonesty that is enshrined in the dreary old slogans about "Art for the Masses' Sake" or "Art for Politics' Sake." And the same dishonesty would be contained in anything like the formula "Art for Religion's Sake." For the province of aesthetics is properly controlled by its own inner necessities, and, when painting or poetry, with prompt obedience, answers the beckoning of this commissar or that divine, she has simply become a whore.

[49]Ibid., p. 108.

Yet the slogans of nihilist aestheticism are quite as dreary and quite as deceiving as those of political or religious zealousness. And, however skillful and even magisterial may have been the finest artists nourished by the modern mystique of "Art for Art's Sake" (Mallarmé, Valéry, Rilke, Stevens), theirs is an art that does finally strike us as having a certain unreality at its very center. For whenever art has *added* wealth of the richest kind to the life of the human spirit, it has done so because it has fed and fattened on something other than art itself. And the greatest literature of the Western tradition (say, Dante's *Commedia* and Shakespeare's *Lear* and Goethe's *Faust* and Melville's *Moby Dick* and Mann's *Doktor Faustus*)—the literature that gives us what Arnold called our "touchstones"—is a literature that is a *response* to the interpreted world.[50]

But—in the particular case of the dialogue that, hopefully, can arise from time to time between literature and the Christian theological community—how may the theological mind go about offering an *interpretation* of the world to the literary imagination, and do so with such manifest respect for the integrity of art as will persuade the writer to give his attention to what is being conveyed? This is doubtless a question to which no one is wise enough about the politics of culture to give a finally definitive answer, though at least we can be certain that the right procedure will not involve gathering poets and novelists around a conference table to discuss the kinds of issues which occupy Oscar Cullmann and Rudolf Bultmann. For, if there is to be a conference table, the talk that goes on around it must have as its immediate subject perhaps not theology but literature. Yet it may well be that, if the right models are contemplated there, with intelligence and liveliness of imagination, this may be a dialogue that does at last *move* its participants from one point to another.

[50]I have in mind the passage in Erich Heller's *The Disinherited Mind* (Philadelphia: Dufour and Saifer, 1952), page 136, in which he says: "In the great poetry of the European tradition the emotions do not interpret; they respond to the interpreted world."

Into such a dialogue as is here being imagined one could not, of course, import the assumption that what is defective in the modern sense of time has utterly disabled our literature, for that would be patently nonsensical, since much of the writing that one has to cite as exemplifying the problem—Proust's *A la recherche du temps perdu*, Joyce's *Ulysses*, Faulkner's *The Sound and the Fury*—is (to paraphrase a line of Yeats) chiselling on the hardest stone and must, in the splendor of its art, evoke astonishment at the sheer magnificence of its lordship over language. But surely it is permissible to believe that, other things being equal, the artist in whom there is a profound acceptance of *temporalitas* may have a better chance of winning "surprises of grace" than he who rebelliously refuses the human condition. So it may therefore be an important part of the Christian's vocation toward the literature of our period to cherish and to admire, and thus indirectly to commend, some of the great examples, wherever they can be found, of the modern imagination reckoning with the world out of an acceptance of the fact that human life is indeed irrevocably committed to time and to history.

In this connection, there is perhaps no modern text that asks to be studied so deeply as that great tetrad of poems which T. S. Eliot completed in the early forties, the *Four Quartets*. And, here, the decisive consideration is that, for Mr. Eliot, "the problem of time" is not a problem of metaphysics but a problem of charity, since, as we are led to see under his guidance, what we confront is not any ontological deficiency inhering in time as such but rather the moral necessity and obligation of making love the mode of our temporal orientation—"not less of love but expanding/Of love beyond desire," and this in order to "redeem the time."[51]

Mr. Eliot does not take the high position of denying the

[51]In the field of systematic theological thought, no one has explored the problem of time as a problem of charity and love so sensitively as the distinguished Japanese thinker, the late Seiichi Hatano, in his profound and moving book *Time and Eternity*, trans. Ichiro Suzuki (The Japanese National Commission for Unesco, 1963).

actuality of flux or of claiming that time is somehow finally
unreal. As *Burnt Norton* says in its opening passage:

> What might have been and what has been
> Point to one end, which is always present.
> Footfalls echo in the memory
> Down the passage which we did not take
> Towards the door we never opened
> Into the rose-garden.

And, in this remorseful glance back at the unhappy decisions
of the past and at the opportunities that were thereby lost, the
fateful irreversibility of time is hinted at. We do not, in other
words, live above time or outside of time, in a timeless eternity:
our human condition commits us to a world that passes cease-
lessly. But, though time is not illusory, it can on occasion be
lost, and this may indeed be at the heart of the pathos of modern
spirituality—that, in an age of extreme secularity in which the
world has been emptied of all radical significance, time is often
lost, in this "place of disaffection," where there is

> Only a flicker
> Over the strained time-ridden faces
> Distracted from distraction by distraction
> Filled with fancies and empty of meaning
> Tumid apathy with no concentration
> Men and bits of paper, whirled by the cold wind
> That blows before and after time,
> Wind in and out of unwholesome lungs
> Time before and time after.

And *Burnt Norton*'s images of *lost* time are matched by similar
images in *The Dry Salvages*, where "the river" of time "is
almost forgotten/By the dwellers in cities. . . . By worshippers
of the machine" and where, as a consequence,

> . . . time [is] counted by anxious worried women
> Lying awake, calculating the future,
> Trying to unweave, unwind, unravel
> And piece together the past and the future,
> Between midnight and dawn, when the past is all deception,
> The future futureless, before the morning watch. . . .

Man recurrently supposes, of course, when his time has been lost, that it can be recovered through some wizardry of calculation, of science or of pseudo-science; and most especially does the rationalist technicism of the modern consciousness make the men of our age susceptible to such a superstition.

> To communicate with Mars, converse with spirits,
> To report the behaviour of the sea monster,
> Describe the horoscope, haruspicate or scry,
> Observe disease in signatures, evoke
> Biography from the wrinkle of the palm
> And tragedy from fingers; release omens
> By sortilege, or tea leaves, riddle the inevitable
> With playing cards, fiddle with pentagrams
> Or barbituric acids . . .

—here, says the poet, are the

> . . . . usual
> Pastimes and drugs, and features of the press:
> And always will be, some of them especially
> When there is distress of nations and perplexity
> Whether on the shores of Asia, or in the Edgware Road.
> Men's curiosity searches past and future
> And clings to that dimension.

But *The Dry Salvages* wants to remind us that "redeeming the time" is not the work of the astrophysicist or the psychoanalyst: it is, rather, says Mr. Eliot,

> . . . . an occupation for the saint—
> No occupation either, but something given
> And taken, in a lifetime's death in love,
> Ardour and selflessness and self-surrender.

And "a lifetime's death in love" brings us immediately to the center of the *Quartets*, for what all these poems are proposing is a kind of death, an act of *kenosis*, a true emptying—but not for the sake of annihilating time: for this is an existential discipline whose goal is moral, not metaphysical:

> In order to arrive at what you are not
> You must go through the way in which you are not.

The *via negativa* that is being recommended here is not, in other words, conceived to be an *askésis* that will enable us to slough off our time-ridden finitude: it is, on the contrary, a discipline designed for right action "in the meantime," in the concrete Now in which we work and worship and hope, for, as the poet says in *Burnt Norton*, "Only through time time is conquered." There is much talk of descent into "darkness, deprivation/And destitution of all property" and of "abstention from movement." But it is not any kind of indifference to the happenings of historical time that is being advocated, not the attainment of some point outside of time, some point of "fixity,/Where past and future are gathered": it is not detachment from responsible involvement in the human community that is sought, but from the tyrannizing power of concupiscence, of self-will, of rampant egoism. As Mr. Eliot says in the opening lines of the third section of *Little Gidding,*

> There are three conditions which often look alike
> Yet differ completely, flourish in the same hedgerow:
> Attachment to self and to things and to persons, detachment
> From self and from things and from persons; and, growing
>   between them, indifference
> Which resembles the others as death resembles life,
> Being between two lives—unflowering, between
> The live and the dead nettle.

The practicing of this discipline of detachment, of submission to the will of God, is not, however, as we are told in *East Coker*, an affair of "the intense moment/Isolated, with no before and after,/But a lifetime burning in every moment"—"a lifetime's death in love." And, as *The Dry Salvages* reminds us in a crucial parenthesis, "the time of death is every moment." As for the rest: it "is prayer, observance, discipline, thought and action"—and, as *East Coker* says, ". . . if we do well, we shall/Die of the absolute paternal care." The alternative is clear: we either lose our time or we redeem it, that is, take hold of it again and restore it to "a condition of complete simplicity" which is the condition of love, so that

> . . . all shall be well and
> All manner of thing shall be well . . .
> And the fire and the rose are one.

But, now, a quite different kind of example of commitment to the timescape of history and to the work of "redeeming the time" can be adduced in one of the most remarkable playwrights of our period, the German Bertolt Brecht. The harshly secular and brutally protestant character of Brecht's Marxist vision will, of course, make his work seem to many of his readers a particularly strident expression of what is *désacralisé* in modern life. Yet surely it can be said that here was a brilliantly gifted artist who spent himself in "shouting from the center of man's lonely and beleaguered heart, uttering *de profundis* what it means to be human in an age like this, confronted by a startling and unmistakable vision of its raw contingency, without having within easy reach the ancient and well-remembered mercy of a God who no longer seems to be here."[52] And in the conviction that is expressed in many of his finest works for the theatre, that man's most essential and arduous task is that of transmuting the contradictions and inequities of history into new patterns of order and justice and freedom—in this his is a secularity that is at least inclined towards the Christian vision of the redemptive power of the spirit amidst the structures of historical time.

Brecht's theatre, with its "un-Aristotelian" or "epic" bias, does not, of course, conduce towards the usual dramatic catharsis. It is not a theatre of the-fourth-wall-removed, and every last illusion of actuality is ruthlessly expunged. For Brecht believed that, when drama devotes itself to the gradual exposition of a realistic plot and invites the audience to identify with the protagonist,

[52] Samuel H. Miller, *The Dilemma of Modern Belief* (New York: Harper & Row, Inc., 1963), p. 104.

the result is merely a kind of hypnosis that may involve a purging of the emotions and a certain consequent refreshment of spirit but that cannot, in the nature of the case, lead to what ought to be the final effect of a socially dedicated theatre—namely, the energizing of the audience to go back into the world to enter into the class struggle and to engage in social revolution. So he undertook to rule out of his plays all the "illusionism" of the bourgeois naturalist theatre, in order that, instead of creating a specious present, they might simply register as accounts of happenings in the past from which a lesson may be learned about the meaning of contemporary life. He wanted his audiences to think, not to enjoy an emotional binge. And, to this end, he forbade the actors working under his direction to identify sympathetically with the characters of the play who were to be "shown," not impersonated; and all the various eccentricities of his dramaturgy—the actors' addressing the audience, the advance tips that are given the spectator on how things will end, the episodic character of the action, the use of décor as a commentary on the dramatic situation—were intended to be a part of this campaign of "anti-drama." In his own summary,

> *The audience in the dramatic theatre says:*
> Yes, I have felt that too.—That's how I am.—That is only natural.—That will always be so. . . .
> *The audience in the epic theatre says:*
> I wouldn't have thought that.—People shouldn't do things like that.—That's extremely odd, almost unbelievable.—This has to stop. . . .[53]

And he conceived it to be the purpose of a truly modern theatre not to be a "moral institution," not to moralize about the hurts and dislocations of twentieth-century life, but simply "to make visible the means by which those onerous conditions could be done away with."[54]

As Martin Esslin has observed, however, in his excellent book

[53]Bertolt Brecht, "Theatre for Learning," *The Tulane Drama Review*, Vol. VI, No. 1 (September, 1961), p. 20.
[54]*Ibid.*, p. 24.

on Brecht, the bitter ironies of many of his finest plays are turned not merely against human nature under capitalism but against human nature itself, and

> . . . only occasionally is there a qualifying clause: "man in these circumstances," "the world under this system," etc. Even then the truth of the proposition that the world can be changed for the better is never demonstrated. "Change the world: it needs to be changed!" is an exhortation that runs through Brecht's plays like a refrain. But he never succeeded in convincingly demonstarting *what* he wanted the world to be changed into and *how* it could be changed.[55]

Yet, despite the pervasively corrosive pessimism which Mr. Esslin justly remarks, Brecht's genius as an artist was such as to make it impossible for his vision to be contained within the tight Marxian dogma of the class struggle or within his metaphysical nihilism. He was (as Cleanth Brooks has said of Ernest Hemingway) "too thoroughly committed to naturalism and too honest a man to try to delude himself into thinking that one can ever get outside the dimension of time."[56] And in play after play he gives us some of the most memorable images that modern drama has anywhere produced of man launching his full human stature into the task of making the world give way before his demand for accommodation: the Joan Dark of *Saint Joan of the Stockyards*, the Shen Te of *The Good Woman of Setzuan*, the Grusche of *The Caucasian Chalk Circle*, and the great old woman who occupies the center of the stage in *Mother Courage* are all exemplars of what Paul Tillich calls "the courage to be," and their purpose is to "redeem the time."[57]

[55]Martin Esslin, *Brecht: The Man and His Work* (Garden City, N. Y: Doubleday Anchor Books, 1961), p. 260.

[56]Cleanth Brooks, *The Hidden God* (New Haven: Yale University Press, 1963), p. 18.

[57]When the Pauline phrase is used at this point, the intention, as at all previous points where it has occurred, is that the term "redeem" should be thought of not in the sense of making good something that is bad but rather in terms of its most primitive meaning, of regaining or of recovering that of which possession

The circle of definition, then, that needs to be drawn about how the literary imagination and the Christian faith are related to time has now been finished. We have noticed how great the divide is at this point between authentic Christian belief and the crypto-Gnosticism that informs so much of the literature of the modern period. For Christianity has a deep and unbreakable commitment to the temporal order: it recognizes time to be a fundamental structure of creation, and since it is therefore of God, it is declared to be essentially good; and, being the basic category or dimension of man's finitude, it is also recognized to be inescapable. And though "the men of the infinite would have us believe that at least in prayer, at least at the moment of union with God, time is transcended and . . . some kind of quasi-eternity is reached," the Christian man knows that "time [itself] . . . *is* a kind of ontological prayer. . . . [and that] there is no other form of union with God."[58] This is the testimony that is recorded in the canonical literature of the primitive Christian community, as it is also again the testimony that is being made with increasing force by many of the major theologians of our period. So the profound lack of faith in time and the great craving for a timeless eternity that are so noticeable in our literature do not represent even a rough approximation of any distinctively Christian impulse: indeed, Fr. William Lynch goes so far as to say that this modern impulse to forsake the temporal order "represents a disease of the feelings and a collapse of the true metaphysical mind": it is, he declares, "a fraudulent aping of religion and Christianity. . . ."[59]

Two radically different writers of our age, however—T. S. Eliot and the late Bertolt Brecht—have been submitted as evidencing the possibility of the literary imagination's reconstitut-

had been lost. It is only in this sense, certainly according to the perspective of Christian theology, that time can ever be thought of as needing to be redeemed: for it never needs to be made good, since there is nothing at all intrinsically evil about it.

[58]William F. Lynch, S.J., *op. cit.*, p. 50.
[59]*Ibid.*, p. 44.

ing itself and rediscovering grace and glory not in infinites and
eternities but

> . . . in the moderate Aristotelian city
> Of darning and the Eight-Fifteen, where Euclid's geometry
> And Newton's mechanics would account for our experience,
> And the kitchen table exists because I scrub it.[60]

That city may not be so "moderate" for a writer like Brecht,
but the important consideration is that he—like the O'Casey of
The Plough and the Stars, the Carlos Williams of *Paterson*, the
Joyce Cary of *The Horse's Mouth*, the Silone of *Bread and
Wine*, the Hemingway of *The Old Man and the Sea*, the Camus
of *La Peste*, the Auden of *New Year Letter*—knows that man
has no other place except the place that he is granted in his time,
in his moment of history. This is, of course, an extremely heterogeneous group of writers—Eliot, O'Casey, Brecht, Joyce Cary,
William Carlos Williams, Hemingway, Silone, Camus, Auden—
and they do not all represent one rank; but, in their unquerulous
acceptance of the irrevocable temporality of the human condition, they do all in various ways furnish examples of that apart
from which any greatness in the things of literary art must be
a very unstable thing indeed: and, for this reason, it is to such
artists as these that the Christian critic of modern literature
ought perhaps to turn for his proximate models of health and
sanity of spirit.

[60]From "For the Time Being," copyright 1944 by W. H. Auden.
Reprinted from *The Collected Poetry* of W. H. Auden, by permission
of Random House, Inc.; in Canada, Faber and Faber Ltd., London.

NATURE, LOVE,
AND ROBERT FROST

H. GRADY DAVIS

NATURE, LOVE,
AND ROBERT FROST

Robert Frost is no votary in a cult of nature. He does not spell nature with a capital N. He does not talk about nature in the abstract. He does not romanticize or sentimentalize things or people. He holds that if we love them at all, we love them for what they are in themselves. This is the first reason why I want to take texts from him, borrow a few of his thoughts and images to illuminate the theme of nature and grace. The aim will not be so much to throw light on Robert Frost as to let him throw light on us.

Creation comes in the concrete. Abstraction is the work of the human mind. Creation comes in an infinite variety of things and forms. Every single thing, every tree, hill, stream, plant, bird, animal, appears as a separate and nameless entity. Each thing comes as a work without a title, an anonymous work, not bearing the signature of its maker, with no directions for its use, its purpose unannounced.

The thing is given just as it is, but its name is a human invention, its use a human discovery. So is the similarity of one thing to another and the difference between them. Theology affirms that all natural things as they are, in their kinds and relationships to one another, are the creation of God. But the abstraction called "nature" is a creation of the human mind. So is every thought about everything, every system of thought, every philosophy and theology.

That is the trouble with nature in the abstract. A theology of nature, even a good one, is not nature. A theology of nature may get between us and the things which constitute nature. When that happens we are dealing no longer with created nature, but only with a creation of our own minds. Not only have we abstracted nature from things that exist as God makes them; we have mentally abstracted ourselves from the creation of which we are a part—apart from which we do not exist. This is the kind of thing Robert Frost does not do.

The creature we call primitive man believed that everything he saw or touched was personally related to him. He believed that when he spoke the name of a thing, he evoked its presence in all its reality and power. The Egyptian, for example, even believed that to speak the name of a dead person was to make him alive and present again.

With the sophisticated, rational persons we try to think we are, it is almost the opposite. Everything is impersonal. Nature above all is impersonal. We call the name of a thing without looking at it or really thinking about it at all. We use names as mere counters, ciphers in a mental game. We speak of the birds of the air and the lilies of the field as mere topics for all kinds of speculative, moralistic, or romantic thoughts, but we do not see them. The one thing we will not do is what Jesus said we should do, namely, look at them. Who looks at birds except a poet or some other oddball with nothing more profitable to do?

Thus we have a science of nature and a theology of nature, both creations of the human mind; but we no longer have a reverent awareness of our bond with natural things. Deep in our institutions and emotions—in our hearts, as Frost puts it—we feel that bond, of course. But "The mind—is not the heart,"[1] as Frost says, and as Pascal and Nietzsche and many another, including Freud, had said before him.

[1] "Wild Grapes," p. 243 in *Complete Poems of Robert Frost*. Copyright 1916, 1921, 1923, 1930, 1934, 1939, 1945, 1949 by Holt, Rinehart and Winston, Inc. Copyright 1936 by Robert Frost. Copyright renewed 1944, 1951, © 1962 by Robert Frost. Copyright renewed © 1964 by Lesley Frost Ballantine. Reprinted by permission of Holt, Rinehart and Winston, Inc. All references not otherwise indicated are to this volume and quoted by permission.

NOT TO LET GO WITH THE HEART

I had not taken the first step in knowledge;
I had not learned to let go with the hands,
As still I have not learned to with the heart,
And have no wish to with the heart—nor need,
That I can see. The mind—is not the heart.
I may yet live, as I know others live,
To wish in vain to let go with the mind—
Of cares, at night, to sleep; but nothing tells me
That I need learn to let go with the heart.

This is the ending of the poem "Wild Grapes." The adventure of a five-year-old girl with a birch tree gives Frost an occasion and a figure to express his determination to hold on, not to nature, but to the heart's experience of life as love and faith, whatever the hands and the mind learn to do. I do not claim that this is unique with Frost, but it is certainly one of the most constant and stubborn of his traits. For him "The Road Not Taken" was the road most people take. He set his feet on "the one least traveled by." He was a "West-Running Brook" in a region where all other streams ran eastward. He believed that to let go with the heart is a betrayal of oneself.

Ah, when to the heart of man
    Was it ever less than a treason
To go with the drift of things,
    To yield with a grace to reason,
And bow and accept the end
    Of a love or a season?[2]

And what is the drift of things, the road most people go by? Is it not just the way of letting go with the heart? The heart is awakened by things as they are; not by nature in the abstract, but by concrete objects and persons, though as yet nameless, unclassified, and unlabeled. This is so not only in the childhood of the race but also in the infancy of every one of us. All that we know of wonder or of love has been born of our intercourse

[2]"Reluctance," p. 43.

with created nature, including people. Who does not recall from his own youth that almost unendurable ecstasy of mingled joy and pain?

> Love at the lips was touch
> As sweet as I could bear;
> And once that seemed too much;
> I lived on air
> That crossed me from sweet things
> The flow of—was it musk
> From hidden grapevine springs
> Down hill at dusk?[3]

Not every reader, alas, has smelled the indescribable fragrance of blossoming wild grapes. And not every sophisticated reader will be honest enough to admit that he ever had such feelings as these. That just proves my point: that our accepted notion of growing up includes letting go with the heart. Yet although he may never admit it to himself or anyone else, every normal adolescent has known these raptures and agonies. The images of a city youth would no doubt be very different, but the experience is the same.

> I had the swirl and ache
> From sprays of honeysuckle
> That when they're gathered shake
> Dew on the knuckle.
>
> I craved strong sweets, but those
> Seemed strong when I was young;
> The petal of the rose
> It was that stung.

Many a poet besides Robert Frost has thus looked back on his youth and found there something precious that has been lost, something that seems better and more real and true than anything that has since come to take its place. The commonest feeling is merely a sense of loss, deprivation, a nostalgic regret for a

[3] "To Earthward," p. 279.

happiness too fine for this world, which first gets darkened by the shadow of disillusion, as we call it (probably backwards), and then disappears behind what we supinely accept as reality. Nobody has put it more succinctly than Frost.

> Now no joy but lacks salt
> That is not dashed with pain
> And weariness and fault;

I repeat: the commonest mood is merely one of regret for the loss of wonder, rapture, uncalculating love, imaginative vision, spontaneous adoration, instinctive worship, all that goes with the first meeting with things when it is not spoiled by persons. The great artists and poets go farther than regret. Wordsworth made a theology of immortality out of it. Dylan Thomas made of it a liturgical anthem, a canticle of praise. W. H. Auden goes back to the completely honest egoism of the smallest infant, (who does not lie because he cannot think) and says that no such honesty exists in any other human being except in the greatest of saints, who have got "past reflection into a passionate obedience in time."[4] Jesus said that the kingdom of heaven belongs to such people as children, and that no one will get into the kingdom unless he becomes as a little child.

It is in this connection that holding on, not letting go with the heart, becomes the decisive issue. The issue is whether one will have the determination to find out who he is and what he is for, have the courage to be what it is given him to be, and not for any consideration to seem to be what he is not. The normal thing, the thing we all seem to do, is to surrender, compromise, capitulate to what is normally considered reality, practical necessity, expediency, common sense. Not only the mind but the heart lets go, or tries to let go, of the things we love. We "grow up," as we call it, which usually means that we grow old, cold, calculating, conniving, incapable of joy or peace.

This is what Robert Frost steadfastly refused to accept in

---

[4]"Mundus et Infans," *The Collected Poetry of W. H. Auden,* (New York: Random House, 1945), p. 72.

principle and tried with all his power to avoid doing. While attaining intellectual stature and economic security, he retained his awareness of the bond that unites him with all things human and nonhuman. The poem I have been quoting is called "To Earthward." Frost was forty years old when it was written, and long accustomed to the taste of joy that lacks salt and is dashed with pain and weariness and fault. The game is half over, and he knows the rules by which it is played. This turning back toward the earth for something more than poetic images is deliberate and final. From here on the words are for the present and the future.

> I crave the stain
>
> Of tears, the aftermark
> Of almost too much love,
> The sweet of bitter bark
> And burning clove.
>
> When stiff and sore and scarred
> I take away my hand
> From leaning on it hard
> In grass and sand,
>
> The hurt is not enough:
> I long for weight and strength
> To feel the earth as rough
> To all my length.

Love is a costly thing in this rough world. It strikes us with a wound that has in it all we ever know of joy and pain, inseparably joined. There are times when it "seems too much," and we could wish not to love. It leaves its aftermark of tears, of sweet and bitter burning. Its wounds leave us scarred and stiff and sore.

The difference between us is in what we choose to do, or try to do about it. If we try to escape, if we let go with the heart, if we busy ourselves with what the hands and the mind can do, and try to forget what the heart knows, that sets the course of our whole existence in one direction, and there is no return. If we have the courage and faith to hold on, not to let go with the heart, then afterwards we shall know that the love which "seemed too much" was not too much but only seemed so. It was "almost too much," sure enough, because it was real. It was our participation in reality itself.

Robert Frost at forty knew this because he had chosen to hold on with the heart. He had learned that the heart's adherence was the single bond that held him to all reality, to the earth and to heaven alike, to nature, to his family, to humanity, and to the Eternal—one undifferentiated bond. He had known that bond when young, when the rose petal stung. He does not renounce it now when joy is dashed with weariness and fault. He wants it still, not in spite of the tears, bitterness, and scars. He craves these too because he wants love real, and these are part of its realness. What he wants is to feel the hurt, not for the hurt's sake, but for the earth's sake. He wants to feel it all over and to all the length of his days.

This is not the road most traveled by. The masses of humanity choose the way of escape. We see the tragedy playing itself out all around us every day of our lives. There is no time here to review that pathetic drama, much less to write a theological commentary on it. I leave the reader to do that if he must. But the main lines of the script are plain.

We learn to think impersonally of the earth and everything in it, to avoid seeing it in relation to a Creator's purpose or to ourselves as part of it. When caring about things hurts or seems to serve no practical purpose, we stop caring. We take no interest in anything for itself, only in what we can gain by it. We pay it no other attention. When the wonder, the visions and adorations of youth do not forward our schemes, we try our best to put them out of mind. We have learned to treat all but a few people in the same impersonal way as we treat things. When love wounds us, exacts its costly tribute, we run away and forget it. We settle for sweet kisses and successful copulation. We let go with the heart of everything, or try to think we do.

For of course we do not succeed in this colossal folly. We cannot break the bond that holds us to life and therefore to nature. We can only reject it and ignore it by a determined operation of the mind. But when rejected, our attachment to nature does not die. Our unacknowledged earth-link is merely banished into the limbo where our primitive feelings and unreasonable desires live on as lustily as ever. There they must remain forever primitive and unreasonable, because they can never know the discipline of love deliberately chosen and endured in courage and faith. To reject love is to reject oneself.

One result of this attempted self-rejection is the strange thing a human being can be. At the level of rational processes he may be a highly intellectual person with a thoroughly modern outlook. In his submerged feelings and desires he is as primitive as a member of the most primitive society. He may reject all the legends and myths of humanity, but the forces in him will have constructed his own private system of myths, dreams, symbols, surrogates, metaphors, and rituals concerning his existence in nature: ingestion and excretion and the organs thereof, his mother's breast and womb, his origin, parents, sexual organs and functions—everything.

Another result is that it impoverishes and desolates the life. When the heart goes out of work, it becomes drudgery. When it lets go of natural things, country things or city things, they become so much debris. When it lets go of people, they become nuisances or rivals. Worst of all, when the heart goes, the imagination goes, and with it go the delights of both memory and anticipation, as well as the tenderness and grace of the present. There is no longer the ability to feel anything enough to matter. There are no more tears, either of joy or of sorrow. There is no more genuine laughter. The nervous cackle and the dirty guffaw remain, but there is no more laughter when the heart has let go.

If I needed any justification for saying such things in this place, it would be this: that when one has let go with his heart, there is no longer in him the possibility of either worship or art. The artist, be he poet or painter or musician or whatever, knows that he cannot work without caring deeply, that he can work only by his heart. But by what fatal break with our own existence have we come to suppose that the love-tie with creation is a special thing for poets and other such extraordinary characters, but which normal people have neither time nor need to be concerned about? Oh yes, we can approve star gazing or bird watching or plant study as a hobby, not that we see anything important in these things, but because every man needs a hobby to keep him up to his best speed in the acquisitive rat race, the really important thing.

The net result of this withdrawal from the true state of existence is that worship too, along with music and literature and all other such unnecessary luxuries, has become a special interest for a comparatively few people, or to a somewhat larger number who choose occasionally to add a new taste item to the diet of boredom. Having insisted on our divorce from nature, few of us take time to figure the heavy price we have paid. The pain of love would be small beside the ache of this absurd emptiness. It would have cost us less, in the hurt we tried to escape, to have held on with the heart.

WE SPEAK THE LITERAL

Robert Frost believed and taught that every true poem is a revelation, a real disclosure of truth, not by a poet but to the poet as much as to the reader. The revelatory experience in which a poem comes into being he called "The Figure a Poem Makes."[5] I have claimed in a book[6] that the best sermon a man can preach comes into being in an experience of the same kind, that the figure a poem makes is the same figure made by a preacher's most authentic sermon. It too is a revelation to the preacher as much as to the hearer. It is a fresh gift of grace to him too, as is every fresh work of the mind and imagination. I

---

[5] "The Figure A Poem Makes," p. v.
[6] *Design for Preaching* (Philadelphia: Muhlenberg Press, 1958).

have supported this thesis at greater length in a work not published. But that is not the main point here.

In case you may be thinking that this experienced revelation is a special gift granted only to poets and preachers and other creative (?) artists, let me tell you another thing Robert Frost says about this figure a poem makes. He says, "The figure is the same as for love." That puts it where it ought to include every one of us, for everyone is called to love. Does this not mean that everyone is called to art too, and we miss our calling to both at once?

Frost does not explain how the revelatory experience is like love. How could either poetry or love be explained? One who does not know love can be given no explanation, one who knows love needs none. So he says it as simply and as reticently as possible: "The figure a poem makes. It begins in delight and ends in wisdom. The figure is the same as for love."

Frost's subject in this essay is poetry, not love. He does not describe love. But he does describe the poetic experience. It begins in delight, in "a glad recognition of the long lost," in "the surprise of remembering something I didn't know I knew." And it ends in wisdom, "in a clarification of life—not necessarily a great clarification," but at the very least, "a momentary stay against confusion." After an illuminating discussion of the whole experience, he says it again for emphasis: "The figure is the same as for love." He takes it for granted that one who has had the experience of love, in which the heart holds on and sees it through to the end, will know how love begins in delight and ends in wisdom. The hint is enough for those who will take it. He even nudges us with the same hint a second time, but it remains only a hint. That is a mark of Robert Frost's character and of his work.

He put it deliberately in a poem, to which he just as deliberately and seriously gave the title "Revelation."[7]

[7] "Revelation," p. 27.

> We make ourselves a place apart
>   Behind light words that tease and flout,
> But oh, the agitated heart
>   Till someone really finds us out.
>
> 'Tis pity if the case require
>   (Or so we say) that in the end
> We speak the literal to inspire
>   The understanding of a friend.
>
> But so with all, from babes that play
>   At hide-and-seek to God afar,
> So all who hide too well away
>   Must speak and tell us where they are.

Our problem of communication with one another falls, I suppose, somewhere between children playing hide-and-seek and the self-disclosure of the hidden God. But the problem in all personal relationships is essentially the same, of course, though that fact may be glimpsed only in a clarifying moment at the end of a poem. I doubt that we have a chance to comprehend what our real problem is apart from the other two, both of them. We try it, but we do not seem to get far, unless it be up blind alleys. I am all for the context Frost has given to the problem. He himself is here speaking in light words that tease and flout, but he wants us to understand that he is speaking in dead earnest about his life work. He hopes we will find him out.

I am not certain I know exactly where Frost stands in the second stanza. His "if" and "or so we say" might seem to indicate that he does not agree with the conclusion expressed. Does the case, the human condition, require that we speak the literal to inspire the understanding of a friend? Stanza one suggests that meaning. He says it is a pity if it is so, and I go along with that. It may be that the "so we say" means his rejection of the notion that we use literal words on purpose to obscure our meaning, because we do not want to be understood by anybody but a friend. Perhaps we cannot resolve the question until we have examined more closely what Frost means by the literal. Possibly he is still teasing me.

At any rate, the literal with Frost is not opposed to the figurative. He always writes of actual people and concrete things, and writes factually about them. This is his literalness. But there is hardly a concrete image in his work which is not also a metaphor. One who has found Frost out knows what he means by speaking the literal to inspire a friend's understanding—that side of it at least. One who has not found him out sees only the literal and stops there, as he easily may do.

In stanza two, Frost may be flouting his critics who complain that he speaks only the literal, deals only with the surface of things, like a man looking into a well "wrong to the light" and seeing only the reflection of his own image,[8] whereas he is never speaking only the literal, and his friends know it. The deeper question is whether the speech of any human being with character ever stops with the literal, whether language is ever rightly understood without its symbolic and metaphorical overtones.

There is another side to this. The great realities of the heart, of love, truth, wisdom, can neither be known nor communicated in exact, literal words. There are no literal words for them. There are symbols for those who can see the reality beyond the sign. There are metaphors, that is, transfer words, across-carriers from the seen to the unseen, for those who can afford the trip. (Note how the word *metaphor* is itself a metaphor.) There are analogies for those who see both things compared. There are parables for all who not only have ears but hear.

But these are the only words there are. Every image is a nature image, an earth image seen with the natural eye. Every symbol, metaphor, analogy, parable rises from actual persons or concrete things. The reality it evokes is still not seen with the eye. It is seen only in the earth image, and when the earth image is no longer seen, the reality is no longer seen. That is why abstract concepts serve so poorly for heart communication, though they are useful for the swift operation of the mind. That is why Frost insists that the only vitally important thing in any

[8] "For Once Then, Something," p. 276.

poem is its subject matter and context—the context of actual persons and things.[9]

What is our problem of communication then? Is it language? I do not think so. I think it is a very old problem: eyes that see not and ears that hear not because the heart, having let go of nature, no longer has a vocabulary of workable images in which to recognize and through which to share its deep realities, and has little or no commerce with them. I think the debased currency of contemporary speech is the direct result of bankrupt hearts, bankrupt because cut off from their sources of supply in nature.

For the grace and truth of life, love, and wisdom are made known and conveyed to us through natural things in the first place: through actual, "literal" things, earth things. The mother's love does not come in abstract propositions. It comes in a breast with milk, in warm enfolding arms and soft bosom, in ministering and caressing hands, in tender eyes and gentle voice tones. Life itself comes from parents not only in the act of procreation, but quite as indispensably in bread and meat on the table and clothes and shelter. Life, love, and wisdom come through the literal, and when divorced from the actual, they disappear.

This is just as certainly true of a God "who hides too well away." He too must speak and tell us where he is. He is not nature; he is "God afar." But if he is to be heard by us at all, he too must speak the literal, must speak in actual things of the earth of which we are a part, in times and seasons, in nations and generations, in blossom and fruit, flesh and blood, love and hate, life and death, in a baby in a manger and a man on a cross.

The language of this speaking is always metaphorical actuality. There are only parables. No one is forced to look beyond the literal. No matter how agitated the eternal heart till he is found out, no one is compelled to look for him. God can no more speak to us except by analogue than we can think or speak of him except by analogue. Grace and truth can reach us only in

[9] "The Figure A Poem Makes," p. v.

natural and human words and forms. The literal fact has the
best possible chance to inspire the understanding of God's
friends. But no one will see who does not want to.

> I turned to speak to God
> About the world's despair;
> But to make bad matters worse
> I found God wasn't there.
> God turned to speak to me
> (Don't anybody laugh)
> God found I wasn't there—
> At least not over half.[10]

I had resolved not to talk like a theologian in this piece. Let
me get back to the way Frost speaks the literal that is always
metaphorical. Here in eight lines Frost speaks of two light-
hearted farm chores in which he wanted companionship, obviously that of Elinor Frost. It is on the face of it a charming
romantic interlude in a bucolic setting, in the spirit, say, of
Virgil's Eclogues, or other Latin and Greek poetry that influenced his.

> I'm going out to clean the pasture spring;
> I'll only stop to rake the leaves away
> (And wait to watch the water clear, I may);
> I sha'n't be gone long.—You come too.
>
> I'm going out to fetch the little calf
> That's standing by the mother. It's so young
> It totters when she licks it with her tongue.
> I sha'n't be gone long.—You come too.[11]

When, not old myself, I first read this printed somewhere,
I took it as the idyll I supposed it to be and liked it well enough,
but was not deeply moved by it. Only later, a good deal later,
after I had owned a copy of *North of Boston* for some time,
after I had been teased and flouted by his seemingly literal words
in numerous poems, did I pay any attention to the title he had
given this poem, or what he had done with it. He called it, "The

[10]"Not All There," p. 408.
[11]"The Pasture," p. 1.

Pasture," left it unlisted in the table of contents, put it on the preface page as a foreword to the whole book, as a personal invitation to the reader. Without much fear of intruding where I was not wanted, I took him up on his "You come too."

Then for the first time I began to see this field stretching north of Boston, north or south of anywhere. I saw the spring of life-sustaining water that makes it a pasture for living creatures, saw young life getting precariously on its wobbly legs, needing to be licked gently and brought in out of the weather. I saw how a long winter's accumulation of blown dead things chokes the spring, and how, when the leaves are raked away, the blessed water comes and keeps on coming of itself until it is clear again.

I had then and now have no doubt that this poem was born of the love between Robert and Elinor Frost. But the love between them could not have been what it was if the poet's whole life of love and work had not been one with their private love as well. And that in itself, it seems to me, has much to say about what love is.

NOTHING ELSE IS LOVE

I have Frost's own authority for saying that the love between him and Elinor White Frost and the love in his life and work as a poet were one and the same. In his *Complete Poems*, he again left the above lines unlisted in the table of contents and set them as a preface to the whole. He ended "The Lesson For Today" with a proposal of his own epitaph, "I would have written of me on my stone: I had a lover's quarrel with the world." He made it explicit at the end of "Two Tramps In Mud Time,"

> Only where love and need are one,
> And the work is play for mortal stakes,
> Is the deed ever really done
> For Heaven and the future's sakes.[12]

This is no easy idealism. It is the faith that sustained him

[12] "Two Tramps In Mud Time," p. 357.

through the loss to insanity of his only sister Jeanie during the
general madness at the end of World War I, the death of his
daughter Marjorie from complications following childbirth in
1934, the loss of Elinor by heart failure in 1938, the insanity
and suicide of his son Carol in 1940, and all the rest of it.
Talk about grace in the abstract! Talk about the courage to be!
Talk glibly about it as an impersonal, theoretical formulation!
Just at this point, courage merely to be, even to be oneself,
seems a selfish thing, in face of the courage to love.

If we were talking about love in the abstract, I could easily
and quickly say what I have to say about it. I would say that
love has two dimensions: one is eternity, the other is the immediate here and now. I would say, furthermore, that love is in
both these dimensions at the same time. That would be spouting
a philosophy or metaphysics of love. It would be playing a
mental game with more or less definite concepts as pieces.
Though played with skill according to the rules, it need not
touch the heart at all. There is no necessary coexistence between
love and a metaphysics of love, as there is none between faith
and theology. The heart loves: the mind tries to explain. The
heart trusts: the mind theologizes. I can know faith only by
trusting, love only by loving. This is the difference between
grace in theology and grace in nature. A theology of love is
"works"—love is grace.

Robert Frost tasted the grace of love in both these dimensions,
and both as inseparable and indistinguishable. That is the key to
all he has to say about it, and that is what makes him so useful
for my purpose here.

To express the time-transcendence of courage to love, suffer
and say "yes" to it all, Frost combines the trial God made of Job
with the myth of preexistence that Wordsworth used in his
"Ode: Intimations of Immortality." As in the prologue of Job,
life, "existence," is a trial, a testing of human courage and
integrity and faithfulness through loss, sorrow, and suffering.
But in Frost it is not just one human existence that is so tested,

but every human being. As in Wordsworth, every soul pre-
exists in heaven before being born on this earth. But the difference in Frost is momentous. Wordsworth has us all bringing
memories of heaven that dim and fade into a common earthly
existence (which is thereby disparaged). With Frost the essence
of the thing is that we must not remember or have the faintest
inkling of our heavenly connection. If we did, earth could not
be what it is: the place where love is seen at its best, that is, in
its heavenly dimension.

Late in life, Frost wrote "A Masque of Reason," a dialogue
between Job, his wife, and God, thousands of years after the
events. Here in light words he has an amusingly defensive God
say to Job:

> Too long I've owed you this apology
> For the apparently unmeaning sorrow
> You were afflicted with in those old days.
> But it was of the essence of the trial
> You shouldn't understand it at the time.
> It had to seem unmeaning to have meaning.

Job had evidently said nearly the same thing to his wife, for
she tells God:

> Job says there's no such thing as Earth's becoming
> An easier place for man to save his soul in.
> Except as a hard place to save his soul in,
> A trial ground where he can try himself
> And find out whether he is any good,
> It would be meaningless. It might as well
> Be Heaven at once and have it over with.[13]

This was written when Robert Frost was about seventy. At
twenty-one he had already said as much and more, in what is
for me one of his most movingly beautiful poems, "The Trial
By Existence." The scene is paradise, and the theme is valor to
choose existence just as it is on earth, including the obscuration
of its heavenly connections. The souls for birth are assembled

[13] "A Masque Of Reason," p. 587.

around the throne. God reads out a human life with all its particulars in full, and some soul volunteers to live it just like that.

> And none are taken but who will,
>   Having first heard the life read out
> That opens earthward, good and ill,
>   Beyond the shadow of a doubt;
> And very beautifully God limns,
>   And tenderly, life's little dream,
> But naught extenuates or dims,
>   Setting the thing that is supreme.
>
> Nor is there wanting in the press
>   Some spirit to stand simply forth,
> Heroic in its nakedness,
>   Against the uttermost of earth.
> The tale of earth's unhonored things
>   Sounds nobler there than 'neath the sun;
> And the mind whirls and the heart sings,
>   And a shout greets the daring one.

It is not a theory of preexistence that Frost is advancing here, of course. He is trying to imagine and describe how a human life must look in the eyes of God and his angels while it is being lived and willed in the obscurity of the earth. However, the choice is not confirmed yet.

> But always God speaks at the end:
>   "One thought in agony of strife
> The bravest would have by for friend,
>   The memory that he chose the life;
> But the pure fate to which you go
>   Admits no memory of choice,
> Or the woe were not earthly woe
>   To which you give the assenting voice."

Then the life is chosen again, and this time there is no more shouting. The awe "passes wonder," and "a hush falls for all acclaim." The poem concludes:

> 'Tis of the essence of life here,
>   Though we choose greatly, still to lack

> The lasting memory at all clear,
>   That life has for us on the wrack
> Nothing but what we somehow chose;
>   Thus we are wholly stripped of pride
> In the pain that has but one close,
>   Bearing it crushed and mystified.[14]

It is in the context of this faith, this "philosophy of life" if you will, that we must read everything that Robert Frost says about love in the here and now. We need this warning because many of his poems are deceptively "literal" and naturalistic in their surface appearance.

For love here and now, I want to take as a text a poem which, along with "Trial By Existence" and thirty others, appeared in his first volume, *A Boy's Will*, in 1913. He calls the poem "A Prayer In Spring," and we need not attenuate the word "prayer" in order to apply it to the first three stanzas. The last stanza is a sermon, a very profound one, in my opinion. Nature here is a blossoming orchard, likely an apple orchard, and the bees and birds it attracts.

> Oh, give us pleasure in the flowers today;
> And give us not to think so far away
> As the uncertain harvest; keep us here
> All simply in the springing of the year.
>
> Oh, give us pleasure in the orchard white,
> Like nothing else by day, like ghosts by night;
> And make us happy in the happy bees,
> The swarm dilating round the perfect trees.
>
> And make us happy in the darting bird
> That suddenly above the bees is heard,
> The meteor that thrusts in with needle bill,
> And off a blossom in mid air stands still.

So far, these lines are an almost perfect trap for a romantic reader off his guard. If not taken as a seriously meant prayer, they may seem to be conventional sentimental nature verse, saved from banality only by the extraordinary freshness and exactitude

[14] "The Trial By Existence," p. 28.

of its images. Almost everything in them can be so taken. Almost, but not quite.

It is not the uncertainty of the distant harvest that will spoil today's pleasure in the trees and happiness in the happy living creatures. It is the thinking about harvest at all: what it may bring as well as what it may not bring. Any turning toward the harvest whatever is a turning away from this perfect day in spring. It is a refusal to drink the cup of this day's grace and blessedness simply and heartily as it is given. It is to poison the cup with considerations and calculations.

Our pleasure and happiness are not the primary things. The trees do not exist for our pleasure any more than for our profit. We do not get pleasure in the flowering trees by looking for pleasure. We get it by looking at the trees for what they are and for what they are like: themselves by day, ghosts by night. The bees and the hummingbird are bent on their own happy business, and are not thinking about us. The strange gift of the heart is that we can be happy by looking at them just as they are, for their own sake, not ours. This is no casual felicity. It is worth praying to heaven for. It is also worth proclaiming, as in the sermon:

> For this is love and nothing else is love,
> The which it is reserved for God above
> To sanctify to what far ends He will,
> But which it only needs that we fulfill.[15]

It is not love that looks forward to the distant harvest. The mind looks to the uncertain future as it should, as it must if we are to live human lives. A man does take thought for his life, what he shall eat and drink and put on. Frost tended his orchard lovingly, but he expected apples. To think he means we should enjoy the flowers and not think of apples, is to miss what he is saying entirely. He no more means that than Jesus meant we should not toil or spin.

The mind looks to tomorrow and plans, but the mind is not

[15] "A Prayer In Spring," p. 17.

the heart. Anxiety looks to tomorrow and fears, but there is no love where there is fear. Faith looks to tomorrow and trusts, but faith is not love; we may have faith to remove (or destroy) mountains and have not love. Hope looks to tomorrow and eagerly anticipates, but hope is not love; hope lives in tomorrow, love lives in today.

Love is blessedness today. It is not necessary for the mind to know love's actual worth or plan for its distant and, to us, uncertain harvest. That is God's private affair, Frost says. We do not need to be in on it. We only need to love—now.

We have heard this before. If we love, whether we know what we are doing or not, we are living now in the only God there is or ever will be. We do not have to know it to do it. We only have to love. If we could know what we are doing, a mighty shout of joy would go up to heaven over this grace. It is called for.

But the only place where we ever can love is a little orchard somewhere on this earth with its flowering trees and its busily happy creatures. This is love, and nothing else is love. Here and now, or nowhere and never. Here where love is needed. Here where love and need are one. It could not possibly be in any different sort of place we can imagine. So far as we are concerned, the ultimatum goes like this:

> It's when I'm weary of considerations,
> And life is too much like a pathless wood
> Where your face burns and tickles with the cobwebs
> Broken across it, and one eye is weeping
> From a twig's having lashed across it open.
> I'd like to get away from earth awhile
> And then come back to it and begin over.
> May no fate willfully misunderstand me
> And half grant what I wish and snatch me away
> Not to return. Earth's the right place for love:
> I don't know where it's likely to go better.[16]

16 "Birches," p. 125.

REALITY AND THE CREATIVE FORCE

Siegfried Reinhardt

REALITY AND THE CREATIVE FORCE

"Reality" is a perplexing word—a word that has defied virtually every speculation about its meaning. My own conception of its meaning varies with every new variety of experience. Therefore a dogmatic, consistent, static, and immutable definition of reality is for me a singular impossibility. The reality of the external world as perceived and reacted to through the physical agency of the biological senses is on a fundamental level; and at this level these senses deliver a specific and indisputable form of reality. This is the animal level, the level upon which the protoplastic combinations congeal to produce the form of awareness that characterizes "natural man." Fire, water, earth, and air exist as real forces, providing the basic dynamics which make the human condition possible as a physically unified masterpiece of mobility. The respect which this form of reality deserves is one of endless awe.

For a painter, the endless varieties which matter assumes in the physical world, which are perceived and examined, and finally used, form the basic patterns of response which begin to define the nature of the artist as a physical agent of nature, in nature, and himself as an extension of nature. This reality obviously must have a prior existence in the form of nature (and all that "nature" implies, defines, and otherwise produces) before any other form or conception of reality is possible. Moreover, reality so perceived underlies, as "fact," all systematic conceptions of nature, and as such it is contained in these conceptions. Fact and reality so defined are essentially one and the same. Without the preexistence of the fact, which allows us to say with absolute incontestability that "something is," reality as a material conception of the material world would be impossible.

To attempt to define what a "fact" is, as an absolute and

irreducible means by which reality is apprehended and thus acted upon, is beyond the scope of this paper. Moreover, its controversial character, in the semantic sense, would provoke inexhaustible forms of argument unrelated to these paragraphs. It is sufficient for me to *accept* both "fact" and "reality" in their most popular sense, which is to say, on the level of physical appearances, the one which is least critical. *For me this must be, and is, the point of the origin of life as a painter, both physically and spiritually.* This particular conception of reality as rooted in the brute data of human awareness is basic to existence; it is one form of the so-called higher realities.

A "higher" reality is a form of reality which resides in the human intelligence and which is expressed in ideas and abstractions of thought; it is not articulated through a system of facts, as described above, but rather owes its *Gestalt* to conceptions of truth. Here again, "truth," traditionally acknowledged as the highest form of enlightened reality, assumes, as any study of the history of philosophy at once reveals, an indescribable number of interpretations. Perhaps the most impressive revelation of truth, as an absolute and mystically transcendent reality which must be "spiritually discerned" to be accepted and understood as immutable, is contained in the triune complexity of Jesus Christ. He states, "I am the Way, the Truth and the Life." Such total finality of conviction and purpose, insofar as human experience is concerned, has no parallel in its claim to be "the truth." No human intelligence can begin to grasp even a fraction of such an infinite, divine manifestation of ultimate reality. The most that can be said is that dogmas which enclose the mystery of truth embodied in the triune complexity of Christ are accepted unequivocally in order to disclose the means by which such divine and final reality is at least accessible. The reality of truth on this level of experience, on which the divine is accessible, makes all other searchings seem futile or unnecessary.

CREATIVE FORCE AND CONFLICT

My own personal confrontation with Christ as a final and only answer for life has fluctuated, and is fluctuating, between unquestioning belief and disbelief. The continuous dialogue between the power of the will which seeks to believe, and the will-to-power, which seeks autonomy in itself, and thus to disbelieve, expresses itself openly in probably all of my work. At the root of this duality lies the profound desire to reconcile all human energy, thought, and experience, and that which it produces, with a principle of divinity to which and from which all forces of creation flow. One attitude which I cannot permit myself is to deny or to suppress the existence of conflict, frustration, and failure. It is, essentially, in the acknowledgment of these turbulences of human mind and spirit that my work ferments, until finished surfaces emerge which mirror the emotional and intellectual conflicts by which they are engendered. The reality of conflict (flesh versus spirit, disbelief versus belief) constitutes the basic pattern of my theme as a painter. However, the truth and the reality of conflict are by no means to be construed as the exclusive forces by which aesthetic forms are released. Impulses of an infinite variety stir and flash, in both mind and spirit, and cause the realization of aesthetic form.

The creative force is, as it were, in perpetual motion, and draws its propelling energies from intangible responses to ideas and insights which culminate in a sustaining drive to make a work of art. The creative force further manifests itself in that its irritant capacity in mind and body generates a compulsive energy which causes a work of art to come into existence. It provides a sustaining charge of *Anwendungskraft*, or the ability to perform in direct ratio to what is required to complete the performance. I do not mean to convey the impression that the creative force is lodged in some subconscious sector of the human spirit, and that it functions as an independent spiritual drive which is uncontrollable and fugitive, and which, in turn, exhausts the artist as though he were afflicted with some progressive, fatal disease. On the contrary, although the circumstances of the existence of the creative force in one person and not in another must thus remain mysterious, it is an exalting energy which exacts the highest act of discipline and order in man. From one point of view, the existence of the creative force in one person and not in another is a question of *degree*, since it seems altogether obvious that man at large, in an ideal conception of his state of being, is designed to be constructive, a builder, a creator. In the collective sense, all men enjoy, in varying degrees to be sure, some portion of the creative force operating in them.

THE ARTIST, SYMBOL, AND GOD

The creative force and its ability to inspire in man any given number of actions which transcend his animal-bound nature represents that force whereby some comprehension of divinity is possible. The "image of God," if one can permit such a speculation, seems to me to be the participation of divinity in the spiritual content and substance of man in the form of the gift of the creative force. More extended speculations about the "image of God" seem altogether futile, no matter how subtle, informed, and penetrating they might be. Moreover, they are inconsequential, since descriptive investigations into the nature of God reveal nothing decisive, useful, or valid, except as a symbol. An elaborate system of visual symbols, oriented upon God, has been developed as a substitute for such speculation in an effort to embrace the Godhead and its Christian tri-unity; i.e., to render visible the invisible.

The power of the symbol and its capacity as an interpretive adjunct for any theological system is not only obvious but indispensable. The symbol is, in point of fact, precisely that form by which mystery is disclosed which makes human communication possible. Without the symbol, no form of communication, in any precinct of life, could exist. The symbol is, finally, the only means by which any aspect of life can be comprehended, examined, evaluated, accepted, rejected, or ignored. Whether the symbol be, as Joyce Cary states, ". . . thing, word, gesture, ballet-step, building, [it] is a compound of concept and associations."[1] Life and symbol are, it seems to me, synonymous and

[1]Joyce Cary, *Art and Reality* (Garden City, N.Y.: Doubleday, Anchor Books: 1961), p. 89.

concentrically indivisible. My life, as an artist, is perhaps far more consciously involved with the symbol than that of the non-artist, since virtually everything with which I am engaged is related to the articulation of symbol and symbolic systems. The re-creation of the visible world and its contents on flat surfaces, whether on gesso grounds or colored glass, is essentially an act of transforming disorganized experience into an imaginative system of symbols which are designed to reflect an affirmation of life as it is lived in the awareness of divine control and authority. To be sure, the animal impulses and compulsions in man deny and violate the existence of such divine control and authority; they extract from physical appearances and experience a pattern of living in which "bread alone," as it were, is the ultimate symbol of fulfillment and reality. Such a conception of life asserts that existence alone, as a genetic imperative in the accidental process of birth, is "the way, the truth, and the life," and it acknowledges nothing independent of its decisive principle. Such a view finds it extraordinarily difficult to accept that which is invisible, transcendent, and silent, revealed through the agencies of divinely inspired prophecy, as the one, the only, and the final means by which truth is made accessible. Yet, to attempt to conceive of any system of life without the promise of immortality, predicated on a set of values which elevate animal existence to a state of being in which divinity governs achievement and worth, is equally difficult. Thus, in my own view of life, which relies far more on what I do than what I am, the presence of the divine principle cannot be excluded.

A NON-PHILOSOPHICAL AESTHETIC

This statement is, in fact, considerably less the result of logic than of training—theological "brainwashing," as it has been characterized by some, from the cradle up. No matter what system of philosophy I have examined, no matter how great the temptation to engage my thought in its often profoundly relevant core of revelation and insight, I have found it finally unpersuasive unless the author acknowledged the divine principle as the governing force of life. This is, to be sure, an emotional response, a subjective contraction of responses which mirrors an attitude that is improper for any intelligent and valuable examination of philosophical thought. I must express whatever I consider important enough to express in any definitive form as an artist and not as a philosopher addressing himself to the problems of ontology. Yet, a concern, a kind of nagging preoccupation with the problem of being is contained in most of what I do as an artist. This preoccupation results in a non-philosophical aesthetic. This aesthetic operates on a level in which idea assumes a plastic character, in which a visual resolution is reached in terms of aesthetic principles described in the tradition of art.

In his *Theology of Culture*, Tillich makes a statement, which is developed into a rather extraordinary chapter, concerning Picasso's "Guernica." In the chapter, "Protestantism and Artistic Style," Tillich writes, "Picasso's 'Guernica' is a great Protestant painting . . ."[2] He proceeds to qualify this statement in an effective and penetrating analysis in terms of ". . . the human predicament in our period,"[3] and concludes with, "The only thing we can do is to keep ourselves open for a new rise of religious art through the expressive style in the art of today. . . ."[4] In essence, this brief chapter contains (for me, at least) a lucid examination of content and style in terms of the aesthetic principles which govern a conception of what religious art is. The absurdity of an exclusive, denominationally restricted art is most certainly, and fortunately, dismissed through this thoughtfully exact statement of Tillich's. His statement, as I comprehend it, states precisely what an artist is about when he resolves a series of forms based on a major human theme and conceived within the framework of an allegory. The forms and distortions of form as they writhe, twist, and scream in "Guernica" are not representations of torment, agony and suffering; *they are, in*

[2]Paul Tillich, *Theology of Culture* (New York: Oxford University Press, 1959) p. 68.
[3]Ibid., p. 68.
[4]Ibid., p. 75.

themselves, precisely those negative qualities of power realized in the medium of painting. Destruction, human fear, guilt, and tragedy are contained in the very act of the painting. I wish only to emphasize here that, though I may not agree with the choice of "Guernica" as a "great Protestant painting," I do agree with the *intention* of its analysis since its penetration reveals the intention of the artist in our time as an aesthetic force no longer concerned with neo-classical motives in *search of beauty*. This, to be sure, does not apply to every artist in the same way; the "expressionist style in painting" that Tillich mentions is not the only style through which profound and totally relevant (timeless, if you please) works of art are achieved.

In our time the artist, fully dedicated to the singularity of a great aesthetic achievement through his craft, cannot be disengaged from the physical world of men and events. The "ivory tower" is no longer a habitable domain if significant and relevant works of art are to be produced, which speak of the "condition of man" as both creator and destroyer. Beauty, harmony, order, and balance—words traditionally related to the descriptive examination of works of art—become superficial and altogether meaningless as guiding principles for their production, since they are the by-product of art, and not the means by which art is achieved. The creative force, which is an intuitive mechanism of perception and action, instinctively imposes a system of organization on the unpredictable chaos of human experience whereby selection and rejection of values become automatic and intrinsic to the processes of response. Whatever beauty, harmony, order, balance, and so forth, emerge in and through a work of art, emerge merely as a secondary and unconscious sequence of order which in no way *makes* it a work of art. Neither do style, technique, color, line, form, shape, and all other such means, no matter how brilliantly they may be employed, make a work of art in themselves. Finally, emotion, feeling, articulation of space, energy, intensity, optical dissonance, impact and all other such abstract human qualities, irrespective of combination and effective master, do not make a work of art. A work of art contains, in any given variety and number, all of the aforementioned in a variety of degrees. A work of art is the work engendered through the human spirit and contains the mercurial quality of the presence of a divine force through which all of its elements are magnetized to create a response of continuous as well as sustained revelation. Thus it is, it seems to me, that certain works of art achieve a *divine state of being* which no amount of time, history, or human vicissitude can alter or ignore. The "Isenheimer Altar" by Grünewald is one such miracle, the "Avignon Pieta" another, and the "Ghent Altar" of the Van Eycks yet another. There are others, most certainly, but it seems unnecessary to list them.

THE ARTIST AS EXISTENTIALIST

In conclusion, whatever I have attempted to achieve with this paper is, in the final analysis, *actually* achieved, with varying degrees of success, in the form of painted surfaces. I could not assume to develop an illuminating group of statements and expect illumination to ensue, since, what I have said, is stated from where *I stand*. I wish, however, to make a final statement in the form of a brief summation.

It appears altogether clear to me that the artist, with respect to his biological nature as a human being, must know that his reality as brute *fact* and all the other relationships established by and through it are absolutely imperative to his life as an artist. The physical world, in its endless proliferation of form and matter, constitutes the source of supply through which his mode of production achieves its tangibility as a meaningful work rendered through the gift of his creative force. In this sense I find it difficult to dissuade myself from the idea that fundamentally an artist is an existentialist, and, more specifically, in that form of being characterized in Kierkegaard as "the single one." The frustrations inherent in mind and spirit; the conflict for identity and the struggle for and with faith as Kierkegaard experienced it in his *Fear and Trembling*,"[5] point up for me the

[5]Kierkegaard, *Fear and Trembling*, translated by Walter Lowrie (Princeton: Princeton University Press, 1941).

restless nature of the artistic sensibility and its exhausting attempt to reconcile itself with divinity. The artist, moreover, in spite of himself as an organic accident, reflects the action of divinity by the sheer force of his role as creator; and therefore his creative activity is an inadvertent affirmation of the image of God in man. The reality of his work, irrespective of its form, is the sole preoccupation to which his life is surrendered; and in his work the attempt to reach and embrace a cosmic reality of meaning makes him an agent of visionary proportions. Whether he works in a conscious awareness and dedication to God, and expresses his gratitude through such dedication, or whether he does not, cannot alter or distort the reality of the existence of the creative force in him, which is to say, the active presence of divinity in the flesh of man.

THE MORTALITY OF GOD
AND THE IMMORTALITY OF MAN
IN GREGORY OF NYSSA

Jaroslav Pelikan

THE MORTALITY OF GOD
AND THE IMMORTALITY OF MAN
IN GREGORY OF NYSSA

One of the perennial problems with which the theology of Joseph Sittler has dealt is the relation between what Paul Tillich calls "biblical religion and the search for Ultimate Reality." From the attack directed by his *The Doctrine of the Word* against a propositional view of revelation to his later preoccupation with "Charles N. Cochrane's lucid description of . . . Christianity's penetration of classical culture"[1] Professor Sittler has continually sought to compare and contrast the Christian and the Greek understanding of truth. And although he has referred only occasionally to Harnack's interpretation of the process of the Hellenization of Christianity,[2] it is clear that Adolf Harnack's problem is Sittler's problem—as, indeed, it is the church's problem. This contribution to a *Festschrift* in honor of Professor Sittler, therefore, will be an examination of the problem of "Hellenization" at one of its most acute points, the doctrine of the soul and its immortality in a thinker whose treatises on the subject have been called "the most significant writings on the soul to appear in the Greek church during the fourth century."[3]

Christian treatises bearing the title *De anima* are a fertile field for the study of the influence of Greek ideas upon Christian

[1] Joseph Sittler, *The Ecology of Faith* (Philadelphia: Muhlenberg Press, 1961), pp. 74-75. (In its original form my essay for this *Festschrift* was delivered as the Ingersoll Lecture at Harvard University, May 2, 1963.)

[2] Joseph Sittler, *The Structure of Christian Ethics* (Baton Rouge: Louisiana State University Press, 1958), p. 10.

[3] Heinrich Karpp, *Probleme altchristlicher Anthropologie* (Gütersloh, 1950), p. 242.

theology. For example, Melanchthon's essay on the soul provided him with an occasion for specifying the relation between faith and knowledge and thus for relating Christian revelation and Aristotelian intellection.[4] Even Tertullian, who is usually cited as the archenemy of philosophy, was obliged in his treatise *De anima* to draw upon the theories of pagan thinkers like Soranus of Ephesus, as the commentary of Professor Waszink has shown, although it is also true that Tertullian showed great discrimination in how he adapted Soranus to the purposes of Christian thought.[5] Thus one *De anima* after another, as a recent observation has put it, "carries with it overtones, ultimately coming from philosophical Greek (Platonism) and from Orphism and Gnosticism, which are absent in *nephesh*."[6]

The powerful book *On the Soul and the Resurrection*, composed by Gregory of Nyssa in 380, is replete with such Platonic overtones. The occasion for its composition was the death in 379 of Gregory's sister Macrina. She had been a formative influence in the lives of three brothers who became bishops—Gregory, St. Basil, and Peter. Basil himself had died earlier in 379, in fact on the first day of that year. Now Macrina died too, just when Gregory had stopped to visit her on his way from a council in Antioch. The book *On the Soul and the Resurrection* is put into the setting of a conversation between Gregory and the dying Macrina. Thus in its form it imitates the Platonic dialogue. Its content, too, is in many ways reminiscent of the Plato of the *Phaedo*: Macrina, like Socrates, seeks to comfort her mourners with the doctrine of the immortality of the soul. Therefore many commentators have likened Gregory's dialogue to the *Phaedo*, although the only explicit reference to Plato in

[4]Cf. Jaroslav Pelikan, "The Origins of the Object-Subject Antithesis in Lutheran Dogmatics," *Concordia Theological Monthly,* XXI (1950), 97 ff.

[5]Tertullian, *De anima*, ed. Jan Hendrik Waszink with introduction and commentary (Amsterdam, 1947).

[6]N. W. Porteous, "Soul," *The Interpreter's Dictionary of the Bible* (New York: Abingdon, 1962), IV, 428.

it is a negative comment about the myth of the chariot from Plato's *Phaedrus*.[7] Nor would it be difficult to argue that the doctrine of the immortality of the soul set forth in the *Phaedo* dominates the treatise and transforms the "organic vitality of biblical speech" about the resurrection into a mere corollary of immortality. Thus almost at the end of the dialogue, Gregory expresses some puzzlement that the discussion has not yet dealt with the most important issue, namely, the very *dogma tēs anastaseōs* and the objections that have been voiced against this dogma by the enemies of the faith.[8] When he comes a little later to provide a definition of the resurrection, he speaks of a "restoration of our nature to its original form [*hē eis to archaion tēs phuseōs hēmōn apokatastasis*],"[9] a phrase for which editors and commentators have found a parallel in the *Symposium* of Plato.[10] The definition of the soul itself is given earlier in the dialogue: "A created essence, a living substance, rational, transmitting from itself to an organized and feeling body the power of life and of sense-experience, as long as a nature capable of doing this remains together."[11]

So dominant is the apologetic concern of the treatise that although the objections of pagan thought to the doctrine of the resurrection are sometimes dismissed as "foolish," they are also

[7]See the discussion by Harold Fredrik Cherniss, *The Platonism of Gregory of Nyssa* (Berkeley: University of California Press, 1930), esp. pp. 12-25 on his doctine of the soul. Cf. Hans von Campenhausen, *The Fathers of the Greek Church*, trans. Stanley Godman (New York: Pantheon Books, 1959), p. 109. For the sole reference to Plato, *De anima et resurrectione Dialogus qui inscribitur Macriniae*, in J. P. Migne (ed.), *Patrologia, Series Graeca*, XLVI, 49. Henceforth I shall refer to this treatise as *De anima et resurrectione* and shall use the conventional abbreviation *PG* for Migne. For a detailed bibliography on Gregory, cf. Johannes Quasten, *Patrology* (Westminster, Md.: Newman, 1951 ——), III, 254-96, to which I am greatly indebted.

[8]*De anima et resurrectione, PG*, XLVI, 129.

[9]*Ibid., PG*, XLVI, 148; cf. *De hominis opificio* 17, *PG*, XLIV, 188.

[10]Plato, *Symposium*, 193D.

[11]*De anima et resurrectione, PG*, XLVI, 29.

reinterpreted in order to show that "despite their diverse ways
of looking at things, those who are outside our philosophy [the
gospel] have, one in one point, another in another, approached
and touched the doctrine of the resurrection. While none of
them exactly coincides with us, they have in no case wholly
abandoned such a hope."[12] The Last Judgment is the *sumphōnia
tou pantos pros to agathon*, the festival of the confession of *ho
ontōs ōn*.[13] The analogy between God and the soul is drawn
very far: "The speculative, critical, and world-surveying faculty
of the soul is its peculiar property by virtue of its very nature,
and thereby the soul preserves within itself the image of the
divine grace; for our reason surmises that Deity itself, whatever
it may be in its inmost nature, is manifested in these very activities, namely, universal supervision and the discrimination between
good and evil."[14] Whole paragraphs like this could be cited to
support the thesis of Anders Nygren that in his doctrine of the
soul Gregory "Hellenizes unblushingly" and that therefore
"Gregory's theology is (to use Luther's phrase) a '*theologia
gloriae.*' "[15]

This process of Hellenization, moreover, is all the more pervasive because it is not overt. There is, rather, the calm assumption throughout that notions about the soul which many theologians of the twentieth century would immediately brand as
idealism and rationalism are in fact the teaching of Scripture.
An intriguing illustration of this is Gregory's exegesis of the
parable of Dives and Lazarus, the details of which appeared to
contradict the doctrine of the non-material character of the soul
after death. Dives lifts up his *eyes* and asks that Lazarus dip his
finger in *water* to soothe the *tongue* of the damned, but the
request is denied because there is a *great gulf fixed* between the
two regions of the afterworld. The language of the account is

[12]*Ibid., PG*, XLVI, 108; *ibid.*, col. 136.

[13]*Ibid., PG, XLVI*, 108, 136.

[14]*Ibid., PG*, XLVI, 57.

[15]Anders Nygren, *Agape and Eros*, trans. Philip Watson (Philadelphia: Westminster, 1953), pp. 430, 443.

certainly physical, but it contains many indications that a literal exegesis of this language would be a distortion. For "the bodies of both of them are in the grave, and their souls are disembodied and do not consist of parts either. Therefore it is impossible to make the framework of the narrative correspond with the truth, if we understand it literally. We can do so only by transposing each detail into an equivalent in the world of ideas. . . . If one, then, thinks of those atoms in which each detail of the body potentially inheres, and surmises that Scripture means a 'finger' and a 'tongue' and an 'eye' and the rest as existing, after dissolution, only in the sphere of the soul, one will not miss the probable truth."[16] Thus a parable of Jesus that has become the *locus classicus* in modern theology for the contention that a life of the soul is inconceivable apart from the body, even after death, is spiritualized and idealized to bring it into conformity with a philosophical doctrine of the immortality of the soul.

The only difficulty in interpreting Gregory of Nyssa as essentially a speculative philosopher who bent the shape of the gospel into a Platonic form is that he claims to be doing something quite different. He may have been dishonest or mistaken in this claim; certainly he would not be the only thinker in the history of theology to palm off a doctrine borrowed from philosophy as an essential implication of the Christian gospel. Yet his claim deserves to be heard. A prominent feature of the dialogue *On the Soul and the Resurrection* is its attention to other doctrines of the soul. These, says Macrina, "are as erroneous as they are numerous."[17] Many of these opinions, as we have seen, are interpreted as adumbrations of one or another aspect of the whole truth about the soul and the resurrection. Yet the dialogue does not proceed to demonstrate the superiority of the Platonic theory or its more profound affinity (not to say identity) with the Christian message. On the contrary, Macrina insists that "while [pagan philosophy] proceeded, on the subject of the soul, as far in the direction of supposed implications as the thinker

[16]*De anima et resurrectione, PG,* XLVI, 80-85.

[17]*Ibid., PG,* XLVI, 49.

pleased, we are not entitled to such license, namely, of affirming whatever we please. For we make Sacred Scripture the rule and the norm of every doctrine. Upon that we are obliged to fix our eyes, and we approve only whatever can be brought into harmony with the intent of those writings."[18] Acceptance of the authority of Sacred Scripture as the norm for the doctrine of the soul and its immortality obliges Christian thought to reject with equal vigor both the Platonic theory of the immortality of the soul, set forth in the myth of the chariot in the *Phaedrus*, and the Aristotelian notion of the mortality of the soul, based upon the *technē* of the syllogism, which cannot go beyond the realm of probability. In fact, as Christians "we must put aside everyone before and since the time [of Plato and Aristotle], whether they did their philosophizing in prose or in poetry, and as the guide for our reasoning we must adopt Scripture, which lays down the axiom that there is no excellence in the soul which is not also a property of the divine nature itself."[19]

This last axiom is, of course, Gregory's version of the *imago Dei*, which scholars like Walter Burghardt have related to the development of the doctrine of man in the Greek fathers.[20] Thus even the highly problematical idea of the *imago Dei*, in which philosophical considerations have always been prominent and of which Christian idealism has been especially fond,[21] is to be rooted in the biblical doctrine of creation. Yet Gregory knows from his conflict both with Eunomius and with Apollinaris that to invoke the "usage of the saints,"[22] i.e., the authority of Sacred

[18]*Ibid.*

[19]*Ibid.*, *PG*, XLVI, 51.

[20]Walter J. Burghardt, *The Image of God in Man According to Cyril of Alexandria* (Washington: Catholic University of America, 1957). On Gregory, cf. R. Leys, *L'image de Dieu chez Saint Grégoire de Nysse* (Brussels, 1951).

[21]Emil Brunner, *Man in Revolt,* trans. Olive Wyon (Philadelphia: Westminster, 1947), pp. 92, 93.

[22]*Contra Eunomium Libri,* III, 1, 7, *Gregorii Nysseni Opera,* ed. Werner Jaeger, II, 6. Henceforth I shall refer to this new edition of Gregory simply as Jaeger, to distinguish it from Migne.

Scripture, is no guarantee of the Scriptural character of one's theology, and that the Arian repetition of a biblical term like the *ektisen* in Proverbs 8:22 does not make Arian theology biblical either.[23] Therefore his alternative to the teachings of the philosophers is the doctrine of Scripture as it has come to be understood in the orthodox tradition of the church.[24] Even amid his most generous appraisals of philosophical theories, he takes his stand upon creed and dogma. "As far as we are concerned, we take our stand upon the dogmas of the Church, and we declare that it will be well to accept only as much of these speculations as will suffice to show that those who engage in them are to some extent in accord with the doctrine of the resurrection."[25] In other words, the theologian's attention to philosophy is to be apologetic rather than substantive. The substance of his thought, even about the doctrine of the soul, is to come from the Sacred Scriptures as the church interprets them.[26]

But what is "the orthodox teaching of the church" on the doctrine of the soul and its immortality? During the second and third centuries various Christian images of the soul and of the shape of death existed side by side among both Greek and Latin fathers.[27] Gregory was well acquainted with several of these. Best of all he knew the doctrines of Origen regarding the preexistence and immortality of the soul. In fact, it is to the writings of Gregory that we are indebted for what seem to be verbatim reports of Origen's doctrine of creation and the fall in relation to the pre-existence of souls.[28] Despite his debt to Origen in other doctrines, Gregory parted company from his master at

[23]*Contra Eunomium,* I, 298 ff., Jaeger, I, 114 ff.

[24]*Ibid.,* III, 2, 98, Jaeger; I; 84.85.

[25]*De anima et resurrectione, PG,* XLVI, 108.

[26]Cf. Georges Florovsky, "The Function of Tradition in the Ancient Church," *The Greek Orthodox Theological Review,* IX (1963-1964), 181-200.

[27]Cf. Jaroslav Pelikan, *The Shape of Death: Life, Death, and Immortality in the Early Fathers* (New York: Abingdon, 1961).

[28]*Ibid.,* pp. 84-86.

this point. But the church had not set down what it meant by orthodox doctrine about the soul and its immortality; for that matter, it did not speak out even on the pre-existence of the soul until the sixth century.[29] Patristic debate over the immortality of the soul arose within the framework of controversy over the church's doctrine of the person of Christ. The Christian doctrine of creation asserted that man was made in the image of God. But the question, as Gregory formulated it, was: "How then is man, this mortal, passible, short-lived being, the image of that nature which is immortal, pure, and ever-lasting?"[30] His initial answer to the question is not intended to be facetious: "The true answer to this question, perhaps only the Truth itself knows."[31] Only the Truth in person, Jesus Christ, knew the ultimate answer to the combination of the mortal and the immortal, not only because of his participation in the creation of man, but especially because in his person the mortal and the immortal had come together.

Just how they came together in the person of Jesus Christ was the issue at stake in the Apollinarist controversy. Our concern here is not with the intricate and subtle question of the validity of the accusations directed against Apollinaris;[32] nor yet with the genetic question, so vigorously debated in the last decade or two, of the responsibility of Athanasius for the problematics of the Apollinarist controversy.[33] Apollinarism is relevant to the subject matter of this essay because it evoked from Gregory of Nyssa some ordered reflection on the relation

[29]Cyril C. Richardson, "The Condemnation of Origen," *Church History*, VI (1937), 50-64.

[30]*De hominis opificio*, 16, *PG*, XLIV, 180; cf. also *Oratio catechetica*, 5, *PG*, XLV, 24.

[31]*De hominis opificio*, 16, *PG*, XLIV, 180.

[32]Cf. G. L. Prestige, *Fathers and Heretics* (London: SPCK, 1940), pp. 193-246.

[33]Cf. Jaroslav Pelikan, *The Light of the World: A Basic Image in Early Christian Thought* (New York: Harper & Row, 1962), p. 119, n. 44.

between the mortal and the immortal in the person of Christ, and because that reflection is of value to us in making sense of his doctrine of the soul and the resurrection. The soul of man may have been immortal, but the central proclamation of the Christian church was the declaration that the grace of God had come to make men alive through the death and resurrection of one who was the Son of the living God. The Son of God had died; on the other hand, the souls of those whom he came to restore to life could not die; the mortality of God and the immortality of man thus demanded clarification in the theology of St. Gregory of Nyssa.

Gregory was obliged to understand Apollinaris, or at least to answer the attacks of Apollinaris upon orthodoxy in his *Apodeixis*. As Prestige has said, "it is quite plain that in certain respects his [Apollinaris'] meaning entirely escaped the comprehension of the two contemporary Gregories."[34] It appears that the dominant concern of the Apollinarist position was the unity of the person of Christ. Not two sons of God, one divine and the other human, but the one person, both God and man, had accomplished the salvation of man by his death and resurrection. But two apparently contradictory motifs emerged from this concern. Gregory quotes Apollinaris as saying: "A man cannot save the world if he remains a man and is subject to the common corruptibility of men."[35] This thesis, which Gregory was willing to accept as it stood without the implications that Apollinaris seemed to draw from it, was apparently intended as a defense of the unity of Christ in his saving act: not a human being subject to corruption, but the one incorruptible Son of God achieved the salvation of the world. Thus Apollinaris seemed to be shielding the person of Christ from the implications of the corruptibility and mortality of human nature by fusing the divine and the human as intimately as he did.

The more prominent motif in Gregory's attack upon Apollinaris, however, was to charge him with impairing the doctrine

[34]Prestige, *op. cit.*, p. 105.

[35]*Adversus Apolinarium*, Jaeger, III-1, 217.

of divine impassibility [*apatheia*]. It was the purpose of Apollinaris' statements, Gregory maintained, "to prove that the divinity is passible."[36] In fact, "the entire aim of his treatise is intent upon [showing] that the divinity of the Only-begotten Son was mortal, and that he did not undergo suffering by means of that which was human in him, but that his impassible and unchangeable nature was changed in order to share in the suffering."[37] So far had this gone, Gregory said, that according to Apollinaris "it is the Crucified One who is called the Lord of glory and is referred to by prophecy as the Lord of hosts."[38] In fact, near the end of his *Antirrheticus* Gregory presents the following as a verbatim citation from Apollinaris: "The death of a man does not destroy death, nor does one who does not die rise again. From all of this it is evident that God himself died, although it was not possible for Christ to be conquered by death."[39] As Gregory interpreted him, Apollinaris had not shielded the person of Christ from corruptibility, but had, by his insistence upon the unity of the person of Christ, subjected the divinity of Christ to death and was thus propounding the wicked doctrine of the passibility and even the mortality of God.

The absurdity [*atopia*] of such a doctrine was obvious on the face of it.[40] In a similar argument, Athanasius had set forth the impassibility of God as an "axiom of natural philosophy" [*logos phusikos*].[41] The thought that the nature of God the Creator might be subject to the change and suffering borne by his creation, Gregory wrote, was too absurd to merit serious consideration and too blasphemous to bear Christian repetition. The suggestion of passibility, he said against Eunomius, was a *diabolē*

[36]*Ibid.*, Jaeger, III-1, 182.

[37]*Ibid.*, Jaeger, III-1, 136.

[38]*Ibid.*, Jaeger, I, 166.

[39]*Ibid.*, Jaeger, I, 219. Cf. J. H. Srawley, "St. Gregory of Nyssa on the Sinlessness of Christ," *The Journal of Theological Studies,* VII (1906), 434-41.

[40]*Adversus Apolinarium*, Jaeger, I, 219.

[41]Cf. Pelikan, *The Light of the World*, p. 35.

perigraphē and a *blasphēmia*.[42] Now against Apollinaris he was equally vehement in denouncing the implication of this suggestion. If, as Apollinaris seemed to Gregory to be contending, "the incarnate God always was that which appeared through Mary and if that which appeared was [his] divinity," then it followed that "the divinity experiences all these things. . . . It bleeds, it becomes a corpse, it is buried, it is placed into a new grave."[43] From the presuppositions set forth by Apollinaris it was unavoidable to conclude that "the divinity of the Only-begotten One itself, power itself, the truth itself, and life itself was put to death in his suffering upon the cross."[44] And so Gregory rejected the suggestion that "God himself died, that in his own nature he underwent death."[45] Such an idea as the mortality of God was ontologically unthinkable, for it negated the very definition of God.

Nevertheless, Apollinaris would not be justified in concluding from this rejection, as he did, that according to Gregory "the Crucified One had nothing divine in his nature nor anything Lordly, that is, the Spirit."[46] What was unthinkable abstractly, in the divine *phusis* and *ousia* itself, could be predicated of the concrete person of Jesus Christ, who remained both divine and human also in his death. In the theology of Gregory of Nyssa, as Werner Elert says, "the picture of Christ in the Gospels comes as a corrective upon a Christology constructed onesidedly on the basis of the Logos-idea."[47] Apollinaris, on the other hand, could be accused by Gregory of completely eliminating what was earthly about Christ.[48] From the statements of Scripture about the incarnation, Christian orthodoxy taught that "the

[42]*Contra Eunomium*, III, 2, 11.12, Jaeger, II, 55.

[43]*Adversus Apolinarium*, Jaeger, III-1, 167.

[44]*Ibid.*, Jaeger, III-1, 218.

[45]*Ibid.*, Jaeger, III-1, 219.

[46]*Ibid.*, Jaeger, III-1, 172.

[47]Werner Elert, *Der Ausgang der altkirchlichen Christologie* (Berlin, 1957), p. 49.

[48]*Adversus Apolinarium*, Jaeger, III-1, 138.

divine, which is always unchanging and immutable in its *ousia*, came to be in that changing and mutable nature [*phusis*], so that by his unchangeability our inclination toward evil might be thoroughly cured."[49] The words of Isaiah 53, "He was wounded for our transgressions, he was bruised for our iniquities," did not mean "that the divinity itself was bruised, but it was the man who clung [*prosphueis*] to the divinity through the union, whose nature was capable of receiving the bruises."[50] When one considered the suffering of Christ, who was God and man, one was to observe the axiom: "That which is inglorious about him is completely the passible nature of his flesh; that which is eternally glorious is his impassible and inviolate [*akēratos*] power."[51]

Caught between the Apollinarist theory of divine mortality and a theory that would exclude the divine from participation in the death and resurrection of Christ, Gregory sought to transcend a false antithesis. "Since [our opponents] say that we claim that the man suffered, not God, let them listen to this from us: We confess that the divinity was present in the One who suffered, but not that the impassible nature became passible."[52] Then in what sense could it be confessed that Christ died, rather than that his human nature died, and that Christ has been raised from the dead, not merely his humanity? "The divinity that was joined [*egkratheisa*] from the beginning to the body and the soul [of Christ] and that remained through everything is raised up in the resurrection of him who had been laid to rest; and in this sense Christ is said to have been raised from the dead."[53] In the economy of God's dealing with man through Jesus Christ, the confession of the church spoke about the death of the person of Christ, not about his abstract natures and their essential mortality or immortality. God could not die, but this person who was God did die. Therefore one had to say "both

[49]*Ibid.*, Jaeger, III-1, 133.
[50]*Ibid.*, Jaeger, III-1, 160.
[51]*Ibid.*, Jaeger, III-1, 168.
[52]*Ibid.*, Jaeger, III-1, 223.
[53]*Ibid.*, Jaeger, III-1, 225.

that he was in death and that death did not have dominion over him."[54]

From what has been said it should be evident that none of this was merely academic or speculative for Gregory, but that he was dealing here with the central issues of the Christian message. For example, the reality of the death and resurrection of Christ was a necessary presupposition for the efficacious power of baptism; writing against Apollinaris, Gregory contended that the voluntary character of the death of Christ, as distinguished from the common and compulsory death of all men, was paralleled by the voluntary character of our death in baptism. Hence "we were buried with him by baptism into death (Rom. 6:4), so that the imitation of his resurrection might follow the imitation of his death."[55] As Georges Florovsky has pointed out, for Gregory "all that takes place in the great Resurrection already has its beginnings and causes in baptism. One may say, baptism is an 'homiomatic resurrection.'"[56] Therefore the hope of the resurrection of the body took hold of the resurrection of Christ through baptism. Hence a New Testament statement like the word of Jesus, "Unless a grain of wheat falls into the earth and dies, it remains alone" (John 12:24) had to apply to his human nature, not only because of the ontological fact that the divinity was immortal, but also and especially because of the soteriological fact that men were asked to have a share in this death.[57]

But the relation of mortality and immortality in the person of Christ had an even more profound implication for the relation of mortality and immortality in man. Imitation, even in the far-reaching significance that *mimēsis theou* had acquired in both pagan and Christian Greek literature, was not an adequate cate-

[54]*Ibid.*, Jaeger, III-1, 153.

[55]*Ibid.*, Jaeger, III-1, 227.

[56]Georges Florovsky, "The Resurrection of Life" (Ingersoll Lecture, April 10, 1951), Reprinted from *Harvard Divinity School Bulletin*, p. 23.

[57]*Adversus Apolinarium*, Jaeger, III-1, 178.

gory for Gregory's interpretation of immortality.[58] The human
nature was by definition changeable, and the divine unchangeable.
Because the divine nature could not be made worse and could
not be made better—the first was impossible and the second
unnecessary—it transformed the human nature of Christ "from
the corruptible to the incorruptible, from the mortal to the
immortal, from the short-lived to the eternal, from the corporeal
and structured to the incorporeal and unstructured."[59] This interpretation of the transformation of the human nature of Christ
into something immortal and incorruptible through its association
with the divine is ascribed by Professor Wolfson to Aristotle's
theory of "predominance."[60] Gregory himself, in an earlier
passage, presents this as an exposition of the words of Paul in
II Corinthians 5:4: "so that what is mortal may be swallowed
up by life."[61] (Just where the apostle got this idea and these
terms is, of course, yet another matter!) The immortality of
God had transformed the mortality of man into something incorruptible—first in Christ, then through him in other men, because
he had shared and thus revivified their mortal nature.

In this way the teachings of the church about the life, death,
and resurrection of Christ affirmed both the immortality of God
and the mortality of the Christ who was God; neither of these
could be surrendered without shipwreck to the faith. It is not
doing violence to the thought and language of Gregory if we
follow the distinction of Eusebius between *theologia* and *oikonomia*,[62] or if we distinguish between the immortality of Christ
kat' ousian and the mortality of Christ *kat' oikonomian*. There is

[58]Cf. Paul Friedländer, *Plato: An Introduction,* trans. Hans Meyer-
hoff (New York: Pantheon Books, 1958), pp. 17ff.

[59]*Adversus Apolinarium,* Jaeger, III-1, 223.

[60]Harry A. Wolfson, *The Philosophy of the Church Fathers* (Cambridge: Harvard University Press, 1956), I, 397-99.

[61]*Adversus Apolinarium,* Jaeger, III-1, 201.

[62]Eusebius, *Historia ecclesiastica,* I, 1.7; cf. the comments of G.
Bardy on this passage: Eusèbe de Césarée, *Histoire ecclésiastique,* I
("Sources cretiénnes" 31; Paris, 1952), pp. 5-6, n. 7.

a parallel distinction in his view of the immortality of man, as the researches of Père Daniélou have made clear. Describing Gregory's dependence upon Philo and also upon the theory of Plato's *Symposium*[63] about the androgynous gender of human beings, Daniélou makes clear that "Gregory transposes the theories which he borrows from secular thought in accord with a different perspective, the Christological."[64] Speaking *kat' ousian*, one could say that man was created immortal and sexless; for this was how man was intended to be and how he would be in the final consummation.[65] But speaking *kat' oikonomian*, one could also say that God had foreknown the fall of man and had endowed him with sexual differentiation and with a mortal body in view of this. As we have seen, Gregory did not follow Origen in teaching the pre-existence of souls, but he did teach that "man created as male and female [and therefore also man created as mortal], though first in the order of time, is only second in the order of intention."[66]

In Christ the fundamental intention, [*archē*] of God is established, and through Christ it becomes possible for mortal men to participate in the divine life. Only from this basic insight do the apparently contradictory emphases of Gregory's thought begin to make sense. Thus his individual statements about the parallels between the soul and the nature of God could be quoted to prove that neither Gregory nor the Hellenizing tradition in which he stood took the difference between God and man with sufficient seriousness; as we have seen, the critical and speculative powers of the soul are the image of God.[67] But the point of these statements in the dialogue *On the Soul and the Resurrection* is to

[63]Plato, *Symposium,* 189E.

[64]Jean Daniélou, *Platonisme et théologie mystique.* Essai sur la doctrine spirituelle de saint Grégoire de Nysse (Paris, 1944), p. 57.

[65]Cf. *De hominis opificio,* 17, *PG,* XLIV, 188.

[66]Jean Daniélou, "Introduction" to *From Glory to Glory.* Texts from Gregory of Nyssa's Mystical Writings, tans. Herbert Musurillo (New York, 1961), p. 14.

[67]*De anima et resurrectione, PG,* XLVI, 57.

insist upon the biblical view of the creatureliness of the soul. The *imago Dei* meant that "what is made in the image of the divinity necessarily possesses a likeness to its archetype in every respect. . . . Yet as far as its own peculiar nature is concerned it is something different from that other."[68] To assert the identity of God and the soul was *asebes*. Therefore the first of the differentia in the definition of the soul was that it was an *ousia gennetē*.[69]

It is in this context that we must understand an argument that appears in the *Antirrheticus* against Apollinaris. Discussing the apparent view of Apollinaris that in Christ the divinity had died, Gregory asks: "If our mind [*nous*] remains even after death, impassible and immutable, how does it make sense for Apollinaris's tripartite God of the flesh to undergo death? . . . If our soul is incapable of death, how is [Christ] capable of it?"[70] This rhetorical question is, on the one hand, a proof for the immortality of Christ based upon the general doctrine of the immortality of the soul. Even if one reads it as an *argumentum a minori ad majus*, it still establishes the immortality of man on some other basis than the life, death, and resurrection of Christ. On the other hand, Gregory can also make the immortality of man dependent upon Christ. In the dialogue *On the Soul and the Resurrection* he describes the stages through which the demonstration of the life-giving power of Christ went: the healing miracles; the raising of Jairus' daughter, of the young man at Nain, and of Lazarus; and finally his own resurrection. Thus not by word alone, but by action Christ showed the resurrection.[71]

It is too easy to find contradictions in Gregory, as Harnack, Nygren, and many others have. He himself quite consciously thought and wrote on several levels. There is perhaps no better illustration of this in the theology of Gregory of Nyssa than the very question of immortality. As was pointed out at the beginning of this essay, Gregory's Christian adaptation of the *Phaedo*,

[68]*Ibid., PG*, XLVI, 41.

[69]*Ibid., PG*, XLVI, 29.

[70]*Adversus Apolinarium*, Jaeger, III-1, 178.179.

[71]*De anima et resurrectione, PG*, XLVI, 136.

the dialogue *On the Soul of the Resurrection,* was composed shortly after the death of his saintly sister Macrina. Most of its message is put into her mouth. But Gregory also wrote a brief and beautiful *Life of St. Macrina,* at almost exactly the same time as the dialogue. In fact, in the *Life* he says that on her deathbed Macrina "discussed the future life, as if inspired by the Holy Spirit, so that it almost seemed as if my soul were lifted by the help of her words away from mortal nature and placed within the heavenly sanctuary."[72] This provides the framework for the dialogue. A little later in the *Life* Gregory describes the death of his sister in words that evoked the following, slightly grudging, tribute from Adolf Harnack: "Perhaps the clearest and purest impression of Greek churchly piety is provided by the reading of the biography of his sister Macrina by Gregory of Nyssa. . . . The dying prayer placed into Macrina's mouth . . . expresses the hopes and the consolation of Greek Christianity in an unsurpassed way, without permitting one to miss the peculiar animation of feeling that belongs to the essence of this Christianity."[73] Since it summarizes also what Gregory had to say about the immortality of man, it may fittingly conclude this essay.[74]

"Most of the day had now passed, and the sun was declining toward the West. Her enthusiasm did not diminish, but as she drew near to her departure, as if she discerned the beauty of the Bridegroom more clearly, she hastened toward the Beloved with the greater eagerness. Such thoughts as these she expressed, no longer to us who were present, but directly to Him on whom she had fixed her gaze. Her bed had been turned toward the East; and ceasing to converse with us, she spoke henceforward to God in prayer, making supplication with her hands and whis-

[72]*Vita S. Macrinae,* Jaeger, VIII-1, 390.

[73]Adolf Harnack, *Lehrbuch der Dogmengeschichte* (5th ed.; Tübingen, 1931), II, 60.

[74]*Vita S. Macrinae,* Jaeger, VIII-1, 397-99; for some of the phrases in my translation I am indebted to W. Lowther Clarke (ed.), *The Life of St. Macrina* (London, 1916), pp. 55-57.

pering with a low voice, so that we could just hear what was
being said. Such was the prayer; we need not doubt that it
reached God and was heard by him:

"'O Lord, thou hast delivered us from the fear of death. Thou
hast made the end of this present life the beginning of true life
for us. For a while thou dost put our bodies to rest in sleep
and dost awaken them again at the final trumpet. Our earth,
which thou hast fashioned with thy hands, thou dost entrust to
the earth. Thou wilt take back what thou hast given, transforming
with immortality and grace what is mortal and shapeless about
us. Thou hast rescued us from the curse and from sin, having
become both for our sakes. Thou hast crushed the heads of the
dragon who had seized man by the throat, in the yawning gulf
of disobedience. Thou hast paved the way of resurrection for us,
having shattered the gates of hell and brought to naught him
who had the power of death. Thou hast given a sign to those
who fear thee, in the symbol of the holy Cross, to destroy the
adversary and save our life.

"'O God eternal, to whom I have clung since my mother's
womb, whom my soul has loved with all its strength, to whom I
have dedicated both my flesh and my soul from my youth until
now—do thou give me an angel of light to conduct me to the
place of refreshment, where there are the still waters, in the
bosom of the holy fathers. Thou who didst break the flaming
sword and didst restore to Paradise the man who was crucified
with thee and who implored thy mercies, remember me also
in thy kingdom. For I too have been crucified with thee, having
nailed my flesh to the cross for fear of thee; and of thy judgments have I been afraid. Let not the terrible chasm separate
me from thy elect. Do not let the Slanderer stand against me in
the way; nor let my sin be found before thy eyes, if in anything
I have sinned in word or deed or thought, led astray by the
weakness of our nature. O thou who hast authority on earth to
forgive sins, forgive me, that I may be refreshed and may be
found before thee when I put off my body, not having any
stain on the form of my soul. But may my soul be received into

thy hands spotless and undefiled, as a sacrifice before thee.'

"While she was speaking these words, she placed the seal [of the cross] on her eyes and mouth and heart. And after a little while her tongue dried up with the fever. She could not pronounce the words any longer, and her voice died away. Only from the trembling of her lips and the motion of her hands did we recognize that she was at prayer. Meanwhile, evening had come and a lamp was brought in. All at once she opened the orb of her eyes and looked toward the light, clearly wanting to repeat the thanksgiving sung at the lighting of the lamps.[75] But her voice failed, and she fulfilled her intention in the heart and by moving her hands, while her lips stirred in sympathy with her inward intention. But when she had finished the thanksgiving and when her hand, brought to her face to make the sign, had signified the end of the prayer, she drew a great breath and thus she closed her life and her prayer together."

[75]On the origins of Christian evening prayer, see the note of Joan Hazelden Walker, "Terce, Sext and None: An Apostolic Custom?" *Studia Patristica,* ed. F. L. Cross, V (Berlin, 1962), 206-12.

THEOLOGICAL REFLECTIONS
ON HUMAN NATURE
IN ANCIENT SYRIAN TRADITIONS

ARTHUR VÖÖBUS

THEOLOGICAL REFLECTIONS
ON HUMAN NATURE
IN ANCIENT SYRIAN TRADITIONS

INTRODUCTION

As Christianity expanded in its early years, it very soon established headquarters at Antioch on the Orontes, an important Near Eastern metropolis of Hellenistic culture; at the same time, the early Christians started a vigorous missionary campaign in the Hellenistic world, throughout Asia Minor, Macedonia, and Greece. The main lines of this development stand clearly revealed to the historian. Indeed, the church's victorious spread and large scale success have left unmistakable vestiges in the earliest Christian literature. But the story of this grandiose campaign within the orbit of the Greek tongue has overshadowed another movement which emanated from the Palestinian Aramaic Christian communities and moved in the opposite direction. For emissaries from the small Aramaic-speaking communities quietly carried the message of the good news toward the Orient, to their kinsmen in the Jewish communities and to their Semitic relatives in the Syrian Orient. This phase of the Christian expansion was not so glamorous as that in the Greek-speaking world, nor were its vestiges so revealing. Nevertheless, the traces it has left have not been mere tracks in the sand.

Let us take a bird's-eye view of the area which the Palestinian Aramaic Christian communities regarded as their reserved terrain and into which their emissaries had quietly penetrated, spreading the seeds of the Christian faith.

First of all, let us turn to Mesopotamia—an area with which Palestinian Judaism had historically had relations. Of Edessa, its metropolis, even the literary tradition claims that the origin of Christianity here goes back to the contacts of Palestinian

Aramaic Christians with the local Jewish community. Although most of the traditions in the *Doctrina Addai*,[1] including the conversion of the King Abgar, must simply be discounted as baseless fables, an authentic kernel of the traditions incorporated in this document appears credible.[2]

Nothing prohibits us from assuming that what happened in Edessa occurred elsewhere as well. Moreover it would be strange if the development in Edessa had been an isolated phenomenon. In fact, other traces do appear, for example, in the area under the rule of the Arsacides in Persia—Adiabene, beyond the Tigris, with its center in Arbela. The *Chronicle of Mešihāzekā*—discovered not very long ago—throws some light on this otherwise dark spot. Even if we do not trust everything in this story, only hypercriticism would discount entirely these traditions which leave the impression that the earliest phase in the growth and development of the Christian mission here was of Aramaic Christian provenance. In the light of this document we must conclude that the earliest figures of primitive Christianity in this mountainous area, however dimly they come into our view, were Aramaic Christians who are to be found also in the areas where there were Jewish communities.[3] This is what the chronicle tells in its simple and unmistakable manner and this we dare not reject.

This is not all that can be said on the question of Christian origins in the Syrian Orient. Besides these scanty but direct historical references, preserved in the literary traditions, there is evidence that leads us to the same conclusion by other paths.[4]

[1]*Doctrina Addai*, ed. G. Phillips (London, 1876), pp. 5 f.

[2]See A. Vööbus, *History of Asceticism in the Syrian Orient: A Contribution to the History of Culture in the Near East (Corpus Scriptorum Christianorum Orientalium*, Subsidia XIV [Louvain, 1958]) I, 6ff.

[3]Cf. *Sources syriaques*, ed. A. Mingana (Leipzig, 1908), I, 6f., 13f.

[4]The earliest exegetical traditions rest on rabbinical exegesis. See S. Funk, *Die haggadischen Elemente in den Homilien des Aphraates* (Vienna, 1891).

Certain interesting facts, for example, concerning the Aramaic background of the versions of Scripture used in Syrian Christianity, speak loudly enough.[5]

Thus, at the dawning of Christian history in the lands of the Euphrates and Tigris, we perceive something peculiar to the genesis of the Christian movement. The historical eye can see little, but that which we can see commends itself as trustworthy by virtue of its naturalness. It is natural that the pioneering work in the expansion of the Christian faith in the Semitic areas was carried out, not by Greek-speaking Hellenistic Christianity, but by Aramaic-speaking Christians who possessed the *lingua franca* of their contemporary Orient.

THE EARLIEST TRADITIONS

The development of the views on nature and grace in Western Christianity, and the turn they took after Augustine are common knowledge. The same is not the case with regard to Oriental Christianity. Therefore it is interesting to see how the question of nature and grace was understood, as well as its subsequent history in that segment of Christianity which could develop its theological thoughts in independence from the West.

The first figure we introduce as a witness is Aphrahat[6]—a man whose theology reveals a strongly indigenous character and whose

[5]Particularly telling are the observations made possible by an investigation into the genesis of the Syriac version of the Old Testament used in Syrian Christianity. For it was neither the Greek Old Testament (which became the scriptural authority for Hellenistic Christianity) nor the original Hebrew text which was translated into Syriac, but the scriptures of the Palestinian synagogue, i.e., the ancient Palestinian Targums written in Aramaic. New findings of this ancient stratum in the Syriac text throw important light upon its real background. See A. Vööbus, *Peschitta und Targumim des Pentateuchs: Neues Licht zur Frage der Herkunft der Peschitta aus dem altpalästinischen Targum* (Stockholm, 1958), pp. 105ff.

[6]A. Baumstark, *Geschichte der syrischen Literatur* (Bonn, 1922), pp. 30f.

picture of his church life presents a very archaic pattern.[7]
According to his own dating of his twenty-three "Demonstrations," the first ten were composed in the year 337, the following twelve in 344, and the last in 345.

There have been misleading rumors about the position of Aphrahaṭ in the history of Christian thought about nature. J. Parisot's claim that Aphrahaṭ furnishes "very precious" testimonies for the dogma of original sin does not hold water.[8] There are other similar statements and references which go far beyond the evidence at hand and which are unjustified simplifications of the questions that surround Aphrahaṭ. Therefore some spadework must first be done if we want clarity regarding Aphrahaṭ's thinking on nature and grace.

We begin with the tenet which is the simplest to settle, namely, the effect of Adam's trespass on human nature, as far as death is concerned. Because of Adam's disobedience, says Aphrahaṭ, death was laid not only on Adam, but on his descendants as well. This is what the whole human race has inherited from him.[9] This for Aphrahaṭ is an axiom and requires no further discussion. Having ascertained this, however, we do not yet have sufficient ground for drawing any conclusions. Aphrahaṭ's theological reflection on this question can be seen only when his "Demonstrations" are submitted to a detailed examination.

It is easy to be deceived at this point. There is one paragraph in the course of which Aphrahaṭ speaks in a summary fashion of the results of Adam's trespass on human nature. Here he describes these effects: the trespass darkened the knowledge, overpowered it by concupiscence, made dim the roots of wis-

[7]A. Vööbus, *Celibacy, A Requirement for Admission to Baptism in the Early Syrian Church* (Stockholm, 1951), pp. 49ff.; also Vööbus, "Methodologisches zum Studium der Anweisungen Aphrahats," in *Oriens Christianus* XLVI (1962), 25ff.

[8]"Aphraate fournit de très précieux témoignages en faveur du dogme du péché originel. . . ." "Aphraate," *Dictionnaire de théologie catholique* (Paris, 1909), vol. I, col. 1463.

[9]Demonstrationes, ed. I. Parisot, in *Patrologia syriaca* (Paris, 1894), vol. I. Dem. II, vol. I, col. 49; Dem. XXII, vol. I, col. 992, *et passim*.

dom, and darkened the fundamental truth.[10] *Prima facie* it looks as if here Aphrahaṭ indeed can furnish a "very precious" testimony for the dogma of original sin, as Parisot suggested. However, a careful look advises caution inasmuch as what Aphrahaṭ gives with one hand he takes away with the other. This we begin to see when we examine the component parts of his imagery in connection with the effects produced by Adam's fall.

First of all, we must look at Aphrahaṭ's significant assertions about what took place in Adam's experience. His understanding of Adam's tragedy is that concupiscence made his fall possible. This is made clear by repeated statements. This concupiscence was in Adam already before the fall[11]—an idea that obviously had its roots in the Jewish-Christian stratum of the Syriac tradition.[12] Through the *sudala*, the "wheedling" or "flattery" of concupiscence, sin could enter into the world.[13] But since concupiscence was something Adam possessed already before his fall, the corollary is that the concupiscence in man's nature cannot be something that originated from Adam's sin, and it cannot be something that has entered human nature as punishment. This is a finding which indicates that we should note carefully the restraint that makes itself manifest in Aphrahaṭ's estimate of the effects of Adam's sin on his descendents.

Secondly, Aphrahaṭ makes statements which deal directly with the effects caused by Adam's fall and which thus help us toward greater precision in stating the position of this Syrian theologian. All these demonstrate that Aphrahaṭ reckoned the fall to be of limited effect. The most instructive among these is a statement which depicts sin in its personified form and draws the lines for

[10]Dem. XIV, vol. I, col. 625.

[11]Dem. XIV, vol. I, col. 685.

[12]The concept of *ieser* ("impulse," "drive") in Dem. I, vol. I, col. 416; Dem. XIV, vol. I, col. 744; Dem. XIX, vol. I, col. 848, recalls *ieser haṭob* ("good impulse") and *ieser hara* ("evil impulse"), both created by God, Yoma *69b* and Midrash Bamidbar R.27,8; see A. Vööbus, "Aphrahat," *Jahrbuch für das Reallexikon für Antike und Christentum* III (1960), 154f.

[13]Dem. XIV, vol. I, col. 625.

the history of its operation: "it was wounded by many [i.e., by righteous ones], it has beaten many, and has killed many."[14] The dominion of sin is a fact for Aphrahaṭ. However, as this text shows, he envisaged this rule as one which, regardless of its ravages and violence, was countered by restraining forces and was kept within certain limits. Consequently, sin was not conceived as something that at once entered human nature and permeated it totally.

A closer examination shows that what is expressed in the text just quoted has been the *leitmotif* for Aphrahaṭ's reflections on the question of the progenitor's role for the fate of mankind in its subsequent history. We shall have to adduce tenets which will further substantiate the observations we have already made. This evidence is important since it clarifies the issue under discussion.

As an example, Aphrahaṭ speaks of those whom the wave of rebellion could not engulf. It was thrown back by those whom Aphrahaṭ calls the "seed of righteousness."[15] He finds consolation in the thought that in the face of all perversion, depravity, and rebellion, there were those who remained pure. In fact, in the corrupted generations there have always been righteous ones.[16] Furthermore, Aphrahaṭ frankly reveals his sentiments when he offers the very remarkable suggestion that in the world there have been more good than evil people.[17]

In view of this evidence, the conclusion that Adam's fall could not affect human nature as such appears in a fuller light. But if human nature did not fall victim to the progenitor's misdeed, the only positive explanation of the effect of the fall is that Adam established an evil example by his deed. In fact, Aphrahaṭ calls this the *megariānūtā* (the "instigation" or "assault") which others emulate.[18] This is what has drawn his descendants into rebellion against God.[19]

[14]Dem. VII, vol. I, col. 313.
[15]Dem. XXIII, vol. II (Paris, 1907), col. 40.
[16]Dem. III, vol. I, col. 101; Dem. XXIII, vol. II, col. 21, 24.
[17]Dem. XXIII, vol. II, col. 12.
[18]Dem. XIV, vol. I, col. 672.
[19]Dem. XXII, vol. I, col. 1000ff.

Taking cognizance of all the evidence in Aphraḥaṭ, the conclusion can be drawn: human nature was not submitted to corruption and depravity through the fall of the progenitor, as if this fall had made mankind a mass of sinners. For Aphraḥaṭ there is no original sin. Human nature is not affected by it. He does take seriously the devastation released by the example set by Adam's fall. This very seriousness compels him to look beneath the surface of nature when he views the battlefield of sin.

When we turn to the concept of grace in Aphraḥaṭ, we find that this is understood in terms of the indwelling of Christ's spirit in the believer. In baptism the Spirit descends and takes a place in the believer's life.[20] However, this grace is envisaged as one which enhances ethical sensitivity, thus moving the believer to strive for sanctity of life[21] and ascetic perfection[22] in order to keep the Spirit in human life. For if disappointed and saddened, the Spirit departs and returns to the nature of Christ, and will become an accuser of the believer in whom he formerly dwelt.[23] On the other hand, as long as the Spirit is present in his dwelling-place, Satan fears to attack the believer as the habitation of Christ's Spirit.[24]

Our second witness, who also represents the ancient Syrian thought-world, is Ephrem (d. 373). He lived in the Eastern provinces of the Byzantium, and finally settled down in Edessa, Osrhoene.[25] He represents a form of Syrian Christianity that was closer to Hellenistic Christianity and reveals some contacts with it. Ephrem himself, however, did not know Greek.

[20]Dem. VI, vol. I, col. 292f.

[21]Particularly virginity; see Dem. VI, vol. I, col. 268f., 309; Dem. XVIII, vol. I, col. 840f. Cf. Vööbus, Celibacy, A Requirement for Admission to Baptism in the Early Syrian Church, pp. 49ff.

[22]See Vööbus, History of Asceticism in the Syrian Orient, I, 173ff.

[23]Dem. VI, vol. I, col. 296. In the final resurrection this spirit will not join the natural spirit that will remain "naked" as Aphraḥaṭ says; the Spirit of Christ will absorb only the natural spirits of those Christians only who have remained faithful.

[24]Dem. VI, vol. I, col. 301.

[25]A. Vööbus, Literary-Critical and Historical Studies in Ephrem the Syrian (Stockholm, 1958).

Ephrem paints the result of Adam's fall with very dark colors. This is a theme to which his lamentations turn again and again. He laments the loss of the "garment of glory,"[26] which caused the changes Adam had to experience: his bodily form grew coarser, trouble, hardship, and pain entered his life,[27] with death coming as the final punishment.[28]

Adam's trespass also involves his descendants, who have to taste the fruits of the disobedience of their progenitor. What these results are for the human race Ephrem tells us quite clearly. One primary and obvious result is death.[29] Ephrem speaks frequently of death since for him *meditatio mortis* has a special significance.[30]

When we examine carefully Ephrem's thoughts on concupiscence, we notice that he did not think that it was introduced into human nature from without, as corruption and punishment. Concupiscence was for him a cause of Adam's fall and not a result. The concupiscence that led Adam to his trespass came not from without, but from within.[31] It already resided in Adam.[32] For Ephrem, this is something that has its place in man's person over against the animals which have it in their nature.[33]

Did Adam's trespass affect human nature? Ephrem can, of course, say that the source of thought and action in all men in all generations has become unclean through Adam,[34] and that

[26]*Sancti Ephraem Syri in Genesim et in Exodum Commentarii*, ed. R. M. Tonneau (*Corpus Scriptorum Christianorum Orientalium*, Scriptores Syri LXXI [Louvain, 1955]), pp. 42ff.

[27]*Ibid.*, pp. 44f.

[28]*Carmina Nisibena* XXVII, ed. G. Bickell (Leipzig, 1866), 40f.

[29]*S. Ephraemi Syri commentarii in epistolas S. Pauli* (Venice, 1893), pp. 14f.

[30]Vööbus, *Literary-Critical and Historical Studies in Ephrem the Syrian*, pp. 106ff.

[31]*In Genesim et in Exodum commentarii*, ed. Tonneau, p. 34.

[32]*Sermones de fide*, III, 35 ed. E. Beck (*Corpus Scriptorum Christianorum Orientalium*, Scriptores Syri LXXXIX [Louvain, 1961]), p. 23.

[33]*Contra Haereses*, XX, 1, ed. E. Beck (*ibid.* LXXVII [1957]), p. 70.

[34]*Carmina Nisibena* XXXV, 106ff. ed. Bickell, p. 57.

every human being has a drop of the sea of poison in him.[35] A closer look, however, shows that what he has in mind is not Adam's sin, but, obviously, personal sins.[36] His definition of sin makes it impossible to accept original sin. Sin for him is "a matter of freedom"[37] and its roots are in the will.[38] In another place he gives a fuller definition: "the sin is this, that a nature [furnished] with will, and a being [furnished] with freedom becomes guilty."[39] Sin cannot be located inherently in nature.[40] Therefore one cannot say that human nature has been fundamentally affected by sin or transformed into evil.[41] Thus Ephrem can speak of the innocence of children[42] and of the righteousness and perfection of those in biblical history.[43] Life lived in virginity he can regard as an angel-like form of existence.[44]

Since Adam's fall, outward conditions have experienced catastrophic changes, but neither human nature nor the spiritual-ethical level in human existence has been affected. Man's moral power and ethical strength have received a blow from Adam's example; in themselves, however, they have not been seriously endangered. The reason is that man's freedom has not been affected. Indeed, it is intact: "if our created [nature] is ugly,

[35]*De paradiso*, XV, 15, ed. J. J. Overbeck, in *Ephraemi Syri, Rabulae, Balaei aliorumque opera selecta* (Oxford, 1865), pp. 339ff.

[36]*Carmina Nisibena* III, 80ff., ed. Bickell, p. 8.

[37]*Contra haereses* XVIII, 3, ed. Beck, p. 64.

[38]*De virginitate* III, 8, ed. I. E. Rahmani, in *Hymni de virginitate* (Scharfeh, 1906), p. 9.

[39]*Contra haereses*, XXI, 5, ed. Beck, p. 74.

[40]*Discourse to Hypatius* V, ed. C. W. Mitchell, in *S. Ephraim's Prose Refutations of Mani, Marcion, and Bardaisan* (London, 1912), I, 144ff.

[41]*Hymni de ecclesia* III, 4, ed. E. Beck (*Corpus Scriptorum Christianorum Orientalium*, Scriptores Syri LXXXV [Louvain, 1960]), p. 8.

[42]*De virginitate* VII, 7, ed. Rahmani, p. 24.

[43]*In Genesim et in Exodum commentarii*, ed. Tonneau, p. 43; *S.P.N. Ephraem Syri opera omnia*, ed. J. S. Assemani (Rome, 1740), II, 344ff.

[44]Vööbus, *Literary-Critical and Historical Studies in Ephrem the Syrian*, pp. 102ff.

the reproach falls on our Creator; but if our freedom is evil, the reproach accumulates itself on us."[45] As human freedom, so also the will has remained intact.[46] Thereby men are furnished with qualities which make them capable of cooperation in the saving work of Christ, being able through their ethical strength and will to take on themselves the consequences of their calling.[47]

Again and again statements emerge which reveal Ephrem's keen interest in and his vigorous stand for the freedom of man. The master of Edessa is confident that the reins of the will are laid in the hands of man.[48] The will "born free" is the power that frees from sins.[49] Through free will, sins fall.[50] Although human power is weak, the will guarantees the victory.[51] Much can be accomplished by it,[52] leading to the highest level of perfection in mortification.[53] Ephrem's eulogies end in a powerful orchestration: through the oars a boat can be salvaged from the waves, yet the waves can bring it down; however, faith cannot go down if the will does not desire it.[54]

In reflections such as these, in which Ephrem comes closer to the realm of the responsibilities and the obligations of the Christian faith, we see him opening his heart and exhibiting the things which lay so heavily on it. In his concern for active and vigorous life he can proceed and even come out with the conviction that man through his dedication and perseverance can

[45]*Hymni de ecclesia* VI, 1, ed. Beck, p. 15.

[46]*Carmena Nisibena* XXI, 51ff., ed. Bickell, p. 36.

[47]*Hymni de fide* XXXI, 5, ed. E. Beck (*Corpus Scriptorum Scriptorum Orientalium*, Scriptores Syri LXXIII [Louvain, 1955]), p. 106.

[48]*Sermones de fide* I, 317ff., ed. Beck, p. 7.

[49]*Sermones de fide*, III, 263-64, *ibid.*, p. 28.

[50]*De virginitate* III, 8, ed. Rahmani, p. 9; cf. *S. Ephraim's Prose Refutations*, ed. Mitchell, II (London, 1921), p. 174.

[51]*Hymni de ecclesia* XII, 1, ed. Beck, p. 30.

[52]*Hymni de ecclesia* L, 15, *ibid.*, p. 130.

[53]Vööbus, *Literary-Critical and Historical Studies in Ephrem the Syrian*, pp. 102ff., 112ff.

[54]*Sermones de fide* IV, 75-78, ed. Beck, p. 33.

reach as far as the knowledge of God.[55] However, in Ephrem we have a remarkable symbiosis of expressions and formulations which are not always consistent and not always controlled by the rigid discipline of theological thinking. Although he seldom speaks of grace, it is wrong to conclude that grace did not play any significant role in his religion. As a preacher he does not feel that anything God would offer can be a problem to torment him or his readers. His concern is (and this is the only concern) how man can and should react to God's gracious invitation. Thus grace is usually included tacitly in Ephrem's writings. Those passages in which he does speak about grace reveal what he had in mind. He saw grace in all God has done through the ministry of Jesus, which provides the context without which such vigorous kerygma would not be possible. It is in this sense that we must read what he says about cooperation between the believer and God.[56] The same comes to the fore when we read further that by grace human will receives strength from God,[57] and by grace it can be made perfect.[58]

As this discussion shows, in the ancient Syrian traditions we encounter a Christianity which in its understanding of human nature was eager to preserve the freedom of man and a certain degree of his self-reliance, thereby laying strong emphasis on ethical power and the sense of responsibility.

FURTHER DEVELOPMENT

Subsequent history led Syrian Christianity towards schism. The problem of Christology divided the theologians, and finally worked a cleavage within Syrian Christianity. However, before the formation of eastern Syrian Christianity took place, there was a longer pre-history during which the centripetal forces could crystallize their theological thinking.

In this pre-history the School of Edessa played a very import-

[55]*Hymni de fide*, LXXII, 7 and XLVIII, 3, ed. Beck, pp. 220, 152f.
[56]*Hymni de fide* XXX, 5, *ibid.*, p. 106.
[57]*Hymni de fide* XII, 3, *ibid.*, p. 57.
[58]*Carmina Nisibena* XXI, 95ff., ed. Bickell, p. 37.

ant role, particularly in the later period of its existence.[59] From its inception a contingent from the eastern regions played an important role in this school. The attraction of the school reached even to the Persian territories, constantly drawing students and teachers from these territories under Sassanide rule. In fact, the School of Edessa not only became a rendezvous for all these leaders of thought who were destined later to play an essential role in the formation of the Nestorian church; it was also a clearinghouse for theological thought, shaping theological positions and preparing the way for the time when they could be elevated to an official status.

In this way the School of Edessa, this center of higher learning, became a channel for new stimuli in the theological thinking of the Syrians. In the theological debate a climate ripened in which it was felt that the views and tenets of Theodore of Mopsuestia were most congenial to those reared in the ancient traditions of the Syrians. This is reflected in the changes that took place in instruction. Teaching and study were saturated with the spirit of the Antiochian biblical exegesis and the theology of Theodore. Thus it was natural that the need was felt for the translation of Theodore's works into Syriac. This materialized under the director Qiiōrē;[60] during his directorship most of Theodore's works were translated. This undertaking, which made Theodore's writings available in Syriac, was, historically speaking, a very important event. Thereby an important new avenue was opened to the influence of Theodore, enabling it to extend into a sphere in which it found warm-hearted appreciation and which was ready to offer unfailing loyalty to his convictions.

A further landmark in the history of this development can be seen in the reform carried out in the School of Edessa. The time came when the works of Ephrem, which had served as a basis for instruction, were gradually replaced by those of Theo-

[59]E. R. Hayes, *L'école d'Edesse* (Paris, 1930), pp. 172ff.

[60]Vööbus, *History of Asceticism in the Syrian Orient* (1960), II, 411f.

dore.[61] Edessa thus gave a vigorous endorsement to the dissemination of the theology of Theodore. This new factor entered into the development, and determined the future course, of this segment of Syrian Christianity which was eager to appropriate Theodore's thought. In what way did it contribute to the thought we have undertaken to elucidate?

There has been a confusion regarding the views of Theodore in this respect. Conclusions have been drawn which are contradictory. R. Devreesse's monograph on Theodore established the thesis that the alleged deviation in Theodore's views from traditional theological positions is a myth.[62] According to Devreesse, Theodore's thinking is orthodox in respect to the immortal status given to Adam by creation,[63] and in regard to original sin and its effects on human nature.[64]

This brings up a question which cannot be answered without a reexamination of the evidence. As we have indicated elsewhere,[65] we cannot follow Devreesse's line of argument. The sources themselves say something quite different. In fact, Theodore contradicts Devreesse in every point. Mention of the salient points makes this sufficiently clear. First, Adam was created as mortal, as is evident from Theodore's commentaries on Genesis[66] and Galatians,[67] in his work "On Creation,"[68] and in the excerpts

[61]*Ibid.*, pp. 412ff.

[62]*Essai sur Théodore de Mopsueste (Studi e testi* CXLI [Vatican City, 1948]), pp. 94ff.

[63]*Ibid.*, pp. 101f.

[64]"Disons tout de suite que rien de cela ne se lit dans l'oeuvre authentique de Théodore, absolument rien. Nous l'avons vu affirmer sans ambages l'immortalité primitive de l'homme et la transmission du péché à ses descendants"; *ibid.*, p. 102.

[65]A. Vööbus, "Regarding the Theological Anthropology of Theodore of Mopsuestia," *Church History* XXXIII (1964).

[66]*Fragmenta in Genesin* III, 17, ed. J. P. Migne, in *Patrologia Graeca* LXVI, cols. 640f.

[67]In *Epistola ad Galatas*, II, 15-16, ed. H. B. Swete, in *Theodori episcopi Mopsuesteni in epistolas S. Pauli commentarii* (Cambridge, 1880) I, 25f.

[68]Some excerpts of *De creatura* in *Patrologia Graeca* LXVI, cols. 633f.

in the *Collectio Palatina*.[69] Second, concupiscence already lived
in Adam as in a mortal being, causing the fall; therefore, it cannot be a punishment.[70] Third, death is not a punishment for
Adam's trespass, but something natural.[71] Fourth, sin has nothing
to do with nature; in his exegetical[72] and theological works,[73]
Theodore develops a biting critique of Augustine's view. Finally,
however powerful are the effects of the trespass of the progenitor in intensifying the inclination for concupiscence and
sinning, the free will and the moral ability to make decisions
between evil and good are not impaired.[74]

The impact Theodore's thinking and approach had on the
milieu of the School of Edessa was immense. This can be sufficiently illustrated by what we are allowed to observe in connection
with the most eminent among the leaders in that center of
learning. We refer to Narsai. He played the most important role
among the teachers and students who had come there from
Persia. When after the death of Qiiōrē, the director of the institution, the question of election of a successor came up, the unani-
mous sentiment of the community was that the only candidate
for this position was Narsai. He was invested with the duties
of directorship.[75] Besides all his other qualifications, Narsai was

[69]Novissime vero in hanc dogmatis reccidit novitatem qua diceret
quod ira atque furore deus Adam mortalem esse praeceperit et prop-
ter eius unum delictum cunctos et necdum natos homines morte
multaverit. *Contra S. Augustinum defendentem originale peccatum,*
ed. E. Schwartz, in *Acta conciliorum oecumenicorum,* I,5 (Berlin,
1924), p. 174.

[70]*In epistolam ad Galatas* II, 15-16, ed. Swete I, p. 26; *In epistolam
ad Romanos,* V, ed. Migne col. 796ff.

[71]*Le commentaire de Theodore de Mopsueste sur les psaumes,* ed.
R. Devreesse, in *Studi e testi* XCIII (Vatican City, 1939), p. 481.

[72]*In Psalmos,* L, 7, ed. Devreesse, p. 337.

[73]Photius, *Bibliotheca,* cod. CLXXVII, ed. J. P. Migne, in *Patrologia graeca* CIII, col. 513.

[74]*In epistolam ad Romanos* IX, 14-21, ed. K. Staab (*Pauluskommen-
tare aus der griechischen Kirche, aus den Katenenhandschriften gesam-
melt, Neutestamentliche Abhandlungen* XV [Münster, 1933]), p. 144f.

[75]Vööbus, *History of Asceticism in the Syrian Orient,* II, 411ff.

a man of stature in the literary world, holding a classic position among the greatest masters. Narsai simply absorbed Theodore's theology. In fact, his acceptance was unconditional. Not only did he adopt views which were in general in the same vein as the ancient Syrian traditions; he also took over the most conspicuous element of Theodore's theology, an element which must have appeared as an innovation, namely, that Adam was created as a mortal being,[76] with its corollary, that death was natural and therefore not a punishment for Adam's sin carried over to mankind. This was something that the ancient Syrian traditions, as reflected in their leading spokesmen, do not assert.[77]

Gathering storms around the School of Edessa compelled Narsai to leave soon after Bishop Qūrā's enthronement, about A.D. 471-75,[78] i.e., before the final liquidation of this center of learning. His departure resulted in the establishment of a new school in Nisibis, on the border of the Persian territory. Narsai became the first director of the new establishment. When, as a result of the intensified doctrinal quarrels, the light of the School of Edessa was extinguished, the new school absorbed the best of its heritage. The torch of learning was carried beyond the Byzantine frontier. Soon after the appearance of the new school, it became a center for spiritual renewal. Among the other centers of intellectual and spiritual life, it held the post of preeminence. It treasured all the traditions which had been cherished in Edessa. The authority of Theodore, along with that of Diodor and Nestorius, was established as normative for hermeneutics as well as for theology. Thus Theodore's theological heritage found a safe repository, where it was guarded and cherished by faithful hands.

The establishment of this new school was of utmost importance

[76] Narsai doctois Syri homiliae et carmina, ed. A. Mingana (Mausilii, 1905), I, 100.

[77] Ephrem, In Genesim et in Exodum commentarii, ed. Tonneau, p. 33f.

[78] A. Vööbus, "Un vestige d'une lettre de Narsaï et son importance historique," in L'Orient syrien (1964).

for future developments, for its foundation and consolidation took place at a time when the final preparations were underway for organizing Christianity in the Persian territory under the Nestorian church. The decisions taken by the Synod of Bēt Lāphāt in Persia in the year 484[79] mark the end of these preparations. Seen from this angle, the establishment of the School of Nisibis could not fall into a more important epoch. In all those theological matters and questions in which this strain of Christianity was determined to go its own way, the School of Nisibis, and with it the traditions of the great Antiochian theologians, particularly those of Theodore, became the very heart in the body of the Nestorian church.

CRISIS AND AFFIRMATION

The firmly established teaching of the theologians of Edessa and Nisibis on nature was not spared opposition, however. In fact, resistance exploded in a place where it could be least expected, emerging with such vehemence that it threatened to develop into a crisis jeopardizing the unquestioned position of the ecclesiastically sanctioned doctrine.

This dispute was caused by Hēnānā, the controversial director (c.571-610) of the School of Nisibis. For his admirers he was a leader without counterpart in the contemporary theological scene. For others he was simply an *enfant terrible* who upset all the standards regarded as sacrosanct. In fact, in Hēnānā we have a man who because of his character and spiritual qualities found it difficult to follow the beaten track.[80] Something in him would not be satisfied with the traditional approach. Thus new stimuli, which, at least in part, were enriching, were introduced into the instruction and theological discussion at Nisibis. On the other hand, these were innovations which necessarily meant a departure from the normative pattern and thereby led inevitably into theological and doctrinal entanglements.

[79]*Synodicon orientale,* ed. J. B. Chabot (Paris, 1902), p. 61ff.

[80]*The Statutes of the School of Nisibis,* ed. A. Vööbus (Stockholm, 1962), Prolegomena and the commentary on Chap. iv of the Syriac text.

Hēnānā's different spirit and taste compelled him to depart from the foundation upheld by Theodore's immense authority. He was attracted to different kinds of authorities, such as Origen, Cyril of Alexandria, and John Chrysostom. This loss of loyalty involved not only christological views, isagogic questions, and principles of hermeneutics, but the entire foundation, including also his views of nature.

What Hēnānā actually taught in this respect, and how far he went in his critique of Theodore's position, we are not able to determine as we would wish. All the sources which we need for this task have perished. In this respect Hēnānā's theological adversaries have been thorough. What little has remained in the liturgical domain[81] can offer no real help in this matter. We are forced to consult only Hēnānā's adversaries. Even worse, we have no other choice than to consult the noisy and highhanded Bābai. However, in view of the lack of other sources we must be grateful that even this much is still available. At least we have some official documents at our disposal which somewhat improve our precarious situation.

For Bābai, Hēnānā had upset everything the church had been teaching. He accused Hēnānā of an eagerness for innovations in which he was not able to think through his premises and could not clearly see the consequences.[82] For Bābai, Hēnānā's position is simply fatalism and determinism. If everything is already determined by birth, then judgment and punishment as well as reward become meaningless.[83] As a consequence all laws and norms become superfluous. There is no place any more for the very foundation on which asceticism and monasticism rest, a matter which stood so close to Bābai's own heart.[84] His accu-

[81]*Ibid.*, Prolegomena II, 3.

[82]*Tašʿitā de-Mār Gīwargī,* ed. P. Bedjan in *Histoire de Mar Jabalaha, de trois autres patriarches, d'un preitre et de deux laïques, nestoriens* (Paris, 1895), p. 477.

[83]*Ibid.,* pp. 478f.

[84]*Syriac and Arabic Documents,* ed. A. Vööbus (Stockholm, 1960), pp. 176ff.

sations include the charge that Hēnānā, in his penchant for speculations, had sacrificed Christian traditions to the thoughts he took over from the Chaldeans[85] and from astrology.[86] Bābai also directed his criticism against Hēnānā's view that ascribes to man a divine nature at the Consummation (*apokatastasis*).[87] This obviously means that he was irritated by the contention that Adam was created as immortal.

Of course, we do not believe everything of which Bābai assures us. However, through his exaggerations and twistings of Hēnānā's thought we can see something which still is useful. It is clear that Hēnānā deviated from Theodore also on the question of nature. This we can take from him as certain, and here Bābai still can offer us a service.

That we are on the right track with this conclusion finds confirmation in an official document, a decision drafted for the synodical convocation that took place under the rule of Catholicos Sabrīšōᶜ in 596. One decision rejects those views which abandon the foundation laid by Theodore, namely the tradition preserved by the heads of the school, the champions of orthodoxy. The heart of the decision is the following decree: "We are watchful and remove everyone from our fellowship who has adopted [the view which] says that sin lies in nature, and that man sins not in free will, and everyone who says that the nature of Adam originally was created immortal."[88]

Hēnānā's battle was doomed to failure, although he had powerful friends without whom he could not have held his position as the director of the School of Nisibis until his death about 610. Official decisions by synodical actions renewed the confidence in the position which had endeared itself in the church. Thus the whole battle, although fought with enthusiasm and tenacity on the part of Hēnānā, remained only an intermezzo which the church wanted to forget. Thus the Syrian traditions of Antio-

[85]*Tašᶜītā de-Mār Gīwargī,* ed. Bedjan, pp. 503f.
[86]*Evagrius Ponticus,* ed. W. Frankenberg (Berlin, 1912), p. 264.
[87]*Ibid.,* p. 294.
[88]*Synodicon orientale,* ed. Chabot, pp. 198f.

chian provenance could secure their lasting place.

In Western Christianity the conception of human nature underwent great changes as it developed, even going so far in its willingness to follow Augustine that it was ready to leave the foundation of the biblical witness as well as the tradition. In Eastern Christianity the Syrian Christians have retained their ancient traditions. Amid the whirlwind of controversies, they have maintained their course, remaining loyal to their own heritage. With their emphasis on freedom, the ethical strength and the moral responsibility of man preserves something of that which, in its deepest layers, rests in the gospel tradition itself.

This whole question would have only a limited value in the history of theology if we were here dealing with phenomena which were nothing more than incidents, often barren and sterile. There is more involved here, however, and our results are enhanced by something which calls for special attention. It is not an accident that the Christians we have referred to are the same Christians who have written many of the most beautiful pages in the history of Christendom—pages testifying to the power of the Christian faith in active life,[89] educational institutions,[90] intellectual endeavor,[91] and missionary enterprise.[92] All of this evokes admiration from the student of history. From here special rays of light fall on the questions discussed above and put them into the proper perspective.

[89]Vööbus, *History of Asceticism in the Syrian Orient,* Vol. I, pp. 234ff.

[90]A. Vööbus, *The School of Nisibis: Its history and contribution to the history of intellectual culture (Corpus Scriptorum Christianorum Orientalium,* Subsidia [Louvain, 1964]).

[91]See A. Vööbus, "Mar Abraham de-Bet Rabban and his Role in the Exegetical Traditions of the School of Nisibis," (to be published).

[92]Vööbus, *History of Ascetism in the Syrian Orient,* Vol. IV (in preparation).

THE GNOSTIC VIEW

JOHANNES KNUDSEN

THE GNOSTIC VIEW

In Hans Christian Andersen's fairy tale *The Snow Queen*, the devil constructs a mirror whose reflection distorts everything so that the good and beautiful vanish and the useless and ugly appear even worse than they are. "The most beautiful landscapes appeared like cooked spinach and the best people became hideous or were turned upside down without a stomach." The devil and his cohorts attempt to carry their invention to heaven to make a mockery of God and the angels, but the mirror is shattered and destroyed. Unfortunately billions of pieces are dispersed throughout the world and whenever they enter the heart or the eyes of human beings the victims see only the wrongs in the world.

Andersen was no great theologian and he nourished a romantic view of life. Before using his parable, therefore, it is wise and necessary that we take the safeguards necessary to maintain an adequate doctrine of sin (especially original sin) and the fall. In our day a person who does not make an adequate confession of sin is under suspicion, and one who claims to see and believe the good and the beautiful is often regarded as a hopeless traditionalist or an anti-existentialist. Let us therefore properly confess "that we are by nature sinful and unclean," and let us hope that we are thereby released to make use of the parable without suspicion of heresy or subversion.

When we discuss the problem of Nature and Grace, and "that we should make that effort is," in the understanding of Professor Sittler, "the commanding task in this moment of our common history,"[1] we must allow for the possibility that a certain view of nature and of man, which is held by a great many loyal and

[1] Joseph Sittler, "Called to Unity," *The Ecumenical Review*, XIV (1962), 177-87.

conservative Christians, is a demonic distortion of the world
which God has created and of which he "saw that it was good."
Even considering and confessing that "cursed is the ground
because of you" (Gen. 3:17), it might be possible that many in
the church or many who camp at its edges or share its heritage
are the victims of a demonic view which invaded and infected
the Christian world at the very outset of Christian thinking.

It shall be our thesis that such is the case, and we shall start
out with a postulate to that effect, hoping to document and
demonstrate the postulate in the subsequent argument. The postulate is not new, nor are the arguments new, but the justification
for their reconsideration is that advances in scholarship have
given us a wealth of material which demands attention. In fact,
everything that has been written about our subject prior to 1950
must be read with caution. When we therefore propose to discuss
the gnostic view of the world and of man, and when we postulate
that this view is an extraneous view inimical to the biblical view
of the world and of man and one which has penetrated Christian
thinking and caused a demonic distortion of the biblical view,
we hope that the consideration of new material will make the
pertinence of our effort evident.

We do not propose to discuss Gnosticism. In fact, it shall be
our postulate that there is not, nor has there ever been, anything
that could justifiably be called Gnosticism, unless we speak of it
in general and ambiguous terms such as we might use today in
talking about conservatism or liberalism. If we use the term we
should write it in the lower case and think of it as designating
a "view" found in diverse forms that vary from group to group
or from one individual to another. When Seeberg says that
"Gnosticism was the attempt to establish the universal religion,"[2]
he is making Gnosticism into a corpus in a way which the sources
do not warrant. The sources do not speak of Gnosticism; they
use the adjective gnostic, and they speak of people who were
gnostic (*gnostikoi*). Even Irenaeus prefers to speak of them as
heretics or in terms of the leader of their school of thought,

[2]Reinhold Seeberg, *Textbook of the History of Doctrines* (Grand
Rapids: Baker Book House, 1958), p. 101.

such as Valentinus. "Gnosticism" is a later term, and when we use it to indicate a specific religion with a distinctive body of thought, we are reading our modern evaluation into the sources.

If there is no corpus in the ancient world which could rightly be called Gnosticism, there were ideas and persons aplenty which could be called gnostic. Our first description of these comes through the attack upon them by the apologists of the second century, of whom Irenaeus is the most important. In the writings of the apologists the gnostics are treated as heretics. The apologists' description of the gnostic distortion of Christianity is severely critical, even tinged with horror; their analysis would be more accurately termed condemnation. Of this we must not be overly critical, in view of the situation in which the apologists found themselves; but we must also recognize that their approach to the problem, while justified and necessary, may not be the most fruitful one for us. The apologists viewed the gnostics principally with reference to gnostic denials or distortions of Christology, and they emphasized strongly the falsely redemptive claim of knowledge or *gnosis*. It is therefore only from the point of view of an outraged orthodoxy that the classical sources give us information about the basic view of man entertained by the gnostics. Up to the twentieth century the emphasis has therefore been placed on the alleged redemption through knowledge (hence the term "Gnosticism") and upon the heresy of the gnostic doctrine of creation and redemption. No one approached the problem from the point of view of anthropology and cosmology, to see how the gnostic view of creation and redemption grew out of a view of man and the world. "Gnosticism" was regarded as a philosophical religion, different in nature from the mystery religions and primarily concerned with philosophical speculations and philosophical redemption. The epitome of this interpretation came when the great Harnack, ordinarily an astute judge of issues, called "Gnosticism" an "acute Hellenization of Christianity."[3]

[3]Adolf Harnack, *Lehrbuch der Dogmengeschichte* (Freiburg: J. C. B. Mohr, 1886), I, 158.

In the research carried on in the twentieth century it soon became evident that there was something wrong with this picture. Even though Greek philosophy was inclined to separate the divine from the earthly, this basic dualism could not account for the elements of separation of the world from God which were inherent in the gnostic view. Scholars like Bousset and Reitzenstein therefore brought Persian or Oriental dualism into the picture. Lidzbarsky called attention to the connection with Mandaeans and Manicheans. *Pistis Sophia* and the *Corpus Hermeticum* were taken to be sources for "Gnosticism," which was considered to be a syncretistic religion, in which the primary influence was considered to be oriental (Persian). "Gnosticism is Hellenizing in so far as the problems of Greek and Roman culture influence its course, but the means by which it seeks to solve these problems are of essentially oriental origin."[4] "Gnosticism was the attempt to establish the universal religion, in which the religious problems of the educated world in that age should be answered by means of ancient oriental mythology and magic, with the addition of the gospel of the church."[5]

Hans Jonas' discerning work *Gnosis und spätantiker Geist* (1934) seriously undermined the artificial notion of a religion called "Gnosticism," that is, a delineated corpus with views and convictions peculiar to it and expressed in a distinctive vocabulary. Jonas called attention to the impossibility of a syncretistic combination of the philosophical dualism of Greece, which was highly speculative, and the mythological dualism of Persia, which was cultic and dynamic. The ancient and fascinating game of a theoretical reconstruction of a world religion, which was a rival of Christianity and which could be fashioned out of the various and varying sources available, was shown up for what it was. The significance of the oriental sources had been greatly exaggerated, said Jones, and both the Mandaean and Manichaean sources, while probably providing excellent testimony of a further development of dualistic trends, could not be taken as

[4]Seeberg, pp. 100 f.
[5]*Ibid.*, p. 101.

documentary evidence of first and second century situations. The pendulum thus swung back toward a stronger appreciation of Hellenistic influence, but not so conclusively as to end discussion. The problem was great and the sources were skimpy or prejudiced. Scholars were cautious. But the perspective of the apologists, i.e., from the redemptive or salvatory point of view, still prevailed.

Then in 1947 a collection of documents was discovered in the sands of Egypt near the village of Nag Hammadi. Upon examination these were found to be gnostic documents, and a strong interest in our problem was rekindled. As yet only a portion of documents have been given critical publication, notably *The Gospel According to Thomas*[6] and *The Gospel of Philip*.[7] There are still many aspects to be considered, for instance, the possible relation of the documents to the literature of the Dead Sea Scrolls; but it is evident that we have a significant body of material from the second century which must be used in analyzing and determining the significance of gnostic thought. Already a number of books have appeared in English which must be considered. Foremost among them are those by Jonas, Robert M. Grant, and Jean Doresse.[8] While extreme caution must be exercised, a number of pertinent observations can already be

[6]*The Gospel According to Thomas,* Coptic text established and translated by A. Guillaumont, H. Ch. Puech, G. Quispel, W. Till, and Yassah Abd El Masih (Leiden: E. J. Brill, Ltd., and Harper & Brothers, 1959). The number preceding each passage cited in this essay is the number of the *logion.*

[7]*The Gospel of Philip,* translated from the Coptic text, with an introduction and commentary by R. McL. Wilson (New York: Harper & Row, and London: A. R. Mobray & Co., Ltd., 1962). The number preceding each passage cited in this essay is the number of the line.

[8]Hans Jonas, *The Gnostic Religion* (Enlarged ed., Boston: Beacon Press, 1963); Robert M. Grant, *Gnosticism and Early Christianity* (New York: Columbia University Press, 1959) and *Gnosticism* (New York: Harper & Brothers, 1961); Jean Doresse, *The Secret Books of the Egyptian Gnostics* (London: Hollis and Carter, 1960).

made which help us in our understanding and to some extent change the customary understanding of gnostic thought.

1. The chronology of gnostic influence is authoritatively pushed back into the early generations of Christianity. It is no longer necessary to make elastic conjectures in order to tie in the "gnostic" influences with New Testament writing. It is evident that the terminology and the ideas which we find in John and Paul, and against which these authors argued (even while using them in a familiar way) were commonly known religious concepts in the early days of the church.

2. The description of the gnostics given by the second-century apologists is, in the main, verified. Although the content of gnostic teaching is not nearly as outré or extreme as in Irenaeus' description, the main tenor is the same. Irenaeus knew what he was thinking about. The main difference is that Irenaeus' account was that of an outraged critic and a staunch defender of apostolic Christianity, while the Nag Hammadi documents present us with the actual writings of gnostics.

3. The Nag Hammadi gospels are closer to the Synoptic Gospels than they are to Irenaeus' description of Valentinus' teaching from which they are quite far removed. They use teachings of Jesus, many of which they have in common with the Synoptics. They also use additional material, however, and they distort the material they share with the Synoptics in a way which presents a teaching and a theology impossible to reconcile with the teachings of the New Testament and the Apostolic Fathers.

4. The notion that there was a distinctive difference between gnostic sects and mystery religions in regard to the cultic and sacramental character of their theology must be discarded. One of the surprising things about *The Gospel of Philip* in particular is the emphasis upon sacraments, of which it lists five. "The Lord did everything in a mystery, a baptism and a chrism and a eucharist and a redemption and a bride-chamber" (line 68).

5. The emphasis upon *gnosis* is far less prominent in the Nag Hammadi gospels than we have previously understood it to be

true of gnostic thought. *Gnosis* is a means of redemption, but it is not the exclusive means. "Gnostic" teachings have a strong ethical and sacramental character, and it is perhaps actually a distortion to characterize them mainly by the word gnostic, if by this term we intend to designate an esoteric, philosophical, religious body of thought.

6. As Robert M. Grant has pointed out in his *Gnosticism and Early Christianity* the fourth element in the gnostic emphasis is the Judaistic influence (the other three being the Hellenistic, the Oriental, and the Christian). This is not only, as Grant says, an extremely heterodox Judaism or even Judaism in reverse; this is also a rejection of Judaism. "When we were Hebrews, we were orphans and had (only) our mother, but when we became Christians we obtained a father and a mother."[9]

7. The main emphasis seems to be a sharp dualism, undoubtedly Persian in its origin, by which the whole material world is held to be evil, sinful, and corrupt. The emphasis upon release from the world and from sin, which is manifested in *gnosis* and in the sacraments, takes its character from the underlying emphasis upon the nature of the world and of man. It is therefore important that we approach the gnostics from an understanding of their anthropology and cosmology, rather than from their concept of redemption, especially as this latter is seen through the eyes of the apologists.

If the main emphasis in the gnostic penetration of Christianity is dualism with a sharp condemnation of the material world, then we must be aware of the gnostic description of the world and the gnostic accounts of creation. The most elaborate story is found in Irenaeus' report of the teachings of the disciples of Valentinus. The whole story is too long and complicated to tell, so we must condense and paraphrase it from the account in *Adversus Haereses* (Book I, Chaps. 1-5).[10] (The "they" in the account are the disciples of Valentinus.)

[9]*Gospel of Philip,* line 6.

[10]The passages cited, here and below, are from *The Ante-Nicene Fathers* (New York: Charles Scribner's Sons, 1899).

The first perfect, pre-existent Aeon, called Proarche, Propator, and Bythus, consorted with Sige to produce Nous (also called Monogenes) and Aletheia. These produced other Aeons who again reproduced to a total of thirty. The last one was Sophia. Only Nous knew the Propator, and Sophia, a degenerate Aeon, had a passion to seek the nature of the Father. In her passion she produced an amorphous substance out of her female nature. She was grieved to see it and bewildered. "And hence, they declare, material substance had its beginning from ignorance and grief, and fear and bewilderment." Sophia was purified and returned to the Pleroma but her enthymesis (inborn idea) was expelled. This was called Achamoth and it (she) was without form or figure, until Christ dwelling on high took pity upon her and imparted a figure to her, "but merely as respected substance, and not so as to convey intelligence. Having effected this, he withdrew his influence, and returned, leaving Achamoth to herself, in order that she, becoming sensible of her suffering as being severed from the Pleroma, might be influenced by the desire of better things, while she possessed in the meantime a kind of odour of immortality left in her by Christ and the Holy Spirit. . . . Having then obtained a form, along with intelligence, and being immediately deserted by that Logos who had been visibly present with her—that is, by Christ—she strained herself to discover that light which had forsaken her, but could not effect her purpose. . . ." She was in grief, fear, perplexity, ignorance, and "this collection [of passions], they declare, was the substance of the matter from which this world was formed."

.   .   .   .

"These three kinds of existence, then, having, according to them, been now formed,—one from the passion, which was matter; a second from the conversion, which was animal; and the third, that which she [Achamoth] herself brought forth, which was spiritual,—she next addressed herself to the task of giving these form." She created the Demiurge who was "the Father and God of everything outside the Pleroma, being the creator of all animal and material substances."

.   .   .   .

"Having thus formed the world, he (the Demiurge) also created the earthy [part of] man, not taking him from this dry earth, but from an invisible substance consisting of fusible and fluid matter, and then afterwards . . . breathed into him the animal part of his nature."

.   .   .   .

"This then is the kind of man whom they conceive of: he has his animal soul from the Demiurge, his body from the earth, his fleshy part from matter, and his spiritual man from the mother Achamoth."

The Gospel According to Thomas does not indulge in the above kind of mythologizing, but it does have several passages that show the same kind of criticism and contempt of the world.

(29) Jesus said: if the flesh *(sarx)* had come into existence because of <the> spirit *(pneuma)*, it is a marvel; but *(de)* if <the> spirit *(pneuma)* (has come into existence) because of the body *(sōma)*, it is a marvel of marvels. But *(alla)* I marvel at how *(pōs)* this great wealth has made its home in this poverty.

(56) Jesus said: Whoever has known the world *(kosmos)* has found a corpse *(ptōma)*, and whoever has found a corpse *(ptōma)*, of him the world *(kosmos)* is not worthy.

(87) Jesus said: Wretched *(talaipōron)* is the body *(sōma)* which depends upon a body *(sōma)*, and wretched *(talaipōros)* is the soul *(psychē)* which depends upon these two.

The Gospel of Philip, which R. McL. Wilson says in his introduction "can be located with confidence as a work deriving from the Valentinian school," has echoes of the story we quoted from Irenaeus, and it has the same condemnatory view of the world.

(36) But Sophia is barren, without child.

(39) Echamoth is one thing and Echmoth is another. Echamoth is simply Sophia, but Echmoth the Sophia of death.

(22) So it is with the soul. It is a precious thing and came to be in a despised body.

(63) In this world there is good and evil. Its good is not good and its evil is not evil.

(99) The world came into being through a transgression. For he who created it wanted to create it indestructible and immortal. He fell away and did not attain to his hope.

Irenaeus' main argument against the gnostics has to do with their substitution of *gnosis* for the salvatory act of God in Christ as it is reenacted in the sacrament of the church. He does, however, strongly refute the gnostic story of creation, emphasizing that God created the world, that he created it through the Word, and that man was created in the image and likeness of God. That the latter is significant is seen through the recapitulation of man's creation in the incarnation of Christ. A few quotations will attest to this.

> That God is the Creator of the World is accepted even by those very persons who in many ways speak against Him, and yet acknowledge Him, styling Him the Creator . . . not to mention that all the Scriptures call out [to the same effect], and the Lord teaches us of this Father. . . . For even creation reveals Him who formed it, and the very work made suggests Him who made it, and the world manifests Him who ordered it. The Universal Church, moreover, through the whole world, has received this tradition from the apostles.[11]

> [John], the disciple of the Lord, therefore desiring to put an end to all such doctrines, and to establish the rule of truth in the Church, that there is one Almighty God, who made all things by His Word, both visible and invisible; showing at the same time, that by the Word, through whom God made the creation, He also bestowed salvation on the men included in the creation; thus commenced his teaching in the Gospel: "In the beginning was the Word, and the Word was with God, and the Word was God. . . . All things were made by Him, and without Him was nothing made."[12]

> It was necessary, therefore, that the Lord, coming to the lost sheep, and making recapitulation of so comprehensive a dispensation, and seeking after His own handiwork, should save that very man who had been created after His image and likeness, that is, Adam, filling up the times of His condemnation, which had been incurred through disobedience. . . .[13]

For I have shown that the Son of God did not then begin to

[11]*Adversus Haereses*, II.9.i (*ANF*, Vol. I, p. 369).
[12]*Ibid.*, III.11.i (*ANF*, Vol. I, p. 426).
[13]*Ibid.*, II.23.i (*ANF*, Vol. I, p. 455).

exist, being with the Father from the beginning; but when He became incarnate, and was made man. He recapitulated [*recap-itulavit*] the long line of human beings, and furnished us, in a brief, comprehensive manner, with salvation; so that what we had lost in Adam—namely, to be according to the image and likeness of God—we might recover in Christ Jesus.[14]

Having demonstrated that the gnostic view of the material world is one of condemnation, which ascribed the creation of the material world to an inferior being who was outside the Pleroma, and having shown how Irenaeus, the great contemporary critic of the gnostic views, places over against this the biblical view of creation and incarnation as he understands it in terms of the concepts of his age, we shall test the two postulates with which we started this essay. The one was that there was no religion which could be called "Gnosticism," only so-called gnostic views. The second was that the gnostic views of man and creation, which were contrary to the biblical view, entered into the Christian thought world, perverting the concept of nature as well as the concept of grace.

The view of "Gnosticism" as a religion, that is, as a delineated corpus with views and convictions peculiar to it and different from the three other great factors in the religious world of antiquity, namely the philosophy of the Greco-Roman world, the mystery religions, and Christianity (or Judaism), stems from a failure to see the nature of the religious atmosphere or the totality of the religious world at the time. This failures derives at least in part from the fact that we have for many centuries viewed this world through the perspective (or should we say the spectacles?) of western culture. The intellectualizing of religion in our culture has obscured the possibility that there might have been an entirely different type of religious understanding in the ancient world. When we encounter a type of religious expression which is different from our own, we relegate it to a strange and different (and heretical) corpus of beliefs which we then proclaim to be some kind of religion, a syncretistic religion perhaps,

[14]*Ibid.*, III.18.i (*ANF*, Vol. I, p. 466).

but nevertheless a religion. We look with a bit of suspicion upon Irenaeus, the great antagonist of the gnostics, because he used the same strange terminology, and we gloss over the fact that St. Paul deliberately spoke the same language, something we attempt to conceal in our translations of St. Paul and other New Testament writers.

The fact is that the terminology which the gnostics used was not a "gnostic" terminology; it was a commonly used terminology reflecting a generally accepted view of the world and of religion.[15] The gnostics used it to their own purpose, to be sure. They used it to express a strange and perverted form of Christianity, an unattractive and even hideous interpretation of the world and its life, and we are not trying to say that their particular cosmology and theology was very generally accepted. In fact, it shall be our second point that the gnostics brought an oriental dualism into the religious picture which it is difficult to reconcile even with the dualism found in Greek philosophy. But the terms and the concepts the gnostics used were so generally understood and so commonly accepted that someone from that period would have great difficulty in understanding our relegation of them to some obscure or esoteric or heretical form of religion.

Samuel Laeuchli's excellent study of the problem of language in the early days of Christianity begins with a brilliant chapter which shows how gnostic usage changed the meaning of words. He states that " 'Gnosticism' is thus the structure of thought of which the church becomes seriously aware in the first half of the second century and by which Christianity is profoundly influenced, positively or negatively, in its formulation of church, canon, and theology."[16] It seems to me that Laeuchli misses the

[15]Among the various suggestions that have been made to designate this common substratum without prejudging the case are "proto-gnostic" and "syncretistic." We have tried to call attention to the distinction between the substratum and the gnostic distortions of it by placing ambiguous uses of the word gnostic in quotation marks.

[16]Samuel Laeuchli, *The Language of Faith* (Nashville and New York: Abingdon, 1962), p. 17.

point of the whole problem and of the relation between the church and this structure of thought. The "structure of thought" in the first half of the second century is not gnostic. That structure is a common one in the religious atmosphere of the time, and it is not an invention or a possession of the gnostics. They used the language that was available; they influenced it, changed it, distorted and twisted it, and they exerted a tremendous influence, but their relationship to the language is secondary. The language and the concepts were there before the gnostics made use of them and filled them with their own content.

As was mentioned earlier, one reason we fail to see this is that we are here confronting a whole sphere of religious life or a whole genre of religious concepts which falls outside the religious landscapes which we have mapped out for ourselves in our analysis of the ancient world. The Danish philosopher Svend Ranulf has pointed out that in approaching literary documents from another age one of two approaches can be followed. "One can either interpret each individual text against the background of the civilization in question, and in accordance with everything otherwise known about it, or each text can be isolated from its cultural setting, and be interpreted against the background of the investigator's own civilization and in accordance with it."[17] The latter is the easier course, says Ranulf, and the only one possible in the earlier stages of investigation. When study of the subject has advanced, however, the question arises "whether those passages which in themselves *can* be interpreted from modern points of view cannot also be interpreted in accordance with the alien views which the investigators have been forced to accept in interpreting certain other passages, and, if so, whether this interpretation ought not to be preferred throughout."[18] When we come across varieties of thought differ-

[17]Svend Ranulf, quoted in Johannes Munck, "The New Testament and Gnosticism," p. 237, in William Klassen and Graydon F. Snyder, ed., *Current Issues in New Testament Interpretation* (New York: Harper & Brothers, 1962).

[18]*Ibid.,* p. 238.

ent from those which should proceed from our predispositions, we are inclined either to relegate them to the weird and distorted world of the gnostics, those ancient heretics, or we speak condescendingly of an ancient "mythology" which modern man naturally cannot accept. When in the Bible we catch glimpses of the ancient religious world, we speak of "biblical concepts" and "biblical language," as if we had discovered something strangely unique attaching to God's special revelation to his people.

The truth is, however, that so-called "biblical languages," that is, the language of the Bible, was the religious language common to the whole religious world in ancient times, and "biblical concepts," the understanding of such things as soul and body, spirit, worship, sacrifice, salvation, and a long list of others, were simply common concepts used in religious understanding. It is not strange, nor is it an embarassment, that St. Paul makes frequent and strong use of terms which he is not supposed to use because they are "gnostic." St. Paul had no hesitation or embarassment about the use of such terms. To understand this fully we must examine the Greek words which lie behind our translations; this is especially true of Colossians 1-2, where St. Paul meets the gnostic argument head on. Let us look at some of these passages.

1:12 the lot of the saints in light
1:13 the domination of darkness
1:15 the image of God, the first-born of all creation
1:16 in him all things were created, in heaven and on earth, visible and invisible, whether thrones or dominions or principalities or authorities
1:18 he is the head of the body, the church
1:19 in him the fulness [*plērōma*] was pleased to dwell. (The R.S.V. translates "fulness of God," but the Greek text has only the word *plērōma*.)
1:22 he has now reconciled (*apokatalassō*) in his body of flesh by his death
1:25 I became a servant (*diakonos*) by the economy (*oikonomia*)

of God given to me so that you might fulfill *(plērōsai)* the
word of God

1:26 the mystery hidden for . . . generations

1:27 this mystery—which is Christ in you

2:2   the knowledge *(epignōsis)* of God's mystery, of Christ

2:3   in whom are hid all the treasures of wisdom *(sophia)* and
knowledge *(gnosis)*

2:8   elemental spirits of the universe

2:9   in him dwells the whole fulness of deity bodily *(to plērōma
tēs theotētos sōmatikōs)*

2:10 you have come to fulness of life *(peplērōmenoi)* in him who
is the head of all rule *(archē)* and authority *(exousia)*

This is a fearless and deliberate use of many of the words we
find in the "gnostic vocabulary." St. Paul does not make defiant
use of "gnostic" words. He makes use of words that are common
to all, into which he, like the gnostics, pours a unique content.

The key words of the "gnostic vocabulary" are used frequently in the New Testament. A few statistics will make this
clear. Here are six important words, each followed by two
numbers, the first indicating the frequency of their New Testament use, and the second (in parentheses) the frequency of their
use by St. Paul: *mystērion* 28 (20), *sophia* 51 (28), *plērōma*
17 (13), *gnōsis* 29 (23), *aiōn* 103 (32), *teleios* 19 (8). Of these
mystērion and *plērōma* are perhaps the most telling, because the
others may have a usage apart from their religious usage.
Mystērion is a technical term in the ancient world, referring
always to an act with a salvatory content. Its element of secrecy,
of which we make the most in our translations and commentaries,
is subordinate to the salvatory significance. St. Paul uses it boldly
to indicate the Christian salvation when, in Colossians 1:27 and
2:2, he makes *mystērion* identical with Christ. *Plērōma* is, of
course, the favorite "gnostic" word for referring to divinity. The
fullness of God is his power, his glory, his dominion; and all
the aeons, those many and strange sub-divine creatures who share
the effulgence of God, though they are far removed from him,
are all part of the *plērōma*. St. Paul uses this word without reser-
vation to express his Christian understanding of God. In Colos-

sians 1:19 he says that the *plērōma* dwelt in Christ; he does not
say "the *plērōma* of God," as our translations usually render
plērōma.

In contrast to the approach of philosophy, the religious terminology of the ancient world was not analytical or theoretical.
It was dynamic, corporate, and cultic. Religion was not an
explanation or a principle; it was action, it was contemporaneity,
it was salvation. Cosmology was not a speculative conjecture
as to what a concept has to do with the affairs of the world;
it was a natural and necessary way of saying that that which
happened in the divine order (and this was identical with that
which happened in the worship) in and of itself included all
things in heaven and on earth. That is why the *anakephalaiōsasthai*
of Ephesians 1:10 should not be translated, as is customary, with
the word "unite"—"a plan for the fulness of time, to unite all
things in him, things in heaven and on earth"—but rather: "as
a plan to create anew through Christ, in a decisive and central
act of history, God's order of all things in heaven and on earth."
This kind of terminology is not "gnostic," nor is it specifically
Christian. It is common to all religious expression in the world
of the first two centuries of our calendar.

There is thus no religion or religious corpus which can be
called "Gnosticism." There is no vocabulary peculiar to such
a corpus which can be designated as a "gnostic vocabulary" in
contrast to a "Christian vocabulary" or a "biblical language."
There is, however, a gnostic point of view and a gnostic use of
common words, which is contrary to the biblical view of man
and the world, and which uses the common vocabulary in a
specific way. This use of the vocabulary is in deep contrast to
the biblical usage; it represents a deviation from the biblical
usage which can be called nothing less than a distortion when it
pretends to be the biblical view. This is easily demonstrated, as
one glance at the gnostic accounts of creation will make obvious;
the difficulty comes in the application. In all too many instances
we find a gnostic view of man maintained by Christians in our

own day together with the contention that this view is the biblical view. The slivers from the shattered mirror blur our vision so that we have difficulty recognizing distortions of the biblical view. The devil wins his most important victory when he has convinced us that the distortion is really the biblical view. It is therefore necessary to make a forceful case for that which everyone takes for granted in theory but which is so often unrelated to reality.

According to the gnostic view all material things, including the physical world round about us and the physical side of man's nature, is sinful, unclean, perverted, corrupt, depraved, contaminated. The world is not created by God but by a lower creature who is outside the *plērōma* of aeons or sub-divine beings. In the gnostic view Christ, too, is a lower being, but for the moment we are concerned not with Christology but with the world and man. As a consequence of the gnostic view, all that perpetuates and propagates material nature is sinful and unclean. Sex is thus sinful and unclean. Man is not created in the image and likeness of God. He is trapped in his sordid body and must be liberated, through *gnōsis* or through the sacraments, in order to rise through the aeons and reach redemption. Everything material in man must be renounced and discarded; only the spiritual is good.

The problem with this view is not that it emphasizes man's sinful nature. The Bible does this and does so emphatically. But the gnostic view denounces the physical world completely, and this is where Christian thought begins to get sidetracked, and eventually goes off the track. Because the Bible and the gnostics both speak about sin, it is assumed that they mean the same thing. The gnostics are then followed in their condemnation of human nature and in their belief that man is totally depraved. As a consequence, nature suffers condemnation along with man's sin. Nature becomes a victim of a gnostic interpretation of a Christian affirmation. We abandon the creation by God and condemn nature to sin along with the recognition of our own sinful nature.

What is missing in all this is a doctrine of the fall and of man's persisting disobedience. Gnostics have no doctrine of the fall of man, because they have no doctrine of creation by God and of creation in the image of God. The reason for a similar deficiency in our own situation is not hard to see. So many people have eliminated all consideration of the fall, congratulating themselves on their cleverness which enables them to refute and discard the silly old belief that "in Adam's fall we sinned all." In ridding themselves of an ancient myth, an ancient "superstition," they believe that they have been liberated and emancipated from an ancient bondage to sin. The result, however, has been just the opposite. The moment man dispenses with a doctrine of the fall he is apt to be caught in a gnostic view of unclean and depraved human nature. Experience has convinced man that he is not free and not good. He is thus trapped by his own claim to be free. He either becomes a gnostic or he becomes totally bewildered and uprooted. He is amorphous like Achamoth. Christian pessimists are gnostic by tradition or by choice; non-Christian pessimists are gnostic by self-entrapment.

The gnostic rejection and condemnation of nature and of man is a penetration into Christian thought of the dualism of Persia. It is commonly asserted that this dualism entered through Manichaeism and that it was perpetuated by certain Church Fathers and medieval monastics. But this estimate is three or four centuries behind the times and fails to take account of more recent evidence indicating that Persian dualism entered into the Christian world through the gnostics of the first and second centuries. St. John and St. Paul fought valiantly against them; Irenaeus and Tertullian attacked them violently. But perhaps the gnostics won the battle after all. There is a frightening lot of gnostic thought in the Christian as well as the non-Christian world today. The minute pieces of the shattered mirror are everywhere.

NEW PERSPECTIVES ON NATURE AND GRACE

BERNARD EUGENE MELAND

NEW PERSPECTIVES
ON NATURE AND GRACE

I

Since the Enlightment much of the discussion of the theme nature and grace has paralleled that of reason and revelation. The underlying assumptions controlling these discussions have arisen from a conception of nature as being a realm of orderly, predictable motion in which occurrences are determined in the imagery of a mechanism. Insofar as the term grace has had any meaning at all in this context it tended to merge with the notion of freedom, thus becoming metaphorical in meaning, expressing unexpected respite from the determinacies of nature. But for the rigorous thinker, grace in this context, like the word revelation, was expendable. The discourse in vogue did not demand it for conveying what was involved or implied.

Kant's formulation of a critical philosophy, providing for a distinction between the noumenal and the phenomenal realms, fixed the imagery that was to inform such discussions throughout the creative period of liberal theology. One can, in fact, see this imagery persisting in modified form in certain neo-Protestant theologies of our own time.

Although it was Kant's intention to establish critical bounds for scientific inquiry, and legitimate grounds for the pursuit of religious inquiry, the implications of his distinctions were to lead to unfortunate results. On the one hand, it became the basis for defining the religious life over against nature, the assertion of our life of freedom in decision and moral will against the automatic and mechanistic occurrences of nature. In this kind of differentiation nature was to be made the "fall-guy" in theology, and any condescension to nature's claims or concern with its destiny was looked upon as a "falling from grace." On the other hand, Kant's critical distinctions became the grounds for asserting that pure reason, capable of producing factual knowledge, could be employed only by the sciences in the study of phenomena. The sciences thus appeared to receive a kind of accrediting from Kant's analysis which no other area of inquiry could claim. And this, in turn, was to give to the sciences an independence from theology, philosophy, and other humanistic studies, even in areas where, presumably, mind and matter, body and spirit, intermingled. Scientists were thus set free to pursue their tasks, unmolested by theologians, unperturbed by ethical questions, undeterred by the moral consequences of their inquiries. As persons, of course, they were responsible to these concerns. As scientists, however, they had no responsibility for them. By the same token theologians were freed from being concerned with the implications of scientific findings, and thus could pursue their task with seeming indifference to intellectual changes indicated by such findings. This was to have serious consequences for theology and for religious thought.

But the implications of this strategy of thought were more devastating with regard to understanding man and his world. For the release of the scientists from involvement with the attending mystery of the noumenal and personal aspects of existence enabled them to construct an ever more complete and unyielding image of nature as a world machine. Descartes and Newton had provided the initial impetus to think of nature after this fashion, and the name of Newton was to be linked with this image, thus giving to it the authority of his immense prestige in modern Western culture. Yet the scientific vision of nature that was to emerge in the nineteenth century went far beyond Newton in elevating the technical and the mechanical aspects of nature to the detriment of all human interests which looked to the free world of spirit for its mode of justification. When Charles Darwin's *On The Origin of the Species* (1859) demonstrated man's linkage to this vast world of mechanism, the threat to a "spiritual" interpretation of man and history seemed complete. For many of Darwin's contemporaries who felt the force of his theory, religion and all idealistic interpretations of man pointing to a dimension and destiny beyond his physical existence, clearly seemed to be on the way out.

The philosopher who did the most in the nineteenth century to temper and redirect this flood-tide of mechanism was Rudolph Hermann Lotze, whose *Microcosmus* (1856-64) had in some respects anticipated Darwin's theory. Insofar as liberal theologians of that period were able to cope with this advancing and ever more demanding mood of mechanism they drew heavily upon the philosophy of Lotze.[1] Lotze was a medical scientist and philosopher at Göttingen and later at Berlin. He encountered human beings both as persons and as organisms, and he never lost sight of the fact that, while the organism as a system of mechanisms was indispensable to the life of the person, its mechanisms nevertheless were instrumental to what occurred at the level of personal existence. Underlying both mechanism and personality, he pointed out, is the Creator who cherishes and works through both of these levels. That the influence of Lotze's thought was to issue in an exaggerated valuation of the person, and thus fashion God and Spirit in the image of man or of the human equation, need not detract from the steadying role he played in this crucial period when a growing scientism was in the ascendancy.

It must be said too that, in the face of an ever perfecting method of prediction and verification that was being developed in one science after another, the appeal to less certain and more tenuous lines of argument in philosophy and religion in behalf of man's "higher nature" could only become, at best, a dubious alternative. Philosophical idealism labored valiantly to counter the claims of a committed scientific naturalism; but it never was an even match for its adversary in academic circles when the

[1] This is paticularly evident in the theology of Albrecht Ritschl and the American Ritschlians, as well as in the writings of the American personalist, Borden P. Bowne. Lotze was the major stimulus back of much of the personalistic theism that was to follow.

going got rough. One of the pathetic aspects of the history of higher education in this country is the way one discipline after another succumbed to the seduction of the vogue of emulating scientific method. This became the way to knowledge *par excellence*.

But whether idealism or scientism prevailed in this contest, the problem of nature and grace, seen in this context, remained in a stalemate. For idealism shared the view of nature that informed scientific thinking, and thus, no less than scientism, contributed to a way of thinking that created the impasse, seeing nature simply as the antithesis of spirit. At best nature could be viewed as the antecedent condition of man's personal existence. And after Darwin, idealists and other theists who employed the evolutionary description of life to expand the story of the human venture made much of the necessity of this antecedent era of jungle ruthlessness in man's climb to his personal level of existence.[2] Liberal theologians were able to find a new rationale for the doctrine of sin in thus correlating evolutionary and idealistic thinking. Sin was seen to be the persistence of this jungle heritage in the person. As Shailer Mathews once put it, "Sin is the backward pull," "the persuasions of animal impulses" in man, or "the survival in man of his bestial background."[3]

II

Our generation, it seems, has had to go the full length of the road in idealizing man and personality in order to catch a glimpse of the limitations of his characteristic structure. Other factors have entered into the story of this reaction. The process of idealizing man by defining him against nature was to run down of its own accord; but at the same time it was being steadily undermined by undercurrents of dissolution which had begun as minority voices of protest during the heyday of Hegel—notably Marx and Kierkegaard, and later Nietzsche and Freud. But that

[2] Cf. John Fiske, *Through Nature to God* (Boston: Houghton, Mifflin Co., 1899), pp. 54-56.

[3] *The Gospel and the Modern Man* (New York: Macmillan Co., 1910), pp. 164f.

is another story. The undermining of modern idealism by recalcitrant forces born of its own intellectual ferment, however, does not account fully for what has happened in our era to alter our thinking about the problem of nature and grace. What is decisive here is the radical revision of our understanding of the human structure of existence itself. This change in perspective goes so deep in the forming and revising of present-day presuppositions that it readily escapes attention. The obscuring of it is further facilitated by the fact that modern thinkers in various parts of the Western world, working within various disciplines, have come upon the basic insight in this change in different ways. In my *Realities of Faith: the Revolution in Cultural Forms*,[4] I likened this shift in the imagery of our thought to the lifting of a canopy that had circumscribed the modern consciousness for three hundred years, setting it free to move in the wider space of existence, inclusive of but not circumscribed by the demands of our own consciousness. In this new perspective we are left free to be affected by realities other than the formulations of our own making. What is implied here is that once again a dimension of depth has intruded our intellectual inquiry. This change of perspective sets our inquiry in a context that at once demands more critical vigilance, on the one hand, lest we be swept into an undisciplined irrationalism; and, on the other hand, a more open awareness to what is beyond our own measure of what is real and true, so that the immediacies of existence, as conscious experience notes and reports them, can have the depth of an ultimate measure.

This lifting of the canopy of human consciousness has occurred in various places under various auspices, as I have said. Early in the century it began in the writings of Bergson and William James in their critical attack upon Hegelian idealism, and specifically upon the prevailing tendency to limit our knowledge to cognitive experience. Much that has since developed as "process" thinking and neo-classicism, in which the creativities of existence are made central and controlling, owes its initial

[4] New York: Oxford University Press, 1962, Chap. iii.

impetus to these early efforts in radical empiricism. From the stimulus of Bergson there was to develop a movement of organismic philosophy in England out of which emergent philosophy took form. Emergence has undoubtedly been the key notion setting process philosophy apart from older forms of naturalism and idealism. Its recognition of spontaneous innovation in natural structures, giving rise to new levels of existence, broke through the monolithic kind of immanence that had dominated earlier forms of liberal thought. In this mode of thought, discontinuities had to be taken into account along with continuities. The new physics was to make a similar observation following from its theories of relativity and quantum, and in the later process thinking of Whitehead the two paths of thought merged in the way he interpreted creativity.

It is interesting to recall that Rudolf Otto kept a close watch on developments in English thought, as well as in his own country, which moved toward this deeper empiricism. He wrote of the work of C. Lloyd Morgan and others, expressing gratification in the fact that a more profound and open understanding of nature had been made possible in the conception of emergence they were developing.[5] Otto still found this avenue of thought unsatisfactory for the kind of answer he was seeking, preferring rather to pursue the problem within the context of the numinous as this was being noted in ecstatic or charismatic instances of religious occurrences or persons. Otto was thus to choose the phenomenological route rather than that of emergent philosophy.

In a similar way, Paul Tillich, partly under the influence of

[5] Cf. *Naturalism and Religion,* trans. J. Arthur Thomson and Margaret R. Thomson. (London: Williams & Norgate, 1907), pp. 274-75. The major works of organismic philosophy (S. Alexander, *Space, Time, and Deity* [2 vols., 1920]; C. Lloyd Morgan, *Emergent Evolution* [1923]; *Life, Mind, and Spirit* [1926]; and Jan Smuts, *Holism and Evolution* [1926]) had not been published. Otto apparently knew only Lloyd Morgan's article on "Vitalism" in the *Monist* (1899), and at that stage of its development, Otto could readily gather "emergence" into the movement of vitalism as it had developed in Germany under Hans Driesch and others.

Otto's work and of those who had shaped Otto's course, held to a numinous discourse. Yet Tillich was also attentive in a limited way to the literature of organismic and emergent thinking. He had read Bergson and had responded positively to his thought. He had also been associated with some of the founders of Gestalt psychology and had found their way of speaking congenial to his own thought. Thus the concept of depth had come into Tillich's vocabulary through a confluence of innovating developments, partaking both of phenomenology and process thought. I recall an exciting instance in which this duality of influence in Tillich's thought was made vivid to me. I was listening to the initial lecture in the series which Professor Tillich was giving on "Life and the Spirit" in Mandel Hall at the University of Chicago in 1957.[6] Professor Tillich was laying the ground for his subsequent lectures, and on this particular morning he was concerned to show how natural structures in nature had developed along the line of levels of reality. In this part of his presentation he seemed to be drawing upon the familiar notions of emergent evolution. Then, suddenly, he seemed to catch himself up as if realizing that he was making the case appear too literal. "Perhaps," he interjected, "the term 'levels' is too precise a category. I prefer to speak of 'dimensions' of reality to convey this notion of depth in nature and in our existence. And hereafter I shall use the term 'dimensions' instead of 'levels.' "

To be sure, "dimensions" is a more ambiguous category in that it avoids the necessity of making literal distinctions; but more important perhaps for Tillich's purposes, it retains the sense of continuity and participation between all levels without requiring one to be explicit about what this can mean literally. Within a symbolic discourse such a procedure would be fully adequate, and it would certainly be more manageable.

III

What had thus occurred within cosmological discussions at

[6]These lectures have since been published as Volume III of Tillich's *Systematic Theology* (Chicago: University of Chicago Press, 1963).

the turn of the century and after, altering the vision of man and nature, had its counterpart, as we have already indicated, in specific scientific experiments in physics. And these were occurring within about the same period of time. Here too a dimension of depth appeared in the distinction between what scientists, in the use of their models, could apprehend and employ of natural processes, and what actually existed as a space-time continuum. Prior to relativity physics there had been no need to acknowledge this distinction. It had been assumed since the time of Newton that what the sciences set forth as their findings was exact knowledge, not only within the limits of laboratory experimentation and its purposes, but within the natural world as a whole. It was thus taken for granted that what the scientists recorded or formulated was descriptive of the natural order in a precise and definitive sense. The change that came into the thinking of physicists with the discovery of radiation and relativity was to limit the findings of scientific inquiry to specific projects aimed at technical ends, and to resist any attempt to elevate such findings to a generalized view of nature as such. There was even to arise some skepticism about there being such a thing as orderliness in nature, or any justification for speaking of "the Order of Nature." Max Born, for example, concluded that, on the basis of relativity and quantum physics, the scientist can only say that we live in a world of chance.[7] Our intermittent successes in making some mathematical formulas work in releasing natural energies, he observed, are accompanied by numerous failures in which none of these formulas works. But Einstein was not content to let relativity or quantum dissipate all sense of orderliness in nature; hence he continued to hold to a vision of an ultimate order in nature, despite the pressure from colleagues to relinquish it.[8] Order and "harmony of the universe" he considered to be a

[7] P. A. Schilpp: *Albert Einstein: Philosopher-Scientist* (New York: Tudor, 1941), p. 176.

[8] Cf. Albert W. Levi, *Philosophy and the Modern World* (Bloomington, Indiana: Indiana University Press, 1959), p. 263ff.

necessary presupposition of scientific inquiry, and he was insistent upon holding to it as *an act of faith.*

This sense of disparity between human formulations in the sciences and what actually and ultimately exists has introduced into our present-day thinking about the world a note of discontinuity along with assumptions of continuity. It is not that the world of the sciences stands over against the actual world. The one participates in the other. It is simply that scientists, insofar as they take the limitations of human inquiry seriously, and thus are made fully aware of the mystery of the universe, acknowledge their investigations to be successful only as efforts to seize, release, or employ these energies in nature, not in providing observations which may be elaborated into universal judgments about nature.

In this acknowledgment there is indicated, then, the need for distinguishing between the natural world as it may be reflected in the accumulative records, findings, or discoveries of the sciences, on the one hand; and the universe as it is in its ultimate meaning and as it transpires daily through space-time. These are not to be viewed as contradictory visions, the one conveying deceptive appearances; the other, reality. There is genuine, if momentary, apprehension of reality within science's marginal glimpses or encounters with natural forces; but for all its statistical precision within that marginal encounter, its discoveries or findings are not to be understood as concurring directly with these realities. Thus the accumulation of data arising from scientific inquiry and laboratory experimentation within any discipline, or from the sciences all together, presents material, not for a natural philosophy in the way Newton proposed, or as a defined picture of the natural order as nineteenth-century thought assumed; but as a record of successes and failures in apprehending these realities for specific purposes, and as a guide to the formation of subsequent working models for carrying forward such explorations. In the nature of the case, some sense of having attained an intelligible grasp of these natural forces within various areas is achieved as a result of scientific inquiry. Thus some basis for expressing tentative judgments about tendencies, habits, or characteristics of various forms of life and matter is made available. But the word is "judgments," not "facts." And, to borrow the phrases of Professor Ian Ramsey, the models which the sciences employ are "models of disclosure," not "pictorial models." After all the data has been recorded, studied, and assessed, the vision of nature as it actually transpires remains an allure, yet uncaptured and unpossessed by man.

This reflects the new vision of science and nature shared by many of our contemporaries, whether philosopher, theologian, or scientist. Despite their evident differences, one can see affinities between such recent thinkers as Rudolf Otto, C. Lloyd Morgan, S. Alexander, Paul Tillich, Alfred North Whitehead, Nicholas Berdyaev, Martin Buber, Charles Hartshorne, Michael Polyani, Karl Heim, Max Planck, and Albert Einstein, stemming from their reconception of the world of nature and their consequent openness to what has come to be called a dimension of depth implicit in all realities at whatever level they may be encountered.

Before proceeding to questions that follow from this analysis, we would do well to note one further change that has come into our thinking about nature. During the period of our history when the contrast between highly developed centers of civilization stood out sharply against vast undeveloped areas of uncultivated space, it was possible and normal to distinguish between society and nature. Nature connoted the wild, uncultivated expanse of the earth's surface, untouched and unspoiled by human hands, in contrast to society, in which human imagination and energy had wrought their creations as well as their folly. We have now come into a period of religious and cultural history when this distinction simply is no longer true to the facts. For technology and the products of its processes can now be seen to have arisen from man's use of the resources of nature in a highly technical and specialized way. As Joseph Sittler has observed on occasions, science, engineering, and architecture all represent a subtle fusing of human ingenuity and natural resources. To speak of their domains as being distinctly physical or social, human or natural, is no longer either accurate or illuminating. Human art and industry have so intermingled these spheres as to defy any dissociating of them. And the new age of nuclear science and technology has accentuated this fusion, making any separation between the human and the natural world seem arbitrary and unreal.

IV

But we are still faced with the troublesome question as to how, in the face of these developments in science and cosmology, we are to conceive of the term nature. If we must distinguish between the reality of natural forces as they persist within an ultimate vision of existence, and the accumulated data of the sciences recording "the nature of things" as they are filtered through our human forms and formulations, which one is to inform our conception of nature?

If nature is to have the second connotation, namely, the manageable aspect of the experienced world which the various scientific disciplines have sought to understand and to make available for practical ends, then we have to be prepared to speak of nature solely within statistical terms and within an imagery of mechanism that lends itself to such prediction and control. Nature, then, will indeed fit into the description given it by Descartes and Newton, and into the scheme and strategy of thought provided by Kant. But this would be to lose sight of the very insight in the new vision of science that differentiates it from the Newtonian world view, and thus to deprive nature of the dimension of depth which this new vision has brought to it. For this reason, on grounds which modern scientists themselves would insist upon, nature cannot be made coterminous simply with "the nature of things" as scientists have recorded it. On the contrary, it can mean only this scientific description seen in the context of a deeper order of relations and forces which, while they yield intermittently to scientific inquiry and experimentation, in many more instances elude its statistical measure.

Nature, in other words, must be seen to be this created order of life and physical reality exemplified in scientific findings and formulations together with the vision of order that inspires and sustains such inquiry. On these terms, nature is by definition the world of created realities seen within their ordered and orderly existence. Nature is the structured body of existence at whatever level. It is the world, insofar as it proceeds orderly within causal effects. Nature, on these terms, is both a record of events and an expectation yet unfulfilled. Nevertheless, it constitutes a total vision and outlook, committed to the orderliness of relations.

Grace, in this context, is still vague—in fact, undesignated. We have to face the fact that, for some modern minds, even when the new vision of science is acknowledged, the term grace has no meaning. The envisioned orderliness is deemed sufficient to take account of all that transpires, or that conceivably might happen.

But within the perspective that now informs the sciences, this commitment to an inevitable orderliness in nature is confessedly an "overbelief." There are intimations within the processes of nature to suggest that such orderliness, insofar as it persists, does so amidst a creative interplay of spontaneities and indeterminacies that point to a drama of possibility, emergence, and transcendence which is rarely if ever envisionable within the calculations of the structured or orderly existence. Emergent philosophies have cited instances of happenings within natural structures illustrating such overtones of possibility and transcendence. What has occurred as innovation in any structure at any level, so they have said, has appeared incipiently as a feature of the structure that served as a womb or matrix of the emergence. The recognized nature of the structure was in dominance and thus assimilated to itself the innovating features pressing toward novelty. The new was known in terms of the recognized features. Yet this very impetus toward novelty carried with it some intimation of a "More," in S. Alexander's terms, "a nisus toward deity,"[9] toward a level of reality transcending the existing structure.

[9] S. Alexander, *Space, Time, and Deity* (New York: Macmillan Co., 1920; reprinted by The Humanities Press, 1950), II, 341ff.

Attention to the ordered structure does not disclose this movement toward transcendence within it. It is only in retrospect, or in an appreciative awareness that is sensitive to what is incipiently at work in an organized context, that such disclosures are possible.

V

One way to convey the force of this transcending aspect is to speak of structured events as being individuated, that is, as being given an identity peculiar to their own functioning and ordered existence. Such a structure of events has its characteristic features, growing out of the form it has attained, and growing out of its own distinctive vitalities. But every such individuated structure participates in relations and a relational ground. While each individuated self persists with a remarkable degree of independence and self-sufficiency, it participates in and, to a degree which it cannot estimate or even recognize, depends upon these relational aspects of its existence. All of the orderly processes of its actualized and individuated existence can be readily recognized, studied, and, in large measure, described. What eludes such inquiry is this relational aspect that remains seemingly tenuous, even marginal as a "More" in existence that only intermittently enters into conscious awareness, or into events known to be shaping one's existence.

Speaking of man, I have tried to argue that this communal or relational ground of man's individuated existence presents him with a level of freedom that transcends the freedom of his own organism and individuated personality. All that inheres in the gene structure of an individual along with its propensities, giving identity to a particular individuality, provides for a particular route of occasions which can be described as being simultaneously free and determined. The determinations arise out of the route of response that is indicated by the actualized structure of the personality; but a freedom of response is also inherent in the spontaneities that attend each specific occasion demanding judgment and decision. The very flexibility (or instability) of conscious awareness at the human level, together with impulses arising from the interplay of volitional drives, defies the mechanistic pattern of action toward which the physical structure is prone. And when imaginative powers are present and persistent in an individual, this momentary release from habitual action gives opportunity for creative anticipation, and possibly for decisions that reach beyond, or at least away from, the route of occasions normally characteristic of its structure. Bergson saw in this imaginative play of the mind and of the conscious human spirit of man in disregard of its bodily existence, both a venture of possible hope and of betrayal. And insofar as it became purely cognitive, it appeared to him to be dissociated from the vital, forward drive of the organism, and thus unresponsive to the more profoundly perceptive level of the person.[10] However one assesses this thesis, the analysis does make vivid in organic terms a kind of freedom and transcendence which is at work in the human individual, a freedom that is peculiar to its individuated existence.

Yet no individual is left to this single route of occasions for giving concrete actuality to its personal existence. For this particular route transpires within the relations that hold the individual in existence, and which lend depth and opportunity to the person's individuated selfhood. It is at this level of existence that the *nature* of the individuated self participates in resources of goodness and judgment that are not of its own making. This goodness not one's own, offering a surplusage of meaning and opportunity beyond the calculations and effortful designs of one's own inherent nature, is what I see to be the reality of grace, or the sphere in which grace becomes operative.

I have spoken elsewhere[11] of the terms of tension between the individuated self and its communal ground as being two levels

[10]Cf. Henri Bergson, *Creative Evolution* (New York: Holt, 1911), esp. Chap. iii-iv; a somewhat modified version of this analysis appears in *Two Sources of Morality and Religion* (New York: Holt, 1935), and *Creative Imagination* (New York: Philosophical Library, 1946).

[11]*The Realities of Faith: the Revolution in Cultural Forms* (New York: The Oxford University Press, 1962), pp. 237ff.

of freedom—the one being expressive of man's nature as a definitive structure or specific concrete entity, or "concrescence," the
other being expressive of a goodness arising out of relations that
give depth and destiny to one's career as a self.

In this context one could interpret the problem of nature and
grace as an issue between the individuated nature of entities or
selves and their relational ground. Applying this understanding
of the problem to the topic of man, this could mean a distinction
between man's freedom to be himself, acting out of his own
nature, exercising capacities, choices, decisions expressive of that
individuated nature, and his freedom to receive relationships, to
be judged, empowered, forgiven, even transformed by the *grace*
of relationships. This presupposes that man's individuated nature
has emerged and persists within a communal ground, and that his
existence is defined and given qualitative dimensions by the creative tension between these levels of his being. Yet this tension,
however real, does not connote a necessary disparity or alienation.
Individuated freedom in man, expressive of his distinctive nature
(gene structure, inherited characteristics, etc.), can resist, depre-
cate, even violate this communal ground. It can ignore relationships, or disavow their forgiveness and resources of grace, and
in this sense become alienated from the communal ground. This
is an invalidism in man familiar to all who have studied human
nature within the perspective of the Christian doctrine of man.
Yet expressiveness of an individuated freedom as such is not
necessarily alienating or invalidating of man as man. It can form
the counterpart to sheer acquiescence, giving rise to authenticity
and qualitative concrescence in the person, even as the person
remains open and receptive to the grace of relationships. And
conversely, the freedom to be in relationship, and responsive to
one's communal ground, need not mean the dissolution of individuated freedom. In circumstances where individual man has
asserted his freedom to the point of violating the trust and affection of others, wherein guilt and despair arise over which man
himself can have no control, only one thing can save him and

"do for him what he cannot do for himself": namely, the grace that issues from relationships which have become forgiving and supportive of the person in his guilt and despair.

VI

Now the application of this analysis to the wider problem of nature and grace will make clear that a reconception of terms is indicated here also. The common way of conceiving of the world of nature simply as a vast mechanism, devoid of the operations of grace, and as a constant threat to all existence expressive of spirit, cannot be sustained once one takes the history of natural structures seriously. And the assumption that everything instinctual, or below the level of conscious awareness, partakes only of this mechanistic order and is thus dominated by it, must also be revised. For sub-human life, and even inorganic matter, are seen to be at least incipiently responsive to the communal ground of relationships, even though at their structural level the parts appear to be in dominance. What defies a sharp separation of this incipient form of relational existence in natural structures from higher forms of relational existence is this hint of continuity that is prescient of the emergent structure even as it persists nascently as a participant in the antecedent structure. This observation pertains particularly to later expressions of emergent thinking. If one were to reassert the claims of Bergson, and possibly the implications of James' radical empiricism, an even more radical reconception of these natural structures would be indicated. For in their reaction against setting cognitive experience above every other form of existence, they opened the way for seeing identification with the undifferentiated stream as being in some sense a return to elemental depths of one's being and becoming. Bergson was particularly insistent upon this point. He exhibited a marked impatience with the tendency nurtured by philosophical idealism and positivism to make of intellect a towering achievement of the creative spirit, and instead looked upon intellection as a dubious expression of man's sophistication when divorced from its primal depths, capable of high, imaginative achievement, yet prone to falsification, deception, and even tyranny against this shared order of existence. This is another way of noting the peril of individuation and exclusive dependence upon its cherished goods. Reinhold Niebuhr has since pursued this line of analysis with devastating criticism of the so-called higher dimensions of human nature, showing it to be expressive of man's sin *par excellence*. There are veins of process philosophy, evident even in Whitehead's philosophy, which seem to carry forward this intuitive confidence in man's primordial being, and to see bodily feeling, for example, not as a deceptive lure threatening the mind, but as its stabilizer, and as the carrier of perceptual experience as yet uncognitive, and thus rich in qualitative resources.

How far this concern with the deeps of conscious experience in process philosophy can be extended toward the world of nature other than human nature, varies with individual interpreters. William James gave evidence of openness on this point in his appreciative essay on Fechner.[12] Bergson was certainly responsive to it. Charles Hartshorne has been the most explicit spokesman in this respect, embracing forthrightly a pan-enpsychism in the spirit of Fechner. Henry Nelson Wieman has always sought to be more selective in his response to "nature." At times he could be fully open to its "rich fullness," as in his *Religious Experience and Scientific Method*; yet his distrust of what is below the level of conscious response as being automatic and mechanistic caused him to veer away from any such identification with nature. In this he was more expressive of idealistic leanings than of organismic sensibilities. Furthermore, he was intent upon fixing upon that in nature and in the human community that gave evidence of a creative working to which he could apply the name "God." And in recent years, as his concept of God has taken on the connotation of "creative interchange of meaning," he has become even more wary of intruding the world of nature into the discussion of the value-making process.

[12] *A Pluralistic Universe* (New York: Longmans, Green, & Co., 1909), Lecture IV.

What is overcome in all expressions of organismic thinking from James and Bergson through Hartshorne and Whitehead, however, is the doctrinaire dismissal of nature as a realm alien to man and to his spiritual concern. In some instances there is a repossession of the world of creatures as a dimension of all created existence that is almost biblical in its simplicity and naturalness. Creation is seen to be God's handiwork at all levels of reality; and conceivably, from within this perspective, his grace extends to all his creatures.

Grace, then, so understood, is a movement of spirit attending not only our human reality as a redemptive life, but a depth of innovation and spontaneity attending the whole of created realities. It is a resource issuing from the internal depth of creation, judging or fulfilling our human measure of its realities; and in circumstances of brokenness, following from our fragmented and distorted vision of existence, we speak of this resource of grace within the Christian idiom as coming into our experience as "a new creation," redeeming our existence.

Grace is a goodness in relationships, and issues from them; it is a good not our own, doing exceeding abundantly above all that we can ask or think. Grace is in situations of crisis, offering the unexpected, the uncalculated, even the undeserved, as measured by laws of cause and effect. For the latter is a judgment of "nature," either as devised by the inquiries of men, or as being given in the ordered structures of existence; but grace is of the fullness of God, present in each moment of the creative passage as unexpected redemptive power, or as opportunity for a new instance of God's creative act in the light of new occasions.

Grace is in moments of heightening, in moments of release, of freedom and joy when, as it were, we are delivered from the barriers and intimidations of our known existence to experience intimations of the More that is there to be received. Grace is the winged emissary of redemptive love that can bring healing and the consolations of judgment simultaneously to our situations of guilt and remorse, restoring and cleansing the inward parts. But always grace is a good not our own, a measure of reality beyond our humanly formulated plans and devices. It is the reality of any situation speaking out of the fullness and ultimacy of a righteous goodness inhering in the very texture of events.

TOWARD A PIETY OF FAITH

JOSEPH HAROUTUNIAN

TOWARD A PIETY OF FAITH

In the traditional juxtapositions of the words "grace" and "nature," grace stands above all for the power of God which enables men to do his will, and nature stands primarily for the human will or for man as a moral agent. The matter under dispute, with regard to grace and nature, has been the power or ability of the human will or human nature to fulfill righteousness as required by the Law of God, especially as given by the Great Commandment. Nature in this context has to do with human conduct rather than with physical process, and with moral ability rather than with physical power. The common conjunction of grace with free will, of *gratia* with *liberum arbitrium,* in our theological tradition, makes this point quite clear. Of course, it was fully recognized that the body and its passions also are nature or endowments of man. But what makes man human was seen as "the rational soul" which enables man to distinguish between good and evil, and, as willing soul, to choose between them.

In the controversies on grace and nature, it was commonly overlooked that ethical conduct occurs in man's interactions with his physical environment as well as with his fellowmen. The setting of man's social life in which he is to obey God and love his neighbor as himself has been the world of sunshine and rain, heat and cold, summer and winter, seedtime and harvest. The question of the power of the will to obey the law of God has arisen under the perennial temptation to violate one's fellowmen for the sake of life and security in the physical world and the vicissitudes of existence in it. It is in the struggle for life and good in men's natural environment that their apparent inability to love their neighbors as themselves has become a matter of common knowledge. Their "original sin" has emerged as they have trans-acted with their fellowmen in a world where the prize often goes not to the just and merciful but to him who is strong, crafty and ruthless. It is in the same setting that reason has insisted upon man's ability and therefore responsibility to obey the law of God for justice, mercy, and peace. In short, the moral life and the physical life have so belonged together that the agency of man as will and the action of man as a physical organism are unintelligible the one without the other.

The will in human nature as traditionally conceived is the will of a creature; or, it is man the creature who is endowed with a will. The creature is a finite being, and he knows his finitude through the fortunes of his existence as a being dependent for his life and good upon the powers in his physical environment. He exercises his will as a creature. Even while as a will he is a moral being, as a creature he is a "living soul" in the land of the living. He belongs in a system of nature, and shares in the creatureliness of all the things, organic and inorganic, around him. His "rational soul" does distinguish him from his fellow creatures, but it also reveals his kinship with them and his involvement with them. He, like them, lives and dies, and is subject to powers which bring upon him good and evil, not always according to his will and often to his great loss and misery. He does his willing in interaction with creatures which act in ways both beneficent and deadly, and are both his kin and alien to him. While these creatures sustain his life, they also are sources of his suffering and despair. They are blessings to him, and they also bewilder him. They mystify him and turn his very existence into a mystery. His thinking and his willing are caught up in this mystery, and his soul is suffused with a piety which is natural both as evoked by nature and as a fitting response to it.

Natural piety is no simple feeling or attitude. It includes an awareness of living as the primal good. The experience of being as good is the basis of piety and the power of piety. The pious man takes his life as the unique gift without which he can enjoy no good, and he is absolutely grateful for it all his days. He knows that he did not give himself life, and that he is absolutely dependent for life upon Power or Powers capable of taking his life as they have given it to him. He finds this Power in the physical world which provides him with his food and raiment and shelter and whatever prosperity and comfort he may have and enjoy. He properly turns to the obvious sources of his blessings in the heavens and on the earth, finding everywhere Power which constrains him to gratitude and worship. He seeks the favor of this Power, or these Powers, and tries in every way to avoid their displeasure. He receives his pleasures from their hands, and attributes his sorrows to their disfavor. He regards them as benevolent and just, and is driven to blame himself for the evils which befall him. Thus he experiences the Powers as wills, and tries to know how he may obey them and receive the benefits of their justice as well as their benevolence. And in all his dealings with them, he seeks to please them; and this seeking to please them is the heart of natural piety or the piety of gratitude. Whether the objects of natural piety are one or many is not of decisive consequence. The decisive thing is that they are the sources of human good, signified by the physical world or nature, and the powers in it.

Now, our problem is that natural piety which, as we have tried to show, is inseparable from willing or not willing to obey the law of God, has lost much of its logic and power in the life of the civilized man. The "nature" of natural piety, either as the physical world or as man's response to it, is no longer a matter of absolute concern to men whose minds and hearts are formed and informed by modern civilization. The truth appears to be that there has occurred a radical change in man's relation to the physical world. Between the natural objects of man's environment and the things which sustain his life and provide him with his goods, there is the massive realm of human enterprise. Man no longer receives the things he enjoys from the hands of a beneficent nature. The things which belong to his way of life are not out there to be picked up gratefully or even

extracted from the earth. They have been produced by methodical and cumulative effort, and from materials which bear no
resemblance to the things themselves. Neither the men engaged
in modern technology nor those who traffic in and use the goods
they produce can be reasonably expected to be grateful to nature
for the goods of modern life; and they can hardly be expected
to treat their "machine works" with the piety which was natural
to the uncivilized man. Their position with regard to nature is
one of initial and not direct dependence, and they are masters
and not the beneficiaries of the things around them. They are
the beneficiaries of the scientific, economic, political institutions
of our society whose beneficiaries they are, and their piety is
affixed to their way of life. The very basis of natural piety in
man's dependence upon the physical world has in effect been
removed, and it has been replaced by autonomy and power which
have become the basis not of a piety of gratitude but of a spirit
of exploitation. The physical world is there to be altered according to man's designs, and not as a sign of divine providence.

It is true that the sun still rises and sets. There are summer
and winter, seedtime and harvest time. Men still have to eat and
drink and be clothed; they have to lie down and sleep, and rise
up and walk. The regularities and irregularities of the physical
world are with us, and the organic processes spell life and death
to human beings. The civilized man has not rescinded the laws
of nature, and he has not ceased to be an organism with his
needs and satisfactions, his pains and pleasures.

Nevertheless, natural law as experienced by the civilized man
is not an occasion for submission to Providence, nor is it an
occasion for the unveiling of an alien Power. It is an invitation
to the use of intelligence and to the devising of instruments of
power for bending nature to the will of man. Cosmic order has
receded in favor of clusters of institutions and organizations
growing out of technology, and natural law has given way to
the ways of machines. Neither the rising of the sun nor its setting
prevents man from the construction of his things or the pursuit
of his goods. In the summer there is air conditioning and in the

winter central heating. Seedtime and harvest time alike are
greeted with machines, and the earth is made to yield where and
what it would not, in man's measure and at his pace. It is the will
of man and not the ways of nature that forms and qualifies the
world of the civilized man. Natural law is of little help for
understanding the ways of things or for making proper use of
them in this world.

Our religious tradition saw the law of nature as the law of
God, and accepted the things that happened by natural law as
having happened by the will of God. When nature yielded its
goods, that was a sign of God's benevolence. When it withheld
its goods, or destroyed existing goods, that was a sign of God's
displeasure. Natural law operated by the will of God, and the
will of God followed his justice and mercy. It was providential
and subject to the providence of God, both for the creature's
good and in the interests of moral government.

But since natural law is now largely replaced by the habits or
ways of things made by man, God's providence no longer dominates the life of man, and the will of God revealed by God's
providence no longer governs the actions of men. Men build up
and destroy not by the will of God but according to human
purpose. The goods and evils of our lives occur neither by natural
law nor by the will of God, but respectively by the intelligence
and the stupidity of men.

Thus it is that man's reason is not subject to a cosmic reason
and his will is not subject to a cosmic moral will. Man is no
longer a more or less anxious spectator of nature, or reality,
which metes out good and evil, life and death, according to a
logic which escapes understanding, and leaves man a bewildered
if sobered suppliant. Passive rationality has been demoted in
favor of an intelligence which is engaged not in contemplation
but in a methodical remolding of the external world. In man's
changed relationship with reality, knowledge occurs not by the
perceptions and intuitions of a passive mind, or by conceptions
which present the mind with the coherences of ideas, but by
more or less complicated processes of methodical inquiry, leading

to consequences which are constructed effects rather than objects of intuition. It is not the business of reason to present the mind with the "given," nor is it the business of the wise man to "accept" it. Reason has become intelligence engaged in creating the "City of Man," and the wise man has made it his business to increase good and decrease evil in the same City.

Human nature is constituted not by reason and will, but by the exercise of intelligence in which thinking and willing are continuous and oriented together toward human good. Insofar as, to the civilized man, there is no alien Mind or Will which demands "obedience," there is no longer a question of the power of the will. The will follows the greatest good as established by the intelligence, and the power of the will is the power of the good upon the imagination of man. Hence the traditional question as to the power of the will, as argued under the heading of "grace and nature," is superseded by the question of methodical inquiry or an intelligent pursuit of good things in the civilized way of life.

HUMAN ENCOUNTER AND NATURAL PIETY

The problem before us is that insofar as the recognition of divine grace depends upon natural piety, with its gratitude for the good things of life, it is no longer logical. Therefore, it is no longer rational to speak of obedience to the will of God, and the power of the will to obey God is no longer an issue among us. Neither gratitude nor obedience can issue from natural piety, because such piety is incongruous with the civilized way of life. If there is such a thing as grace, it has to be discerned not in natural process as such, but in social process which has assumed a peculiar quality and weight in our civilization. It may be that the solution of our problem is to be sought in an understanding of the human community itself as both the locus of grace and the occasion of gratitude, without which there is no knowledge of God or obedience to God.

Our confession of God's presence in nature depends upon a prior self-communication of God which occurs in men's life together. The very act of confession presupposes men's communion one with another by which they exist as human beings. But communion is by way of speech, by the hearing and speaking in which men recognize one another as fellowmen, and in so doing exist: exist not only one to another but also in the physical world. Although physically the organism is prior to the fellowman, logically the fellowman is prior to the organism called a human being. A human being is an organism who acknowledges himself as such. But it is the fellowman who acknowledges that he is an organism, because it is the fellowman who uses speech, and speaking is a function not of the organism but of the fellowman. Even though there is knowledge of a sort that is non-verbal, there is no acknowledgment that is not by hearing and speaking; not even an acknowledgment of the world of physical objects. "Nature," as men speak of it and live in it, is the physical environment of fellowmen who exist by their mutual communications. It is a realm of objects to a community of subjects who exist in their trans-actions by way of speech as well as in an organic process. Whether as a beneficent "mother," or as a repository of materials for human alteration and use, nature is known by a community of inquiry whose very methods in dealing with it depend upon a disciplined use of words which are social entities. In short, natural objects belong in a world of fellowmen, who experience them as things they have in common, know in common, and respond to variously in common. Nature is the public environment, and it is public to men who communicate one with another with denotative and connotative language.

The mutual communication of fellowmen is the logical ground of human existence, and of human experience as a whole. That this truth has commonly been obscured in our philosophical and theological traditions is no decisive argument against it. For reasons which we need not explore in this place, in the quest for knowledge, our thinkers have been preoccupied with the world as the object of human thought, rather than with the social context in which thinking takes place. They have failed to reflect in a sufficiently illuminating way upon the existence of the knower as a fellowman, and upon the objective world as the scene of a common life and operation for fellowmen. Much as people commonly ignore the natural processes by which they live as organisms, so people, as thinkers, have ignored the communion by which they live as fellowmen. It has been habitually assumed that human society is to be subsumed under natural process and understood under "being in general," in which nature and society are continuous. With their minds turned upon "universal Being," our thinkers have seen themselves as thinkers first and as fellowmen secondly; from which it readily follows that reality is made up of subjects and objects. More recently, we have been led to think of the world in terms of organisms and their environment. Thus it is that the origins of knowledge in the trans-actions of fellowmen has been obscured, and man's vision both of himself and of his world has been distorted.

The mutual communication of fellowmen is the logical ground not only of human existence but also of man's knowledge of his world. There is no knowledge without experience; no experience without language; no language without the trans-actions of fellowmen. The society of fellowmen is given before the knowledge of natural process, and the objectivity of the latter is presupposed by the mutuality of the existence of fellowmen. Our very world is a gift to us of the people who are in communion with us. We exist and know and act and enjoy because we are spoken to by our fellowmen, and may in turn speak to them. So it is that we have neither life nor light without them, and have our good and hope of it by them. If as organisms we are quickened to a natural piety toward the physical world, this is because we are fellowmen whose very piety is made possible by their mutual communications. When we reflect on the matter, we must recognize that piety is a human response which belongs in the context of a communion and a common life formed and informed by language.

It is a failure in discernment to respond to nature and not to one's fellowmen with gratitude. It is nearsightedness to acknowl-

edge one's dependence upon nature, but not upon one's fellowmen. A man's life is a continual gift in communion, and his goods
subsist by communion. The unique and priceless gift of being
occurs by the trans-actions of fellowmen, and every work and
enjoyment grows out of it. It is true that the light and heat of
the sun, and the fruits of the earth, are in their orders gifts, not
of man but of nature. But man's experience and enjoyment of
these things, together with the piety they evoke, are rooted and
flourish in the communications of fellowmen one with another.
This is especially evident in civilized life. Civilized beings neither
eat nor drink, neither enjoy nor suffer, neither hope nor fret, as
do the beasts of the field and the birds of the air. They do them
in their own human manner, with qualifications of them which
depend upon human enterprise and not upon natural process.
This their manner is their life as human beings, and for both
manner and life they depend absolutely upon their fellowmen.

Natural piety is evoked not only by the givenness of the good
things of life, but also by the existence of men as "finite beings."
The man of piety acknowledges himself a creature; and in his
creaturely sensibility, his finitude is a determining fact. His mind
and heart are impressed by grace because he is—a finite, contingent being who is neither his own maker nor the master of
his future. He has no security against fortune and no guarantee
of permanence in his own person. He lives and dies, and leaves
his world behind him. He knows that he will be cut off from
the land of the living and from experience itself. Things and
enjoyment will remain, and he himself will be reduced to nothing.
There will be light and darkness, action and passion, loving,
knowing, and hoping in this wonderful world. But he will be
gone, and he will never again be in it. All this is true, and it is
integral to his natural piety. The life he enjoys and suffers is
not at his disposal, and his piety is a sorrow as well as a
celebration.

In this respect also, natural piety is a quality of being which
belongs in the society of fellowmen. The human being, in his
finitude and anxiety for his life, is a fellowman; and it is as

fellowman that he feels the "ontological shock" by the co-mingling of being and nonbeing in his experience. Anxiety is a function of human existence, which in turn is a function of the trans-action of fellowmen. It is true that it is the organism who lives and dies and is finite both in being and in power. It is true that if a man were not an organism, he would not have the sensibility of a creature. Nevertheless, human contingency, temporality, finitude, with the corresponding anxiety and dread, are qualifications of the mutual dependence of fellowmen. These things are experienced by beings who are posited as "intelligent creation" in their trans-actions one with another. It is in communion that physical finitude evokes the "sense of creatureliness," and the natural piety that goes with it.

The sense of finitude with respect to power also is a human phenomenon. Power over against our own, which calls us to a halt and forbids progress, belongs first to our fellowmen. It is our fellowmen who resist us, and in resisting us show forth their power. They confront us as "wills" who may or may not be present to us; who may or may not trans-act with us, acknowledge us, posit us. They express their power not merely by their mass and weight but also, truly, by the grace they exercise towards us and the demands they make upon us. They limit us by calling upon us; by demanding our fidelity and justice. They are not at our disposal, and they will not tolerate our power if we seek to dispose of them. They posit our finitude by their willing toward us and limit our power under the covenant of truth. Thus they endow our existence with a peculiar finitude, and give rise to a piety which goes with the grace or power of our fellowmen towards us.

Natural piety which, more or less clearly, depends upon the grace of its object, responding to it as to a will, has its logical ground in the mutual communications of fellowmen. The strange and rather uncritical attitude of human beings toward nature as beneficent and just, or towards God as the Power behind nature, is not due merely to the anthropomorphism of alogical minds. It is due not to nature in its sub-human primitivity, but to our original experience of reality in the trans-actions of fellowmen. It is because human beings exist by their mutual willing that they experience grace and judgment in their dealings with the physical world. It is fellowmen that believe in gods and God, and are incurably anthropomorphic in their beliefs as well as their piety.

THE PIETY OF FAITH IN SCRIPTURE

Natural piety has encountered the Holy and Mysterious in intercourse with nature rather than in the communion of fellowmen. Even though natural religion has had its sacred persons, its shamans, priests, and sundry mediators of sacred Power, it has located the numinous not in a "holy people" but in their physical environment. Natural piety has been attached to the sun, the sky and the earth, animal life and vegetation, rather than to fellowmen; even though piety has commonly endowed natural objects with the likeness of humanity and men have universally been engaged in some species of "communion with God."

It is therefore not without reason that the biblical prophets, and the Fathers and Reformers of the Christian church, have denounced natural religion as idolatry and repudiated its gods as fictitious and demonic. It has been altogether clear to them that the living God of the Bible, who is the covenant-keeping Lord of a holy people, is a God altogether different from the gods or God who have been the objects of natural piety. The God of a holy people and the Holy experienced in the physical world are two different gods. Even though both gods may be anthropomorphic, they are not anthropomorphic in the same way. The living God is the God of communion; whereas the God of natural piety is a sacred Power. The One reveals himself in men's communion one with another under his law. The Other is experienced in the vicissitudes of men's interaction with the physical processes and powers around them. The living God is the God of his people as fellowmen; whereas the Power is the God of human beings as organisms. In a sense, the issue between biblical faith and natural religion is the issue of man himself:

of whether man is first a fellowman or an organism. If it is true that a man is a fellowman who exists by and for his faithfulness, then the true God of man is the living God of the Bible; and the gods of natural religion are misleading if not false gods. Such an insight is integral to the insistence of prophet and Father that biblical faith is true religion, whereas the religions of the "nations" are false or superstitious. Perhaps, it is thus that we are to understand the perennial vituperations of Fathers and Reformers and theologians against the idolatries of natural religion.

This is not to deny, or even to minimize, that the God of the Christian faith is "God the Father all mighty, maker of heaven and earth." The point rather is that the Bible knows no true God who is the Creator and not the Covenanter. According to the biblical faith, the Lord God of heaven and earth is the God of Abraham, Isaac, and Jacob; the God who brought his son out of Egypt and bound him to himself with the covenant of truth and justice. He is the God of the law which is the way and the life of his people for their prosperity and peace: the law of the life of fellowmen who live by faithfulness and perish by untruth and oppression. It is this God who "sits upon the circle of the earth" and makes all things as well as all people to subserve the covenant under which fellowmen both exist and see good or evil. In short, in the biblical view, it is the God of a people or of fellowmen who is the God of nature.

The New Testament confirms the logic of the Old. Jesus' God, who makes "his sun to rise on the evil and the good" and sends "his rain upon the just and the unjust," is the Father of his people who in doing good or evil exist under the covenant and law of the God of their Fathers. The apostle Paul could say, as though uttering an axiom, "for us there is one God, the Father, from whom are all things and for whom we exist, and one Lord, Jesus Christ, through whom are all things and through whom we exist" (I Cor. 8:6). The Gospel of John begins with the hymnic confession, "In the beginning was the Word, and the Word was with God, and the Word was God. He was in the beginning with God; all things were made through him, and without him was not anything made that was made." The God of the New Testament is the Father of his Son Jesus who is the Lord and head of his people the church, who, in him and through him, exist under covenant to love God with all their mind, soul, and strength, and to love their neighbor as themselves. Once again, as in the Old Testament, God is the God of his people first, and of "all things" secondly. He is identified as the Father of his Son and people, and as such confessed as being God "through whom are all things and through whom we exist."

It has been a fixed point of Christian piety that Jesus Christ is "the Incarnation of the Word of God." Whatever else this expression means, it does mean that we know God in this man Jesus and his people first, and in "all things" or the "cosmos" secondly. The doctrine of the Incarnation is, in one effectual sense, the triumph of biblical anthropomorphism. The critics of Christianity have not, at this point, been altogether wrong-headed; and the apologists of Christianity, who have denied the charge of anthropomorphism, have not been altogether clear-headed. When we acknowledge that the God of the Bible is the Father of his Son and people, or of a people who are his son, in his image and likeness, it is hard to avoid anthropomorphism and the charge of anthropomorphism. The God of the Bible is the Father who is faithful toward his people, and subsumes all things under his faithfulness. All things exist in the interests of his faithfulness, and have their origin as well as their end in it.

It is, therefore, not inappropriate for a Christian theologian to say, in line with biblical religion, that the living God reveals himself in the covenanted life of fellowmen, which is the logical ground of men's finding him in the physical world. It is a matter of history and fact that the confession of God as "the Creator of the ends of the earth" occurred in a community of people who had long since become a people by a call to live by the Law of God and by their accepting that call. It is of more than historical interest that God the Creator was the God of a covenanted people. The confession of the covenant-making

God in the Bible may well be understood as an intuition of the logical priority, in human existence, of communion to physical interaction. The priority given, in the Bible, to the Word of God and the law of God, over the phenomena of the physical world, as self-manifestations of the living God, signify a peculiar kind of "ontological" awareness. The biblical preoccupation with the Word of God as the primary mode of divine self-communication, applied in the New Testament to the person and mission of a fellowman by the name of Jesus, indicates an awareness of the communion of fellowmen as the locus of the life and light of men. The conviction that prosperity and peace alike depend upon obedience to the law of God by hearing of the Word of God, suggests an ontological understanding of communion as the ground of human existence and the source of human good. It was the peculiar good sense of the biblical mind to recognize that human life, human light, human truth, human blessing, appear and are realized in keeping covenant, which is man's being, in and by doing. This is how the biblical man saw that "in the beginning was the Word," and that "without him was not anything made that was made."

It must be acknowledged, not grudgingly but joyfully, that the Bible, from the first chapter on, is suffused with the marvel and glory of the physical world. Thanksgiving to God and praise of God for the things in heaven, the things on earth, and things under the earth, belong to the mainsprings of biblical piety and are at the core of it. Still, natural piety in the Bible is expressed as the praise of God, and the God who is praised is the God of Moses and the Father of his people: God who is faithful in his works and righteous in his deeds. It is God who is praised, and he is praised as the faithful God. Biblical piety is first of all faith, and its first object is not nature but the God of his people. It is a response to the faithfulness of God, and its proper expression is obedience. It is the piety of obedience according to God's truth or faithfulness, and it partakes of the faithfulness of God. Piety is formed by his people's obedience to the law of God, which is the very self-expression of the living

God. But the law of God governs the trans-actions of fellow-men, and obedience to God is expressed in "justice, mercy and peace," which are elements at once of faith and piety, and constitute the very life of fellowmen. Faith, through the law, transmutes natural piety into a praise of the covenant-keeping God, and makes it an occasion of the fellowman's fidelity to his neighbor. Such fidelity expresses a piety which is social before it is natural, and natural because social.

In a sense, it is the peculiar accomplishment of the biblical mind that it conjoins natural piety with the piety of communion; or that it conjoins piety toward natural objects and processes with piety toward one's fellowmen, their words and actions, without which there is neither human existence nor human good. The biblical mind was impressed first with the existence of God's people, and saw in it the prime act of divine grace. This people existed by and under a covenant, which posited the fellowman as a being whose very existence is by and for faithfulness and the piety that goes with it. There is in the Bible no gift that takes precedence over the fellowman; no faith without faithfulness toward fellowmen; no piety that is good without men's keeping covenant. When covenant replaced nature as the first locus of divine faithfulness, there emerged a new type of piety in which a man's trans-actions with his fellowmen took precedence over his inter-actions with nature, and gratitude for the good things of life was subsumed under a grace which works by justice, mercy, and peace.

Thus, there is in the Bible a piety of faith which is logically prior to natural piety, and radically qualifies it. The piety of the biblical man is not the piety of an organism as such who is happy over his food and shelter. It is the piety of the fellowman who is an organism; who, as he seeks to satisfy his organic needs, is under covenant to love his neighbor as himself. There is no biblical piety apart from the acknowledgment of the fellowman as "living soul," as "flesh and bones," or as "body and soul." The fellowman is a fellow organism, and a man is bound to his neighbor with a covenant which binds his fellow "flesh" to himself in the quest for prosperity and peace. His awareness of fellow flesh as existing before him under the covenant of justice and mercy is at the heart of his piety, which must therefore express itself in faithfulness. By divine constitution, he has no life which is not the life of a fellowman. He may neither eat nor drink except as a fellowman. This means that he may, rather must, acknowledge his fellowman in his eating and drinking as his fellow organism; that he must have eyes to see flesh, and ears to hear the word of flesh. He must be just and merciful, and thus it is that he must be pious and grateful. Natural piety in the Bible is still "natural," but the bearer of it is a fellowman and an organism as a fellowman. Thus, faith and piety, although not the same, are inseparable.

GRACE AND NATURE RECONSIDERED

In the Bible grace and nature are distinguished one from the other, not as two powers but as faithfulness and flesh. God exercises grace in his faithfulness, and the object of his faithfulness is flesh. Nature is not first of all the opposite of grace, but the object and recipient of grace. The God of covenant is gracious toward his people who are flesh: who are living souls, organisms, who live by bread and have peace when they are healthy and prosperous. Indeed, God is spirit and strong; and man is flesh and weak. However, "grace and nature" is another matter. God's grace points first neither to his spirituality nor to his power, but to his faithfulness; and man's nature points to his fleshness, not first in his weakness but as the object of divine grace. Neither God's ability nor man's inability comes logically first. First comes the communion of God with man, in which the grace of God posits man as fellowman and flesh, that is as flesh in communion.

By the grace of God, the people exist under the grace of communion. Grace is exercised, therefore, not only *toward* flesh but also *among* flesh. Men who exist by communion one with another, exist by the grace they exercise toward one another; and without grace among themselves, they do not exist. They communicate by speech. By speech, they communicate as selves, which means that they communicate in the freedom of fellowmen. Their communion arises not from an organic necessity but from grace among them, by which they *may* communicate under the law of human existence. The communication of each man's fellowman with him is an act of grace. In the meeting of flesh with flesh, there is no necessity by which fellowmen must speak and hear, or acknowledge one another and care one for another. Communion confronts one fellowman with the grace of another, and demands from him the response of gratitude with grace. Speaking and hearing, by word and deed, by which we exercise our humanity, belong in the realm of grace and under covenant. Therefore, we meet grace when we meet our fellowmen who acknowledge us as fellow flesh, and speak to us and act toward us by this acknowledgment. We are posited as nature or flesh by the grace of our fellowmen; and they exercise grace as fellow flesh. We ourselves receive this grace by ourselves exercising the grace of fellow flesh; so that our fellowmen live by our faithfulness, even as we do by theirs. But they, as representatives of God, come first, logically and in fact.

The traditional contrast between grace and nature may now become more intelligible to us. The Augustinian thesis of the inability of "nature" to fulfill the law of God goes with the truth that outside of communion we have no power to do good as fellow human beings. Where the grace of communion is lacking, there is only weakness and futility. Human power, or the power of a fellowman, comes from communion, and communion is by grace. And since communion is under God's covenant of grace, "nature" without the grace of God, neither wills nor does the human good. Thus it is that the grace of God is the power of God working in the communion of the faithful, who care one for another as organisms or living souls. In short, the ability to do justly and love mercy is by communion, and communion is by grace toward nature.

Finally, we need to return to the human situation with regard to physical nature considered early in this paper. Since man today lives in dependence upon human powers, artifacts, and institutions in a new and radical way, the natural piety of his forebears is not natural to him. He no longer sees the blessings of his life as benefactions of nature or its God. He lives not by a "sacred" Power exhibited in natural phenomena, but by the powers of his science and engineering, in an environment of artifacts. He makes the good things of life and prevents evils as enabled by his intelligence. Nature to him is a repository of materials for his artifacts, and not an object of piety.

Lacking natural piety, there is, for this man, no way from nature to God, and no point to the contrast between grace and nature. Unless he exercises piety of faith towards his fellowmen, he barely has any piety at all. Unless God finds him in his dependence upon his fellowmen for life and good, he hardly seeks after and does not know where to find him.

The impulse for natural piety in civilized men depends upon the meeting of fellowmen as flesh. The awareness of "organic life" and the sense of "the vitalities of nature" may now come from the mutual acknowledgments of fellowmen as "flesh and blood." A lively piety toward the physical world is evoked not by the individual's participation in natural process, but by the communion of fellow flesh in it. Nature is the milieu of human life, but human life is the life of fellowmen. Hence communion is the basis of natural piety in a civilized society and comes alive by justice, mercy, and peace.

We are unquestionably called upon by Scripture to exercise the piety of gratitude for the wonder-full world of nature in which we exist as flesh and our souls are satisfied with good things. The insensibility of the civilized man toward his fellow creatures is an ignorant and wicked thing. It is not a good but evil thing that our natural piety is greatly diminished; for without it we are neither flesh nor fellowmen. However, the logic of civilized life makes it necessary that the piety of faith take precedence over natural piety, both as the ground and as the fullness of it.

NATURE, GRACE, AND THE CHRISTIAN INDICATIVE

Philip J. Hefner

NATURE, GRACE,
AND THE CHRISTIAN INDICATIVE

I. THE STARTING POINT FOR CHRISTIAN THEOLOGY

The Christian faith originates in the redemption which is unshakable and concrete reality in the lives of Christian men and women. The starting-point for Christian life and belief is not in ideas or principles, or even in a sacred book, but rather in the actuality of redeemed existence in this world. This assertion, together with the structure of thought that underlies it, is of fundamental and even urgent importance for Christian theology and preaching as they essay the relationship of nature and grace,[1] because this affirmation of the reality of redeemed existence furnishes the only adequate starting point for reflecting upon that relationship. From this starting point it follows inescapably that Christian awareness begins with the conviction that nature and grace have already been related meaningfully and constructively by God's own action. There is something incongruous, therefore, about Christian theological discourse that concerns itself with the *possibility* of relating nature and grace meaningfully. Whether nature and grace can be united is not a question for the Christian; he knows that they have been united already in the redemptive reality which forms the matrix from which his own existence has emerged. The questions which exercise Christian reflection are rather these: What are the relative positions of nature and grace in the unity which God has forged? And what are the implications of this unity of nature and grace for every realm of truth and life?

[1] In this essay, "nature" is used in a broad sense, to designate the whole created order as it stands in distinction from God. Therefore, "nature" refers to the structures of society and culture, as well as the non-human creation of animal and inorganic life. "Nature" is at times almost synonymous with "the world" and "the age we live in."

The assertion that Christian discourse presupposes a unity of nature and grace rests upon a certain understanding of what is constitutive for Christian life and belief: that for the Christian the first fact of life and belief is the actuality of reconstructed human existence. There are several forms in which this primary datum of redeemed existence can be Christianly stated. One statement of it has been the affirmation (in the Old Testament) that human existence entails life within the covenant that God has made with man; this covenant creates a *community* with God and men,[2] outside of which one cannot properly speak of "life," because this covenant community is the only enfolding ambiance which sustains life that is fully human. The earthiness of the Old Testament witness leaves no doubt as to the concrete, this-worldly character of the life which the covenant engenders. Christians have also given expression to this primary datum of their life by asserting the reality of the Incarnation in Jesus of Nazareth. This proclamation of the Incarnation asserts a fundamental penetration of the structures of nature by divine grace. The one truth that shines through all of the Christological debate that exercised the church for centuries is that the *reality* of the penetration remains unshakable in Christian awareness; the reality is prior to all reflection upon it, as well as to all attempts to demonstrate its plausibility.[3] Still another form in which the primacy of redeemed existence has been put is in the confession of Christians that they have found new life in this world through the Spirit who came at Pentecost and in the

[2]See Genesis 15:4-5 and the account of the Sinai covenant in the book of Exodus.

[3]It has become commonplace for interpreters of Chalcedon to assert that Leo's *Tome* and the *Chalcedonense* answer no questions, but rather merely underline the central problem of Christology (namely, how the man Jesus of Nazareth could be called God). Even if this critical judgment is accepted, it must be acknowledged that the very embarrassment evident in these documents testifies to the consensus among Christians that the reality of the union of nature and grace in Jesus is prevenient to theological and metaphysical speculation concerning the Incarnation in two natures.

resurrection of Jesus of Nazareth to which that Spirit points.[4]

Each of these assertions—concerning the life in the covenant, the Incarnation in Jesus, and the power of Jesus' resurrection in the Spirit of Pentecost—concerns the reality of divine grace which has unfolded within human existence (although, to be sure, not there alone) and transfigured it. Furthermore, these are the root assertions of Christian faith; no other assertions can claim the preeminence enjoyed by these. The basis for their preeminence is that they articulate that which constitutes or engenders all of Christian life and belief, the principle or power of its unfolding, namely, the reality of redemption that has engaged men in their concrete existence and reshaped that existence. The images of "constitutive," "engendering," and "principle of unfolding" are important because they imply not only that the actuality of redeemed existence stands at the beginning of Christian faith, but that it accompanies Christian faith in every moment of its career, giving it substance and nerve and shape. In other words, the starting point for Christian faith is the actuality, the "happenedness" of redemption at the hands of God—the fact that men, unlikely candidates for sainthood that they are, have been given a new possibility for life, and that the entire creation shares in the destiny which is shaped by this new life.[5]

'Peter's sermons in Acts, the witness of the Fourth Gospel, and many sections in the Pauline epistles make it clear that we use the Pentecost affirmation wrongly if we allow it to lead us towards a disengagement from the present world. The Spirit's testimony to the resurrection affirms the reconstruction of life here and now.

'The Roman Catholic theologian, Karl Rahner, has given clear expression to this in his book, *Maria, Mutter des Herrn* (Herder: Freiburg, 1962), pp. 33, 34: "Christianity perfected must consist in this, that man receives this gift from the eternal God—which is God himself—in a freedom which is itself the product of grace, with his body and soul and with all the power of his total being, with all that he is and has, all that he does and suffers, so that this reception of God takes up the total being of man and his history into the eternal life of God. . . . [Christianity is] receiving God, not just in

The significant implication here is that an *indicative* stands at the basis of Christian existence. The indicative implies that redemption is already a fact; a fact of the past in that creation and establishment of the covenant with Israel, as well as the renewal of the covenant in Jesus Christ, reveal that God has already acted decisively to effect redemption; a present fact inasmuch as it is the realization and recognition of this decisive redemptive action that makes our Christian existence and hope possible even now; a fact that is future because this redemption is not yet fully realized.

The fact that God's action engenders redemption as a concrete reality in human existence leads inescapably to the assertion that somehow grace has already penetrated decisively into the realm of nature. It is true that some Christians have traditionally argued that the presence of grace emphasizes the discontinuity between God's gracious action and the structures of this world, that grace does not *penetrate* nature so much as it enables our *retreat* from nature. These Christians look to grace to rescue them from this evil world. Such a position may be plainly contradictory in that the very presence of the knowledge of God in the person who asserts this discontinuity is a denial of that discontinuity (inasmuch as such an assertion implies the penetration of grace into *his* world at least); this position is also a denial of the Pauline attitude (discussed below) found in passages like Colossians 3 and II Thessalonians 3.

INDICATIVE-CENTERED REFLECTION

The proper methodology, therefore, of reflection upon the so-called problem of nature and grace (and upon our Christian life generally) is informed by the awareness of this indicative.

an abstract ideality, but in the concreteness of history, in his human Word, in his grace that transfigures the world, in short: in man's corporeality." (This book is now available in translation: *Mary, Mother of the Lord* [New York: Herder and Herder, 1963].)

Rahner considers this to be the basis of Roman Mariology. Other Christians would be more inclined to say that it is the basis of Christology.

Such indicative-centered reflection is marked by several notable characteristics: it is permeated by the unity of nature and grace as a reality that the Christian, whether in life or theology, works *from* and not *towards*, a reality animating Christian awareness rather than constituting a goal to be grasped. Attempts to grasp or demonstrate this unity of nature and grace are futile from the outset because they automatically call into question the vivifying reality which is prior to all grasping and demonstration. This helps explain why attempts at demonstration and calls for decision are peculiar and occasional phenomena in the Christian community, employed in very special apologetic and evangelistic situations, and not universally. Traditionally, Christian converts have affirmed that the new truth which once seemed to be demonstrable is really a mystery, and that the new life which before appeared to be an option for human choice is really a gift bestowed by God. It was in this way that the power of Jesus' resurrection manifested itself in the first-century Christian community. If it had been a matter of human decision, men could have avoided the perplexing and at times preposterous consequences that accompanied their adherence to the kerygma concerning Jesus' resurrection and the descent of the Spirit. But it is in the very nature of the indicative that it leaves no options to those grasped by it and that it cannot be avoided, because it is the very breath of reality itself. The first Christians found that a new possibility for life was present which before had been either unknown or unthinkable. The only way that they could account for this new possibility of life was in the life, death, and resurrection of the man Jesus of Nazareth. This resurrection power, so we say, grasped them and henceforth animated their existence.

This indicative-centered approach in no way overlooks the fact that Christians continue to sin, nor is it unaware that the world continues to be filled with evil. The biblical witness itself seems to suggest at times a thorough-going dualism between good and evil, nature and grace. But the Christian finds himself grasped by the concrete reality in which these dualisms, rooted as strongly as they may be in human awareness, are overcome. The Christian's affirmation of victory over evil and sin, therefore, grows not so much out of a naivete in the face of evil, as out of allegiance to an unshakable reality which has transfigured his life. On the basis of this reality, he is forced to conclude that evil is the deviation from essential reality, from the true destiny of man and the world. As such, the presence of evil poses a problem which has exercised every generation of Christians. But it always remains a problem and not the answer to a problem; the Christian as a Christian is rarely tempted to succumb to dualism as the final metaphysical answer, or to evil as the essential nature of man and the world, because succumbing to such temptation would be in flat contradiction to the concrete reality which as indicative in his life is prior to all doubt. Many centuries of Christian speculation make it clear that Christian faith simply cannot account for evil; rather, following the lead of Genesis 1-3, it asserts the prior reality of grace in nature, the redeemed existence engendered by Christ, and then proceeds to give an honest description of the devastating effects of evil which persist in opposition to the prevailing power of God. The integrity and persuasiveness of Christian faith do not rest on the ability of faith to account for evil; rather, this integrity rests on the faithful exposition of what Christian existence has discovered, namely, that in it grace has penetrated nature, thereby defeating sin and evil. Paul Tillich has expressed this succinctly: for the New Testament, "evil has no ontological, but only moral, foundation."[6]

THE INADEQUACY OF IMPERATIVE-CENTERED THEOLOGY

This methodology of the indicative stance opposes rather sharply a life and theology which is based upon the imperative aspect of Christian faith. This imperative-centered reflection is keenly aware of the possibilities of grace as they stand over against man, not as the animating principle of his existence, but

[6]Paul Tillich, *The Protestant Era* (Chicago: The University of Chicago Press, 1948), p. 29.

as a task or responsibility which must be discharged. This approach grows out of a tortured dialectic between sin and forgiveness which, even though it is a pure gift of God, nevertheless demands man's decision to accept it. This imperative stance is expressed in a network of assertions which are widespread in Protestant circles today. One of these is the contention that the first fact of Christian life is a call for decision, repentance, and conversion; such a note dominates the preaching and strategy of certain evangelicals, and it is accompanied by great emphasis on conversion. Decision (to be sure, of a different sort) figures prominently in Christian existentialism also, together with its nearly overpowering emphasis that man's authentic existence is an entity set over against him, a reality which teeters on the brink of an agonizing and dramatic entrance into his personal world, which he cannot hope to seize, but which, if he relaxes his frantic grasping, will be his as a gift. A variation of this last theme animates much of the so-called new quest of the historical Jesus, which, on the basis of the Synoptic Gospels, distills the message of the Nazarene as the dramatic announcement that authentic life is even now imminent, breaking in upon man and eliciting his decision for or against it.[7] In its most extreme form, this existential concern with the Synoptic Jesus asserts that the *announcement and description* of this possibility of new life is sufficient, quite apart from its actualization in

[7]See, for example, James M. Robinson, *A New Quest of the Historical Jesus* (London: SCM Press, 1959), pp. 121-25. Robinson carries this out even more explicity in "The Formal Structure of Jesus' Message," *Current Issues in New Testament Interpretation*, ed. William Klassen and Graydon F. Snyder (New York: Harper & Brothers, 1962), pp. 99-110. It must be said, however, that Robinson has a clear vision of the power that is actual in Jesus; the question is whether this vision can be communicated through the explicit polarity which is involved in the existential dialectic that Robinson adopts as the formal criterion of Jesus' message. This position is maintained also (although modified somewhat) by Günther Bornkamm in *Jesus of Nazareth* (New York: Harper & Brothers, 1960), cf. pp. 64ff., 82f.

Jesus' own life.[8] The traditional Reformation version of imperative-centered Christianity lies in the well-worn formula that the proclamation of the law, with its condemnation, precedes the offer of the gospel which can alone lift the creature who groans under the curse; from which it is often concluded that the law's imperative must be preached with special force so as to drive man to the gospel.

Such an imperative-centered methodology raises many questions. Perhaps the most serious is whether such a methodology can really be a vehicle for the reality of grace that it is so eager for men to accept. Throughout the proclamation of the Christian imperative, one feels the plight of man bent forward in striving towards a destiny which is not yet real, but which is within grasp. Even though the existentialist or traditional Lutheran asserts that this destiny is a gift which we cannot seize by force, the reception of the gift is described in an imagery so muscular and tortured as to stand in contradiction to the prevenience of grace which the imagery intends to exalt. Such an imagery can scarcely speak with conviction concerning a positive interaction or unity of the realms of nature and grace; because of its starting point in the imperative, it seems structurally incapable of illumining the actual redemptive possibilities which broke in upon the early Christians through the resurrection of our Lord and the outpouring of the Spirit. These imperative versions of the gospel do affirm a positive relation between nature and grace; they assert the victory of God over all evil. But they remain unconvincing because the centrality of the imperative poses too great a tension between nature and grace,

[8]This view grows out of a method that makes a formal concept of authentic existence the "essence" of Christianity. It may have its basis in Bultmann himself, particularly in the methodology of his *Jesus and the Word* (New York: Charles Scribner's Sons, 1934), which claims no interest in the life of Jesus himself and proceeds instead to distill his message into terms that inevitably become formal. Even though this message has concrete, existential impact upon those who encounter Jesus, the tendency is to divorce it from Jesus' own achievement in his earthly life.

even a contradiction, so that the two cannot stand in any effectively positive or constructive unity. Furthermore, because the logic of the imperative position often holds that redemption can be real only after the law has done its work, faith appears as a human achievement, brought to completion by man's wrestling with the law and by his final submission to Christ; as an achievement following upon the law, the indicative reality of grace is all but repudiated.

The adequacy of this imperative-centered reflection comes further into question in the face of its inability to deal with the social-ethical issues which always attend the Christian faith. The current social-ethical dilemma grows out of a cultural situation in which the old imperatives are strange and unpersuasive to people for whom new modes of technology and thought have reshaped reality in a bewildering way. In this situation men and women seek first of all an affirmation of life which will overcome the estrangement they know. It is singularly unimpressive to reiterate in these circumstances the imperative character of grace or to set forth old verities which are waiting to be obeyed. Whether in the personalized realm of a sex ethic or in the public realm of government and technology, our generation feels the curse not so much in the irrepressible impulse to make its own redemption as in the anxious separation from the central dynamic of life itself, from the life which can give meaning and direction in the midst of bewilderment. The primary datum of Christian faith speaks of the fundamental unity of being in grace which makes possible the affirmation of life which can lead out of the maze of contemporary anxiety; and it speaks in a way that does not compromise its essential nature, but rather in a way that brings God's reconciling will to bear upon men's lives in an effective manner. The methodology of the imperative finds it difficult to speak in such a situation because it cannot communicate persuasively the redemptive unity of nature and grace that God has created.

The methodology of the indicative counters this imperative stance at nearly every point. It by no means repudiates the imperative; but it does insist on the priority of the Christian indicative. It suggests that the call to decision and conversion cannot find a response except in the spirit which has a prior vision of the unity of nature and grace which alone can give sense to such a decision.[9] Similarly, one might suggest that authentic human existence is a consummation, a fulfillment of existing humanity rather than a dramatic invasion by an entity which stands over against present man.[10] Reflection which springs from the indicative insists that the Synoptic Gospel picture of Jesus must ultimately be viewed through the events of Pentecost and Easter precisely because, apart from these events, this historical Jesus is himself estranged from the power of the resurrection that informs Christian existence; and in this estrangement he emerges time and again exclusively as a preacher of the imperative. Submission to the Nazarene preacher is a possibility

[9]In this context, one can appreciate even more the profound significance of the theological methodology which underlies the dogmatic construction of Friedrich Schleiermacher and Albrecht Ritschl. Schleiermacher bases his entire system on the antithesis in human consciousness between the inability to realize absolute dependence upon God and its realization in Christ. But he recognizes that this antithesis itself presupposes man's relatedness to God; see *The Christian Faith* (Edinburgh: T. and T. Clark, 1928), pp. 123-24. Ritschl accepted Schleiermacher's methodology, in his insistence that the consciousness of the church (i.e., those who have been reconciled in Christ) is the only legitimate basis for dogmatics; see his *The Christian Doctrine of Justification and Reconciliation* (Edinburgh: T. and T. Clark, 1902), Introduction. Whatever one might conclude concerning the dogmatic edifices that these two men completed, this aspect of their methodology represents a permanent contribution to the Christian theological tradition.

[10]Such a position harks back to patristic theology, e.g., Saint Irenaeus' classic statement: "For the glory of God is a living man: for man, however, life is the vision of God" (*Adversus haereses,* IV, 20, vii). It is interesting to note that the critique which Schubert M. Ogden has leveled at Bultmann points in the same direction: as when he argues that authentic existence, if it is a human potentiality, must rest on an ontological foundation *in God,* which precedes the familiar existentialist dialectic; see his *Christ Without Myth* (Harper & Brothers, 1961), pp. 177ff. and chapter 4.

only because the power of Jesus' resurrection and the presence of the Holy Spirit enable post-apostolic men and women to recapitulate Peter's Caesarean confession.

SOME REASSESSMENTS

Special attention needs to be given to the light which the indicative methodology throws upon the Reformation categories of law and gospel. The customary strategy of law and gospel uses the law as a club to beat sinners into some sort of submission to the gospel, as an alcoholic is purposely driven into despair so that therapy can take hold. This dialectic of law and gospel presupposes a fundamental unity between the realm of nature in which law is operative and that of grace in which the gospel is preeminent. This unity is in the God who exercises both law and gospel. But this unity is also in the created order in which both are operative. Generations of Lutheran theologians, for example, have observed that the dialectic between law and gospel presupposes a man who is malleable, who can be driven by law into gospel.[11] The difficulty is that the preaching of law sometimes rests on a view of man so corrupt that it is impossible to account for his transition to the gospel, towards which he is being driven. The methodology of the indicative reminds us that the first fact of Christian faith is not sinful men laboring under the curse towards the gospel, but rather redeemed men who look back in retrospect upon their life under the curse; even when the redeemed man continues in sin, the Christian considers this, not as a continuation of life under the law, but rather as a manifestation of the ongoing evil that has been decisively overcome by Christ. The Reformation "grace alone" thus assumes its true character as a Christian's way of accounting for the *fait accompli* that sinful men have found God's favor. The formula of law and gospel, therefore, cannot stand alone as an interpretation of Christian faith. It stands rather as the reflection of a man who has already come to know the actuality of the gospel's redemption. The law-gospel formula cannot serve

[11] See footnote 9 above and also Philip Watson, *Let God Be God!* (Philadelphia: Muhlenberg Press, 1947), pp. 80f.

as the sole guide for the church's preaching; rather, it serves as a reminder of the path which the redeemed man has trod and which he looks back upon in retrospect, remembering all the while that the reality of Christ's redemptive work has enabled him to walk that path victoriously.

The underlying logic of Paul's faith certainly points to the priority of God's decisive action over a concern for the law-gospel dialectic. Three important Pauline passages throw light on this point. The extended discourse in Romans 6-8 makes it clear that the wretchedness which the law (here equivalent to the Mosaic law) awakened in Paul (7:13-25) was not the first datum of his awareness, but rather that it stood in the light of the indicative expressed in 6:1-4—"How can we who died to sin live in it?" This is the basis of Paul's "delight in the law of God" which is concomitant at every point to his wretchedness and superordinated to it. This fact may very well be reflected also in Philippians 3, where in verses 6-11 he seems to imply that it was not wretchedness under the law (which here refers to the Mosaic law), but rather the presence of Christ, which brought him to faith. Colossians 3 is one of the strongest Christian statements of the priority of the indicative over the imperative. Here it is unambiguously clear that our death and resurrection with Christ form the background for any consideration of the law (here referring to ethical obligations). These Pauline passages emphasize that the law-gospel dialectic is not considered to be the sum of the Christian faith; rather, consideration of the law follows upon the *fait accompli* of reconstructed existence in the power of Christ's resurrection.[12]

The methodology of the indicative does not stand opposed to

[12] I am grateful to my colleagues, Professors Lorenz Nieting and Cora Klick, for clarifying certain exegetical developments in the interpretation of these Pauline passages, including the current reservations concerning the autobiographical status of Romans 7. See Günther Bornkamm, *Das Ende des Gesetzes* (Munich: Chr. Kaiser Verlag, 1958), pp. 51-70, and Paul Althaus, *Paulus und Luther über den Menschen* (3rd rev. ed.; Gütersloh: Carl Bertlesmann, 1958).

the classic Reformation formula *simul justus ac peccator* (justified and sinner at the same time), even though a superficial
glance might give this impression. This methodology does entail
a new perspective, however, which makes old theological verities
appear in a different light, rearranging their interrelationships.
Thus, reflection on the basis of the indicative actuality of
redeemed existence does not obliterate the fact that the Christian
is a sinner even while he is justified, nor that the gift of redemption is always imperfectly realized in the midst of man's perpetual rebellion. But it does assert that in the dialectic between
sin and redemption there are certain priorities which dare not be
overlooked. In the Reformation formula the terms *justus* and
peccator are not of the same value. As Romans 6-8, Philippians
3, and Colossians 3 testify, the *peccator* is described through the
eyes of the *justus*.[13] It may be adequate psychological description
to assert that the despair of sin is present every moment as a
concomitant to justification. It may be proper sociological and
historical description to assert that man's hands are always dirty,
continually marring the new creation which Christ has brought.
Theologically, however, it must be said that the very concept of
peccator is dependent upon a prior awareness of the concrete
actuality of redemption, and that the phrase *simul justus ac peccator* is itself meaningful only in a community which celebrates
and marvels at the fact that its existence *has* been recreated quite
beyond any reasonable expectations, *sola gratia*. There is a tension between the new life in Christ and the sin which despoils
every human existence, but it is a tension that is played out
within the framework of a decisively recreated existence; and
even if the old Adam should be victorious in any single individual or generation, thereby bringing about a total lapse from the
new creation in Christ, this very fall would itself underline the
preeminence of redemption which shapes the Christian life. This
redemption is present as a concrete reality on the basis of the

[13]See footnote 12, especially the discussion by Althaus and the
sources to which he refers.

unity of nature and grace that God has forged in his own action in man's behalf.

RESHAPING THE REFORMATION PREACHING

When this perspective of the indicative is thus properly understood, it becomes clear that it does not stand in any fundamental opposition to classic Reformation theology. But it does call for a reappraisal of certain popular modes in which the Reformation confession has been promulgated. Certain traditional Protestant habits of expression may have to be reshaped, even fractured, in order to enable the Reformation churches to be faithful to their own best theology and to protect them from distorting it. The Lutheran preoccupation with sin and grace as constituting the dialectic of individual piety may need to be shifted to a greater concern for the reality of the resurrection and the new life in community it engenders as a framework which is prior to the law-gospel dialectic and which is indispensable if that dialectic is to be interpreted properly. It may well be that an unrelieved concentration on sin and grace, law and gospel, cannot escape eventual bondage to the methodology of the imperative which misses the real center of Christian faith. For at least seventy-five years, students of Luther have reminded us that in the *simul-justus* formula he was, after all, speaking of the sinful man who would perish without Christ's grace within the larger society of the covenant community.[14] One has only to read Luther's treatises on the sacraments to see that the acuteness of his insights into man's condition of woe and his thirst for Christ's benefits of forgiveness are inseparable from his awareness of the community, the *koinonia*, in Christ's resurrection, which is prior to human woe and thirst, and which is the basis of the resolution of man's predicament.[15] The question that faces many Protes-

[14]See, for example, Albrecht Ritschl's historical and theological analysis of this aspect of Luther's thought, in relation especially to later attempts to clarify the essence of Reformation faith, in his essay "Ueber die beiden Principien des Protestantismus," *Gesammelte Aufsätze* (Freiburg: J. C. B. Mohr, 1893), pp. 234-47.

[15]See in particular Luther's treatises, "The Holy and Blessed Sacra-

tants today is whether, through some leeching of Protestant piety, they have not thrown aside the Reformers' presuppositions concerning the nurturing matrix of the resurrection community, thus misunderstanding their explicit concern for sin and grace, with the result that the total structure of Protestant discourse is perilously close to irrelevance and unfaithfulness. The provenance of this imperative mode—whether in the faulty exegesis of Paul, in the misinterpretation of Luther's own personal experience, in a vestige of Kantian philosophy (perhaps also misunderstood), or in a Western capitalistic ethos—is a matter for debate; but it is clear that it represents a tendency to permit one valid Christian insight to displace other valid truths, to permit a part to become the whole, thus deceiving both life and belief; a tendency that disrupts the order of faith's logic, threatening to overthrow the priority, the prevenience, of God's grace—the bosom of meaning and being from which all Christian life emerges—in favor of the tortuous existential wrestling with sin from which no Christian life can escape. The repossession of faith's logic of the indicative may indeed call for a redirection of preaching and theology; without such redirection, it is doubtful that Protestantism can be faithful to classic, Reformation Christianity.

Finally, no theologian can escape the obvious ontological implications that are reflected in the foregoing discussion. The imperative mode of reflection seems to presuppose an ontology of discontinuity, in that it depicts the law which orders man's being (as well as the world's being) as lying irrevocably outside that being. It is too easy to assert that this discontinuity is overcome by the abolition, recreation, or fulfillment of the law in Jesus Christ, because this argument allows no underlying structure of being upon which abolition, recreation, or fulfillment could be actual. Christ's work thus becomes a rather unpersuasive *tour de*

ment of Baptism" and "The Blessed Sacrament of the Holy and True Body of Christ," in *Word and Sacrament I (Luther's Works,* Vol. XXV, [Philadelphia: Muhlenberg Press, 1960]), especially pp. 32ff., 56-60.

force. It would be preferable to acknowledge that the tension between law and gospel, between man as *justus* and man as *peccator* is no ontological description, but rather faith's phenomenological description of its own awareness of man as *homo viator.* Such a description is faithful to the Christian insight into man's sinful nature, but it plays out its role against an ontology of continuity, in which God's power is constitutive of all life, as the very order of creation which sustains this world and man in the hand of the Creator. The methodology of the indicative rests on such an ontology of continuity, acknowledging the moral foundations of the traditional dialectic between law and gospel, but refusing to give that dialectic ontological dignity.[16]

II. NATURE, GRACE, AND CATHOLICITY

The foregoing discussion centered on the premise that the primary datum of Christian faith is the actuality of redemption in human existence through the resurrection of Jesus, sustained by the presence of the Pentecost Spirit. This datum was set forth primarily from the perspective of the individual redeemed man. Our understanding of this datum is not complete unless we recognize more specifically its significance within the life of the resurrection community as well.

The Christian community's affirmation of actual redemption in its midst through the resurrection is embodied in its traditional claim to *catholicity;* in applying the term "catholic" to itself, the community celebrates the fullness of divine grace that

[16]See Wolfgang Berge, *Gesetz und Evangelium in der neueren Theologie* (Berlin: Evangelische Verlagsanstalt, 1958), pp. 1-27. It may be that the program of indicative Christian reflection calls for a repossession of the classical Christian sense of cooperating grace, not in the sense that man initiates God's gracious work (a view that the Reformation rightly repudiated), but rather that *God has consented* to work his will within natural structures, thus *allowing* man to cooperate in his plan, in response to his prior grace. Justifying grace, which Reformation Christanity has opposed to cooperating grace, is an action of God that takes its place within the enfolding ambience of cooperating grace, classically conceived.

lives in its midst and asserts that this grace penetrates without limitation every aspect of the existence and the world in which the community fulfills its destiny. Thus, catholicity refers to the unity of nature and grace which the community knows in its own existence. From the beginning of Christian reflection, "catholicity" has been interpreted to refer to the church's penetration or involvement—in one way or another—in the world in which it finds itself.[17] This penetration has its basis in the Incarnation, and for this reason, catholicity, like the Christian life, is essentially Christ-centered. Theologians may differ on the concrete manifestations of the church's catholicity, but they are agreed on its basic character as including the notions of penetration, comprehensiveness, and universality.[18]

The closer determination of just what this catholic penetration and universality imply is a difficult matter. Gustave Weigel is undoubtedly correct when he chides Protestants for their tendency to make catholicity equivalent to a kind of invisible universality in the church. Catholicity is not a disembodied attribute of comprehensiveness; it appears always in the concrete, bound to specific positions in time and space. Catholicity refers to something particular and not to everything in general. On the other hand, its reference to the concrete manifestation of grace in nature also includes a testimony to the penetration of the natural order which is as inexhaustible and irrepressible as the nature of the initiating God himself. Considerations like these prompt us

[17]The earliest use of the term "catholicity" in patristic literature points to this Christocentricity: Ignatius' *Epistle to the Smyrneans*, chap. viii.

[18]One notes this in Roman Catholic, as well as Protestant discussions of catholicity. See Jaroslav Pelikan, *The Riddle of Roman Catholicism* (New York: Abingdon, 1959), p. 22; Gustaf Aulén, *Reformation and Catholicity* (Philadelphia: Muhlenberg Press, 1961), p. 181ff.; Henri de Lubac, *Catholicism* (London: Burns, Oates and Washbourne, 1950); Karl Adam, *The Spirit of Catholicism* (Garden City: Image Books), chap. ix; John La Farge, "The Story of a Roman Catholic," *Between Two Cities*, ed. Thurston Davies *et al.* (New York: The America Press, 1962), pp. 4ff.

to observe that catholicity, like the grace upon which it is rooted, contains within itself the character of a specific, unique substance of redemption, focusing on Jesus Christ, while at the same time including in itself the expansive power which accounts for its ability to be comprehensive. Catholicity is thus constituted by a double thrust, one aspect of which is marked by its Christ-informed identity, the other by its propensity for inclusiveness. On both sides of this equation, however, there is a drive towards completeness, a reflexive completeness on the one side, an expansive completeness on the other.[19]

The reflexive thrust which is inherent in catholicity may be described as the church's obedience to the fullness of God's revelation in Jesus Christ, as that revelation is manifested in the actuality of redeemed human existence. It is in this obedience that the church (and the individual Christian) discovers what it really is and what its existence entails. The expansive thrust of catholicity is constituted by a universal outreach in the fullness of revelation to all the world in all places at all times.[20] It is in this outreach that the church participates in the power of God's own action. The reflexive thrust accounts for the church's continual concern for Scripture, tradition, intra-ecclesiastical affairs, liturgical development, continuing instruction of its people, and the like. Under the rubric of expansive outreach, we account not only for the obvious geographical outreach of evangelistic missions, but also the church's concern for the social order and what Paul Tillich calls "intensive catholicity," which refers to the church's involvement with culture, as for example the penetration of Christian reflection into philosophy and of the Christian Story into artistic achievement.

The affirmation of catholicity appears, therefore, to be essential in any approach to the subject of nature and grace, because it adds a testimony to the corporate, cultural, even cosmic, di-

[19]Karl Adam speaks of a similar two-fold thrust under the terms "internal" and "external" catholicity (op. cit., pp. 154-55).

[20]See my "Catholicity and Liberal Theology," Una Sancta, XX, (1963), No. 4.

mensions of the unity of nature and grace which God effected in his concrete action of redeeming human existence in Jesus Christ. And while catholicity points to this massive character of the penetration of grace into nature, it also carries with it an inherent concern for (even drive towards) the mainsprings of the substance of the grace which nourishes the church, thus preserving it from dissolution and meaninglessness as it penetrates the world. There is a dialectic, then, which binds our consideration of nature and grace indissolubly to a concern for the church and its catholicity: the unity of nature and grace is the presupposition of the church's claim to catholicity; this catholicity, in its own way, points to the fullness of that unity.

Some of the most important implications of this line of thinking appear when we consider that the church's catholicity is not a disembodied concept or simply an abstract way of thinking. Catholicity, as we have noted, takes its source from the action of God in history, preeminently in the Incarnation in Jesus of Nazareth; from this source, catholicity receives a continual impulse towards concrete manifestation. In what follows, we need to consider how this drive towards concreteness holds important implications for both sides of the equation that includes reflexive as well as expansive movement in the church.

CATHOLICITY IN AN AGE OF TRANSITION

When we consider the expansive side of the church's catholicity, we see that this inherent concreteness of expression poses particular problems in periods of historical transition, as the period in which we are now living serves to illustrate. The concrete impulse of the church's catholicity (and of the actuality of redeemed existence which underlies it) leads inescapably to the conclusion that the shape of that catholicity must be affected by the lineaments of the age in which the church lives, i.e., of the nature that forms the matrix for the church's existence. To say that grace has penetrated concretely the realm of nature inevitably precludes the possibility of ascribing to catholicity a shape or configuration which is independent of that realm, even as the very notion of Incarnation entails the full humanity of our Lord Jesus Christ. In ages of stability, this insistence on concreteness causes no anxiety. In an age in which all architecture is informed by a Christian ethos, there is no reluctance to erect sanctuaries in an architectural idiom that speaks to the culture as a whole. Similarly, in a period in which the king is generally held to be God's own delegate, close relationship between church and state raises little controversy. What of an age like ours, however, which is on every hand designated an age of disruption and transition, whether by secular historians as "post-modern" or by church historians as "post-Christendom?" In such a time, the lineaments of the age (which constitute its "nature") are at best bewildering idioms for expressing catholic substance and at worst outright betrayals of that substance.

Certain historical examples offer paradigms for our perplexing situation. The period from Saul to Solomon constituted a transitional period in which the religion of the Mosaic covenant, a religion certainly possessing a catholic thrust, at least as far as Israel's culture was concerned, was faced with a radically new configuration—the Davidic monarchy, with its concomitant upheaval in Israelitic society and religion.[21] Consistent with its catholic thrust, the Mosaic religion proceeded to appropriate the Canaanite-Davidic ethos, utilizing nearly every facet of the new configuration in its own system. For mainline Israelitic piety, the Davidic religion was the continuation and fulfillment of Mosaic religion. A minority, however, never did accept the validity of the new lineaments as a continuation of the former piety. The era of early Christian expansion, in which the religion moved from Hebraic to Hellenistic culture, can also be construed as a

[21]For the pertinent details: Albrecht Alt, *Kleine Schriften zur Geschichte des Volkes Israel* (Munich: C. H. Beck, 1953), II, 61-64; Leonhard Rost, "Sinaibund und Davidbund," *Theologische Literaturzeitung* (1947), p. 129ff; Gerhard von Rad, *Theologie des Alten Testaments* (Munich: Chr. Kaiser Verlag, 1957), I, 113ff.; Leonhard Rost, *Die Ueberlieferung von der Thronnachfolge Davids* (Stuttgart: W. Kohlhammer, 1926).

paradigm. Here too, the catholic impulse appropriated in an amazing way the chief elements of the Hellenistic system, even to the extent that the Hebrew meaning of the term "Christ" became blurred in the popular Christian mind and the term assumed the status of a surname. The overwhelming victory of the catholic impulse is obvious; but it must also be noted that a minority has never accepted this transition. The result has been the dejudaization of early Christianity, and the Protestant concept of the "Fall of the Church," which steadfastly refuses to accept the full legitimacy of Christianity's incursion into Hellenistic Roman culture.[22]

Today, the church is confronted by voices like those of Dietrich Bonhoeffer and Paul Tillich—faithful sons who are calling attention to the radical way in which our cultural forms have been reshaped and the impact which this reshaping must have on the Christian church. These voices have sometimes been welcomed as guides for the church's evangelistic strategy; the church has not failed altogether to adapt its preaching to the urgent needs of our times. But at a profounder level, as a legitimate idiom for the expression of catholic substance, the lineaments of our present cultural situation are at best ignored and at worst utterly rejected. The significance of such concepts as "holy worldliness," "belief-ful realism," "culture as the form of religion," "the new humanity," is little understood.[23] The task which the church faces today corresponds in its urgency and complexity to the task of post-Davidic Israel and post-Apostolic

[22]For a comprehensive survey, see W. Glawe, *Die Hellenisierung des Christentums in der Geschichte der Theologie von Luther bis auf die Gegenwart* (Berlin: Töpelmann, 1912).

[23]For Bonhoeffer's discussion, see his *Prisoner for God* (New York: Macmillan Co., 1957); also, Martin Marty (ed.), *The Place of Bonhoeffer* (New York: Association Press, 1962). Tillich's most important works in this area are *The Protestant Era* (Chicago: The University of Chicago Press, 1948), chaps. iii, iv, v, vii, xiii; xiv; *Theology of Culture* (New York: Oxford Unversity Press, 1959), chaps. i, iv; *The Religious Situation* (Living Age Books; New York: Meridian, 1956).

Christianity. It is the task of preparing the way for the reality of catholic substance to express itself in the idiom of a secularized world. Here Protestants generally are critical of Roman understandings of catholicity (although Protestants have little enough to boast of at this point), because Roman theologians equate Romanism and catholicity in a manner that does not seem to take seriously the creative possibilities of new cultural configurations.[24]

One of the chief problems that must be resolved here is the matter of the *marks* of catholicity. What can one say about the marks of catholicity if the lineaments of nature, i.e., the world in which the church lives, play a part in determining the shape of catholicity? At the very least one must acknowledge that the distinguishing characteristics of catholicity cannot be determined solely by reference to repristinated forms, whether of dogma, liturgy, polity, or piety. This sort of protesting criticism does not furnish an adequate solution to the problem of designating and sustaining catholic substance, however, even though Protestantism has at times seemed to think that such a demurral is sufficient. Today, much more is demanded of Reformation Christians than the stereotyped protest against the absolutizing of historical forms; much more attention must be given to the repossession of the substance of divine revelation that vivifies the church.[25]

[24]The manner in which such theologians automatically identify Roman and catholic Christianity can be seen, for example, in Gustave Weigel's portion of the book he authored with Robert McAfee Brown, *An American Dialogue* (Garden City, N. Y.: Doubleday Anchor Books, 1961), pp. 211-12; the Roman Catholic reaction to the formulation of a sex-ethic that can speak to the problems of our times sometimes reinforces the impression that new cultural configurations are suspect; see, e.g., a series of comments in *America*: D. J. Dooley, "Cauldron of Unholy Loves," Sept. 14, 1963, pp. 262-63; and subsequent comment in "The New Morality," Sept. 21, pp. 277-78; John C. Knott, 'Father O'Brien's Article," Sept. 7, p. 225; and O'Brien's response, Sept. 28, pp. 333-34.

[25]Paul Tillich has indicated as much in his as yet untranslated

In order to determine the substance of the church's catholicity, attention must be given to its reflexive activity as this was outlined at the beginning of this section, particularly as it complements the expansive catholic thrust we just noted. This reflexive aspect constitutes the continual activity of the church by which it clarifies to itself the identifying characteristics of its catholic substance. Here too the church's catholicity is concrete in its expression. In its reflexive activity, the church must establish its identity on the one hand by paying heed to the concrete expressions of God's revelation in actual redeemed existence (and its concomitants) and on the other hand by analyzing judiciously the concrete opportunities available for expressing its identity in its contemporary life.

RECAPITULATING THE HISTORY OF GRACE

The church must heed carefully the concrete expressions of God's revelation in actual redeemed existence, because there is simply no other source for gaining an understanding of its catholic substance. This redeemed existence is overwhelmingly a phenomenon of the past. This redeemed life of the church (which has its origin in God, we must remember) is available through certain monuments or vestiges which have been left: Scripture, dogma, theology, piety, liturgy, polity, ethical actions, and the like. Some of these vestiges are embarrassing reminders that the church has been sub-Christian through much of its history; other portions of this history reveal a faith that counters some of the observer's own cherished predilections, thus reminding him that his own personal "essence" of Christianity cannot serve as a completely adequate principle for interpreting the Christian Story; finally, some of the church's historical witness is unintelligible, and this calls attention to the poverty of any

explication of the constructive implications of the "Protestant Principle" in "Der Protestantismus als kritisches und gestaltendes Prinzip," *Der Protestantismus als Kritik und Gestaltung* ("Gesammelte Werke," VII; Stuttgart: Evangelisches Verlagswerk, 1962), pp. 29-53. See also Jaroslav Pelikan's comments in *The Place of Bonhoeffer,* ed. Martin Marty (New York: Association Press, 1962), pp. 163-64.

age's "existential situation" as a receptacle for divine revelation. The reflexive thrust of the church seeks continually to recapitulate this historical witness to redemption and God's revelation. Only through a recapitulation which seeks to be faithful to the totality of this witness can the church find its true identity. Such a recapitulation is possible *only* by careful attention to, and participation in, the *concrete* manifestations of the Christian tradition (whether Tradition or traditions); it is not enough to effect this recapitulation by recourse to an idealized "essence" of Christianity, even though, ultimately, some such abstraction is inevitable. Any formulation of a "new essence of Christianity" must, however, come to grips with the fullness of the concrete vestiges of redeemed existence that past ages have left for us. Without a recapitulation of the past's fullness, there can be no assurance that the "essence" is faithful to the Christian *identity* that comprises it. Such a recapitulation is beset by imponderable difficulties: it is impossible to recapitulate the totality of the historical witness; a principle of discrimination is inevitable if meaning is to be found, but a principle of discrimination by its very nature must repudiate parts of the witness and thus forfeit universality in the interest of abstractness; the recapitulation of the past witness to revelation is always dependent upon the concrete possibilities for expression that are available in the present. Despite these problems, it seems clear that this reflexive activity of the church is of some urgency for every age, including our own.

One of the most pressing tasks facing Christian theologians today is the refinement of a methodology that is adequate to the task of grasping the essential substance of the catholic faith through a recapitulation of the totality of God's concrete revelation in actual redeemed existence and expressing that substance in the forms given to us today; or, one might say, the task of evolving a theological methodology that can frame a genuinely communicable "essence of Christianity" for our times which does not violate the integrity of the concrete history of redemption that God has wrought. If there is any point where contemporary Protestant theology and preaching has been weakest, it is here.

This is an intramural task, a task of self-understanding. It may be less appealing to theologians today than the more glamorous activity of inter-cultural dialogue, but it is nevertheless urgent enough to merit a programmatic position.[26]

We must draw the conclusion that the church's task today, both in its life and its theology, is to confess in an appropriate way the unity of nature and grace which has engendered Christian faith. This confession entails, as we have observed, careful attention to the configurations of the culture in which the church now lives, as well as a concern for the history of grace in the church's past life. The cultural configurations disclose the shape of the unity in which nature and grace are bound; recapitulation of the history of grace reveals the substance of that unity; shape and substance are inseparably and indistinguishably bound together, so that even our analysis distorts the reality of the nature-grace unity if it presumes to divide them.

CATHOLICITY AND THE CHRISTIAN INDICATIVE

Fundamental to our considerations of nature and grace has been the assertion that their unity is an indicative in Christian existence. This holds true as well for the unity of nature and grace which underlies the church's affirmation of its catholicity. The foregoing paragraphs have spoken of catholicity, both in its reflexive and its expansive facets, as a challenge, which is as yet imperfectly discharged within the church. This challenge, however, must be seen within the framework of the church's existence as it is already radically recreated by God's redemptive action. The church's catholicity is an irrepressible indicative that animates every age of its existence. Even when attempts are made to stifle it, even when this irrepressible dynamic is unnoticed, it nevertheless remains active. Catholicity is not primarily

[26] Professor Wolfhart Pannenberg has taken some steps towards forging such a methodology in "Heilsgeschehen und Geschichte," *Kerygma und Dogma,* V (July, 1959), 281-37; and V (October, 1959), 259-88; also in *Offenbarung und Geschichte* (Göttingen: Vandenhoeck und Ruprecht, 1961).

an ethos to be enforced upon the church; it is chiefly a living power that vivifies the church. Even a cursory glance at the contemporary life of the church will bear out this observation.[27] Here we must be purposely selective, overlooking many of the more obvious signs of outreach.

The expansive thrust of the church's catholicity is unmistakable in the present age. It may be important to suggest that the much-maligned nineteenth century in liberal European Protestant theology be included here as one of the significant contributing factors to the current scene. We are accustomed to harking back to Loehe, Harms, Grundtvig, Mercersburg, and the Tractarians as a basis for a current statement of the church's catholicity, but the nineteenth-century German Lutheran theologians of the liberal school have generally been castigated as apostates or else accounted for as manifestations of the liberal mind in theology. Both of these negative judgments have their justification. It would certainly indicate a peculiar lack of insight, however, to overlook the indicative dynamic of the church's catholicity in the work of Schleiermacher, Baur, Ritschl, Harnack, and the other liberals. In the realms of life and theology, they took particular care to point the way (even if they did so imperfectly) in which classic Christian testimony to God's grace had penetrated the idiom of the modern European culture.[28]

Partly as a continuation of this liberal thrust, partly in repudiation of it, we can point to several facets of the church's life today that constitute the expansive thrust of its catholicity. Dietrich Bonhoeffer's concept of "holy worldliness" is part of this thrust, even though its usefulness is far less than the more thoroughly elaborated thought of Paul Tillich, particularly in

[27]Here I must limit my comments primarily to the Protestant situation. Any comments concerning Roman Catholicism are made in the full awareness that positions are likely to change very quickly in the present state of affairs (the second session of Vatican II is in progress as this is being written).

[28]See footnote 20.

the understanding of the relation between the secular and the sacred which underlies his concepts of belief-ful realism, Protestantism, and in his formula: "culture as the form of religion, religion as the substance of culture."[29] In the same breath, we must mention Rudolf Bultmann's program of demythologizing as it seeks to make cultural configurations effective in the discerning and proclamation of the Christian Story. Of all these frames of thought, Tillich's is certainly the best worked out, and it deserves renewed attention.

Professor Gibson Winter, particularly in his *The New Creation as Metropolis,* represents a current in the contemporary life of the American church that is unusually sensitive to the efficacy of cultural lineaments in the realization of the actuality of divine grace. His suggestion is that the ministry of the church is constituted by the layman's agency of reconciliation in his occupation in the nerve centers of contemporary culture, with the religious professional in the background, offering his resources to the layman. When this is understood, not just as a strategy for the church's organization, but rather as a reconstituting of the reality of redeemed Christian existence in our world, then its profound implications for the life and thought of the church become clear. From one perspective, Winter's work is a cartography of the shape which the church's catholicity will take in its ministry to the contemporary urban world. His attempts at cartography are intimately related to the ministry of the church through its laity, in which the laity, as it permeates the world, is considered not as a tool of the organized church, but rather as an agent of God's reconciliation through the church and its ministry.

Finally, for our purposes here, the work of the more speculative, philosophical theologians must be considered. In a period when more "orthodox" Protestant theologians have largely abandoned the philosophical task in theology, there have been pockets of Christian theologians who have, whether consciously or unconsciously, reflected the catholic insight that grace has

[29]See the works referred to in footnote 23.

indeed penetrated the farther realms of human thought, as well as the farther geographical spaces. Here one must include the theologians concerned with linguistic analysis, Tillich's rapprochement to classical metaphysics, as well as the "process" theologians who are informed by modes of thought stemming from William James, Alfred North Whitehead, and Charles Hartshorne.[30] Even if all of the criticisms which have been leveled at these philosophical attempts were valid, there is no reason to suppose that in the longer view of things theology will refuse to incorporate their achievements into the catholic fullness of its theological activity. The anti-metaphysical phase through which we are moving is not only a passing phase, but also, if its legitimate protest is carried too far, an impossible denial of the catholicity which is an indicative in the church's life.

The phenomena just mentioned are marks of the church's irrepressible surge today towards catholic outreach, the penetration of the natural realm in which we live. The activity of a reflexive catholic thrust is also evident; this thrust represents the community's impulse to probe its own unique identity, so that its outreach does not result in "contourless dissolution." Under this rubric one can include the increased concern for biblical exegesis and "biblical theology," the liturgical renewal in life and theology, the resurgence of interest in the uncovering of the Reformation faith, the ecumenical movement among Orthodox and Protestants, the burgeoning *aggiornamento* among Roman Christians, and the increasing concern of all groups of Christians for each other. The theological understanding of the functioning of these activities is important in the face of the

[30]For a summary of some of these trends in philosophical theology, with bibliographical notes, see Jules Moreau, *Language and Religious Language* (Philadelphia: Westminster, 1961). Special attention should be paid to the efforts of Bernard Meland to deal with the interrelations of the Christian faith with the changing configurations of culture; e.g., his *Faith and Culture* (New York: Oxford University Press, 1953) and *The Realities of Faith* (New York: Oxford University Press, 1962).

"non-theological" interpretations that are rife today. The ecumenical movement is not simply animated by the human trend towards collectivism; the look to our biblical and Reformation heritage is not just an attempt to find stability in times of psychological, sociological, and historical crisis; the liturgical renewal cannot be ascribed to psychological forces alone, nor to a perennial romanticism. These activities are susceptible to such non-theological analysis; but more importantly—for the church, at least—they are to be seen as part of the inherent catholic thrust within the community of grace; a thrust that moves from the presupposition that grace is at work in the realm of nature and that this gracious presence is ultimately oriented upon nothing else than the Incarnation of our Lord Jesus Christ —the Incarnation which animates the Christian cultus and the biblical and Reformation confessions and which is the substance of the unity that all Christian groups seem to strain towards today. These activities are expressions of the almost prerational sense of the Christian community that an understanding and cultivation of the substance of its own self-identity, leading ultimately to the Incarnation, is a necessary concomitant to the catholic outreach into the world; a grasp of this self-identity is impossible apart from a recapitulation of the biblical, theological, and liturgical tradition; this self-identity includes the unity of all members of the body which comprises the community of God's people. The activities we have just noted are part of a vast intramural activity which moves along in its own inscrutable fashion, but which nevertheless aims at enhancing the church's self-understanding. This activity is part of the church's attempt to make what Karl Adam calls "a resolute affirmation of the whole of revelation in all its living fulness," which he considers to be inherent in the catholicity of the church.[31]

As cursory as these comments have been, the scope of the synthesis which they suggest indicates that the burgeoning theological concern for the relations that obtain between nature

[31]Karl Adam, *op. cit.*, p. 155.

and grace will inevitably lead our reflection to the very center of the Christian faith and out from that center to comprehensive systematic elaborations. This concern will certainly extend to programmatic lengths, as the church's theologians recognize that, in our day at least, the unity of nature and grace in God's redemptive action engenders new perspectives through which the core of our faith is to be grasped and expressed. Finally, reflection upon the unity of nature and grace may give us new insights into the functioning of the Christian community, as it lives in the matrix of a nature that has been decisively penetrated by grace.

THE SOCIAL ROLE
OF THE MAN OF GOD

Karl H. Hertz

THE SOCIAL ROLE
OF THE MAN OF GOD

Speaking to a workshop on "Jazz and Contemporary Culture" in 1962 Joseph Sittler observed:

"I sometimes think I have the most nerve-racking job in my church. Time after time I am called upon to subject myself to the data of a specific field of discourse, sit for several days, take it all in, mull it all over, and then, just in time for market, like a theological hen, lay an orotund, complete, and summarizing egg.

"Or, to change the figure to one perhaps more apt in this situation, I am expected to be a kind of shortstop for God ranging back and forth on the baseline, with Roach, Hentoff, Hammond and company at bat, and whether the ball is on the ground or hits a pebble under my nose, or as is more like the case, is quite out of my reach, the extravagant expectation is that I shall cleanly field it and make an out."[1]

These remarks characterize quite well the role Professor Sittler has played in the church. To use a more elegant metaphor, he has in a very striking fashion been a kind of one man scouting party sent ahead to meet, speak with, listen to, and interpret the aborigines on the occupational and social frontiers where the claims of the Word have never penetrated or have been lost or surrendered. Among those outside the pale of respectability, e.g., the jazz musicians, in the company of the student intelligentsia, when the cleansing light of skeptical minds has banished the last misty remnants of old superstitions, this man has come, consciously and openly as a man of God, to converse with these worldlings about nature and grace, to join

[1]Quoted from the taped recording of Professor Sittler's address, *The Village Gate,* New York City, February 28, 1962.

them as a partner in the struggle to discover traces of meaning
and order in their common predicaments.

Such activities breed questions from both sides, questions
which I want to subsume under three general headings, each
bearing on the larger issue of the social role of the man of God,
i.e., of the pattern of life to which a Christian is called as a
citizen of the world. From the perspective of the individual
Christian, this is the form which the question about the relation
of nature and grace will take. How does a man who has known
the gift of grace in the new creation live in a world whose
basic shape derives from the old creation? How does the child
of grace inhabit the domain of nature?

Three major issues are before us. The first and most basic is
whether the religious man should have anything to do with
non-religious activities. Do we not live in two kingdoms which
we must not confuse? Has God not supplied two sets of rulers,
the law and the gospel, each appropriate to its proper sphere
of activities?

A general affirmation of Christian involvement in the world
still leaves many questions unanswered. For in the world itself
it may be possible to distinguish activities which a child of God
may properly undertake from those which are taboo. Thus a
Christian may be a barber but not a bartender, a horsebreeder
but not a horse player, a promoter of subdivisions but not the
impresario of a night club. Or perhaps a Christian may be both.
How does the man of God know and decide?

Finally, we must come to terms with the responsibilities of
the professional man of God, the clergyman or theologian, and
discover whether there are special marks which distinguish his
activities in the world from the work of the Christian layman.

All of these questions arise from the social role which Professor Sittler is playing, arise as issues in the relationship between
nature and grace.

In speaking to the workshop on Jazz and Contemporary
Culture, Professor Sittler made clear a basic position with respect

to nature and grace: "Music is of the body, it's of the world, it's of the world of nature; because that is so, it needs no apologia, it needs no attachment to other things, no legitimation by decent marriage to something else to make an honest woman out of her; with the interior forces and passion of every natural thing, music must at the risk of her life resist reduction to some purpose or end anterior to herself or supposedly superior to herself; it is what it is; its being has its own integrity; it does not have to mean but be, and whatever it means must spring with a kind of lubricated naturalness out of what it is."[2]

Because jazz is not yet a fully respectable occupation in the eyes of many, its claim to authenticity on its own terms may serve as a paradigm for us. For what is involved in the statements Professor Sittler made is an assertion of the autonomy of the natural. But in what sense is nature "autonomous"?

Certain historical observations must precede a direct discussion of this question. In a "religious" society, such as medieval society has been described to be, the natural world is not separable from the sacred. Instead nature is "sacralized," and the divine or the demonic may be at work anywhere. Every occupation, every social stratum, every community has its rituals, festivals, and patron saints. The basic political issue in such a society, that of the "two swords," does not define a dichotomy of sacred and secular.

Even in the early Protestant world, in which "two kingdoms" replace "two swords" as the metaphor, it remains true that each kingdom, whether on the right or on the left, is under God. Different rules apply; love is the mainspring of action in one; justice orders the other. But justice is something God gives and demands. Indeed by its interpretation of Romans 13 the church gives legitimacy to what the state requires. Careful efforts are made, furthermore, to avoid confusion of the two realms; thus Lutheran theologians in particular grapple with the questions of law and gospel.

[2]*Ibid.*

But a problem comes to haunt devout men. For the distinction between law and gospel, the differentiation of love and justice, tends psychologically and sociologically to lead to a divorce between the public and the private, between personal kindness and official rigor. Pietists in particular follow this logic through consistently, even to the extent that some of them deny Christians any proper place in public life. Conservatives, on the other hand, tend to defend *Realpolitik* on religious grounds.

The practical divorce is also an intellectual one. In the dualism of Descartes and in the philosophy of the Enlightenment the distinction between matter and mind, revelation and reason, natural theology and Christian dogma, allows men to mark out "the natural" as an arena in which, paraphrasing Newton, "One does not make hypotheses," in which only what is empirically given, or rationally demonstrable, only that which has reality within the world of space and time, can be taken into account in the ordering of events in the world of nature.

The differentiation which liberates the scientists, which spreads into the domain of politics (where the laws of nature and the rights of man are sufficient ground for good order) and into economic doctrine (where the free market provides for the wealth of nations), serves more and more to limit the scope of the man of God until "pure religion and undefiled" turns into a worship of God by means of liturgies, hymns, and sermons that extol primarily an inner "spiritual" life and the personal piety of the virtuous individual.

The criticism Troeltsch made, so much resented in most Lutheran circles, has its focus and relevance here. True, Luther would not have understood these dichotomies, but in the nineteenth century his heirs in almost all evangelical groups insisted upon this strange divorce between the realm of grace and the realm of nature.

The familiar dualisms of the swords or the kingdoms had meaning in societies in which church and state towered above all else as the dominant institutional realities. But even where "establishment" still exists legally, a pluralistic social order has in fact replaced the old dual structures. The contemporary social world is a vast complex of many major organizations and an almost infinite multitude of minor ones, voluntary or semi-compulsory, varying from local associations to national and international corporate bureaucracies.

If a dichotomy is still valid, that dichotomy cannot order life in terms of church and state—for too much would be omitted. It must distinguish church and community, but once we make this distinction, we are in trouble. Two swords and two kingdoms had meaningful institutional referents; they existed alongside one another in organized form. But within the community we do not have church (singular) but churches—of diverse traditions, sizes, and theological persuasions. We may, if we please, talk about "the coming great church" but that reality is eschatological, not institutional.

The options are few and may be briefly stated. We may still, by some kind of evangelical coalition politics, in memory of a once vital Protestant culture, insist that the community must be ordered under the mandates of God. Given the conservative denial of natural theology, such an order could only be imposed from the outside; it would not grow out of the community in a natural way. In whatever guise it came, the end product would be a theocracy.

We may choose a liberal "way out" and see the churches only as a species of private associations. Then the question remains whether anything legitimates religious demands for social justice; whether the church may speak to the great associations of the public arena.

It is no accident that the founding fathers of the liberal doctrine of the state, Locke and his intellectual heirs, in their pleas for religious tolerance were concerned primarily to get the churches out of their controlling places in the social order. If contemporary religious liberalism now asserts social responsibility, quite often its attempt to legitimate these concerns is

grounded in a general doctrine of justice, in a religiously tinged
humanitarian impulse, in which the distinction between grace
and nature has almost evaporated. Theories of theocracy claim
too much; liberalism comes with too little.

In a strange way the liberal doctrine of the essentially private
nature of religious associations and the Lutheran doctrine of
two kingdoms proved to be functional equivalents under the
pluralistic conditions of American life. For the "life of faith"
defined a private piety; the public sphere, one affirmed implicitly
at least, lay beyond the reach of the gospel. The legislative hall,
the courtroom, the market, the shop, even the school, ran on
their own inherent principles. The logic of the distinction thus
implied the autonomy of the natural, but the compulsive preoccupation of the devout with inner spirituality often led to a
practical disparagement of what had been liberated.

One approach to this dilemma is to suggest a new metaphor.
Grace and nature do not define two realms of human activity,
but two dimensions of a single unity: human existence. They
represent different ways in which we are related, not different
places in which we stand. Like sight and hearing, both grace
and nature serve best to orient us in the world when used
together; yet each defines reality in its own way.

Thus positively and constructively we assert that nature and
grace must be distinguished, that the unique reality of each
must be recognized, and that since every man stands simultaneously in both dimensions, we must understand the relatedness
of the two dimensions.

The knot of our controversy is in the second and third of
these assertions. Here Sittler's reexamination of the old dichotomy under the more universal categories of nature and grace
makes possible a new perspective. Nature is what it is, and it
must be accepted on these terms. As original creation, it was
made for man. In and through its manifold structures man was
to express his humanity. Even as fallen creation, nature remains
the human habitation. In the new creation its restoration is antici-

pated. And man's ultimate destination is a new earth, restored to its pristine perfection.

Now all of these assertions remain true, whether any man believes them or not. For just as man stands in a finite world, ever busy at a multitude of tasks, so he also stands related to God. Whether he knows God or not, God knows him, and God requires that he be a man. Whether he blows a horn, punches a time clock in a shop, wears the wig of an English barrister or the Stetson of an American cattleman; whether what comes out is broken or beautiful, whether the imperfection of his performance drives him to despair or the charlatanry of others provokes his contempt, the burden of being what God made him to be remains inescapable. He may deny it or curse it; he may experience it as the wrath of God and look upon existence as an act of defiance in the face of the unknown; or, without recognizing its origin, or the ultimate direction in which he must face, he may affirm that what has been given him is good and dedicate himself to using it with care and shaping its materials into things of beauty.

This is the autonomy of nature, even in its broken form. The stamp of the Creator remains upon it; the order which his love bestowed may be disrupted but it cannot be annihilated. It is an order of things social as well as things physical, not imposed from without, but as energy, vitality, instinct, motive, purpose an inherent dynamic that must run its appointed course.

To see nature as "autonomous" in these terms is already a gift of grace and therefore never secular. What the man of God has learned, however, is that a man may misread his own humanity; not every claim for integrity is authentic, nor is every passion nor every impulse an unconscious yearning for goodness. The calling of the man of God when, to use an older terminology, he preaches the law is a recalling of man to his authentic being within nature, within the creation. It is a plea for justice, for right relationships within the human community.

We can explicate more fully the meaning of nature we have

sketched out and also the particular character of the relatedness of nature and grace by using the concept of social "role" to look at what the man of God does.

Sociologists use "role" to describe the behavior expected of the incumbent of a social position. Role behavior is both instrumental and expressive. To behave as a husband means to do certain useful things, to earn a living, provide a domicile, accept specific obligations and prohibitions. But to be a husband is also something more. By my behavior towards the woman who is my wife I also *express* the quality of a relationship. What I do not only has instrumental value; it also carries symbolic significance. Indeed, if my conduct towards my wife, no matter how proper otherwise, does not express this relationship, am I properly a "husband"? Even in the most intimate of relationships, it is not (despite the sex manuals) really the mastery of the technique of the sex act which affirms the quality of the relationship, but the quality of the relationship which gives meaning to the act.

The crux of the matter here is not merely that roles may be both instrumental and expressive, but that both dimensions are valid. In our utilitarian culture, with our Puritan heritage, we have not always accepted the expressive. Artistic roles, for example, are generally more expressive than instrumental. In America we have given the artists a bad time, especially in the entertaining arts—actors, jazz musicians, and the like. The insistence of the artist on integrity is in one sense an insistent demand for the freedom of the expressive. Indeed, apart from the expressive, it would be hard to define our essential humanity. We would be means, not ends; things or commodities, not persons.

More has to be said; for I would contend that the essence of a "religious role" is often found in its expressive dimension, for what happens in religious action must always somehow point beyond the immediate function to a larger context of meaning. Even in religions of the law, there is a pointing to the Lawgiver.

In Christianity it is this relationship which is essential; for we are saved by grace, not works. Even in nature a relationship may be expressed—indeed where else, since we are all creatures of flesh and blood. In a "fallen nature" it is expressed partially and incompletely, often with fear and trembling. Yet the demand (when it is valid) for authenticity, for autonomy and integrity, is finally the demand for the right to be a human being.

This demand can be richly documented from the "heretical" literature of the past century. If Matthew Arnold's protest against "faith in machinery" was a mild, culturally genteel brief against reducing man to a commodity, his contemporary Marx filed the same brief in language that was strong and prophetic. To make man a thing, to make labor a commodity, is to do violence to humanity; it is to alienate man from himself. In a similar vein protests can be heard in Tillich and Freud, more recently in Goffman, Berger, and Paul Goodman.[3] To be a man, Goodman insists, is to grow up into a meaningful existence; it is to find work which is not only "useful" in a monetary sense, or instrumental to some other person's purpose; it is to be able in one's work to express manhood; it is a demand for integrity.

Many of the discussions of adolescence, of sex problems, of the odd world of *Playboy*, could thus be illumined. Indeed, many of the demands voiced in "off-beat" literature, in the eccentric and the bizarre, as well as in the exaggerated glorification of "woman as body" and "man as an aggressor" carry, despite all distortions, an undercurrent of protest against the "thingification" of man. Grace demands that nature be set free as a stage on which men may play their parts as men, not as puppets dancing to some absentee power's tune.

The primacy of the personal thus offers the criterion for judging both whether a certain role is acceptable within the

[3]Erving Goffman, *Asylums* (Garden City, N.Y.: Doubleday Anchor Books, 1961); Peter Berger, *The Precarious Vision,* (Garden City, N.Y.: Doubleday, 1961); and Paul Goodman, *Growing Up Absurd* (New York: Random House, 1956.)

human community and which demands for integrity are valid. The perspective of the horse player, consistently applied, would affirm that in its essence, life is a gamble and the universe a random affair. Where randomness prevails, order cannot exist and meaning is impossible. Under such circumstances, man may be one of the possibly more interesting accidents turned up by the ceaseless spinning of the wheel of chance; he cannot be a person—a maker of useful things and the proclaimer of significant propositions.

To be a person is to stand within a network of relationships, relationships which reach far beyond the simple tracing out of social connections. Since man is a part of nature, what a man expresses reveals not only his stance within a community of persons but also his wider kinship with all living forms, with the elemental forces of the universe itself. The integral statement of our humanity is finally always an ontological claim, an assertion about what our being is.

To assert what it means to be a man is not a matter only for philosophers, nor is such assertion limited to discursive propositions. Poets and painters, children at play, and craftsmen at their workbench also have their parts. The deceptive ease with which a superb athlete executes a difficult play, the stylized gyrations of a prima ballerina, the sure hand of the experienced truck driver negotiating a difficult stretch of road, the controlled ecstasy with which a jazz trumpeter takes his solo—all of these are particular ontological assertions through which the meaning of nature is expressed.

Robert Frost once wrote:

> Every single poem written regular is a symbol small or great of the way the will has to pitch into commitments deeper and deeper to a rounded conclusion and then be judged for whether any original intention it had has been strongly spent or weakly lost; be it in art, politics, school, church, business, love, or marriage— in a piece of work or in a career. Strongly spent is synonymous with kept.

. . . Every poem is an epitome of the great predicament; a figure of the will braving alien entanglements."[4]

It has been the particular gift of Joseph Sittler to aid in the recovery of the expressive. His concern with poetry and drama, with contemporary voices in the arts, and also his concern with worship and liturgy has been to understand what these express, how they manifest the predicament, the burden, and the glory of our humanity.

To be a man is to be more than a function; it is to be a person, to be someone who counts, to have a name, a place to come home to. Robert Frost caught this note in "The Death of the Hired Man":

> 'Home is the place where, when you have to go there,
> They have to take you in.'
>   'I should have called it
> Something you somehow haven't to deserve."[5]

From a different point of view Carl Sandburg voiced the same insight:

Shake back your hair, O red-headed girl.
Let go your laughter and keep your two proud freckles on your chin.
Somewhere is a man looking for a red-headed girl and some
     day maybe he will look into your eyes for a restaurant
     cashier and find a love, maybe.
Around and around go ten thousand men hunting a red-headed
     girl with freckles on her chin.
I have seen them hunting, hunting.
          Shake back your hair; let go your laughter.[6]

[4]"The Constant Symbol," introductory essay to *The Poems of Robert Frost* (New York: Modern Library, 1946), pp. xvi, xvii.

[5]From "The Death of the Hired Man" from *Complete Poems of Robert Frost*. Copyright 1930, 1939 by Holt, Rinehart and Winston, Inc.

[6]"Red-headed Restaurant Cashier" from *Smoke and Steel* by Carl Sandburg, copyright, 1920, by Harcourt, Brace & World, Inc.; renewed, 1948, by Carl Sandburg. Reprinted by permission of the publishers.

Grace and nature coexist as dimensions in the being of every man, as dimensions of the creation as well. For every man is potentially a man of grace. The kingdom metaphor in our day becomes increasingly dubious; it is too geographical, too spatial. The tensions are within every man; within each existence the conflict goes on, nature and grace, works and faith, the instrumental and the expressive. Indeed, the unity of these diversities is mirrored in the doctrine of the church, in the paradigmatic New Adam, possessing two natures yet existing as one person.

What we affirm is coexistence; both under God. The labors of man in this world are adaptive, economic, and instrumental; this is part of our long cultural evolution. This is obedience, however partial, to the will of God. But at the same time, finitely, man may express his insistence that life has meaning beyond the immediate utility of things. The man of God will know even in the most utilitarian of tasks that his obedience is ultimately to the Creator himself.

It is proper and valid, therefore, to insist upon the autonomy and integrity of the natural, but the full meaning of what we do comes only when we set our deeds into their full relational contexts. The difference between the "man of God" and "the man of the world" lies not in what they do, but in how they are related, their awareness of this relatedness, and their expression of it. Thus it is not wrong, indeed it may be quite proper, for the jazz musician to express deep and passionate erotic feelings in his music. The "man of God" will recognize the integrity of what is done; he will also know the context within which that integrity exists.

Indeed, the man of God can play his role with an additional perspective. To stand under God in nature is to know one's self committed to use the things of the world within the limits that mark the creation as finite. Many men know this implicitly —as advocates of modesty and moderation, of conservation of resources or consideration for their fellows. The man of God should know it explicitly. Thus he knows that even as he carries out his daily work he is in the hands of God. He makes his decisions in the perspective of this knowledge; though others may neither notice nor know the significance of what he does, the deeds of the man of God express the relationship of grace within which he stands.

It does not follow, therefore, that his deeds or his decisions are salvatory. Quite the contrary. He knows that they are bound to this world, that their meaning, necessity, and purpose lie within nature. This is why they are required, yet insufficient. They are required because man is always related to his fellows and his manhood is expressed through his relationship to them. They are insufficient, for they can define man's relationship to God only in its imperfection and brokenness. The very necessity of the demand for justice is already a recognition that injustice exists, that nature has been violated and the creation betrayed.

The recognition that moral decisions are bound to this world means that within the civic community the debate over justice can proceed on autonomic terms. Autonomy here is not secularism; indeed the social role of the man of God is to point out both what is possible as justice, within the limits of human reason and experience, and what justice cannot do. Even the man who rejects God still stands under God and within the mercy of God. He is entitled to justice. But to him justice may then become the experience of the wrath of God. This is the shattering power of love; for when love demands justice, when love demands that men use the world aright, as God intended it to be used, it may break through the hypocrisy of existing institutions, it may expose respectable oppressions and uncover how charity serves to camouflage exploitation.

Grace thus breaks into nature, not as a set of rules, not as a system of doctrines, but as a pointing to a new relationship, the recognition of a lordship, indeed as the affirmation that the only God we know even in nature is the Father whom the Son has revealed to us.

The social role which Professor Sittler has played has been

precisely to express through the integrity of his utterance the authenticity of nature and to set it in its proper relational context. The man of God neither rejects nature nor defies it. He accepts it for what it is. To know nature finitely can at its most articulate lead to a calm acceptance of one's fate. Even in the blues, for example, there is an implicit joy. They express man's predicament, yet they also face that predicament with honesty and courage. To do this is no mean virtue; it is this integrity which allows a man to sing even in the midst of sorrow.

In all of this the professional man of God, as distinguished from the layman, has a particular calling, an instrumental role to express the demand that no role is ever purely instrumental. No man is ever just a means to other ends; freedom remains, integrity remains.

Indeed, grace remains; for a breakthrough is always possible. As I recognize that in a broken world and as a broken man I cannot fully be what I am called to be, at the same time I know the joy that I am called to be "a man," a "new Adam," giving authentic expression through my work to what God has made me. To know suddenly that what I am doing is more than handling a cash register, or blowing a horn, or coming home to die, that as a man I am always called to be a man of God, to see beyond the utilities and the calculabilities of what I am doing to the dimension of depth: this is to take nature gracefully, rather than morally; to treat nature gracefully, rather than solemnly. To be a man is to possess a kind of grace, to express a graciousness. This is the social role of the man of God, whatever his worldly calling. To announce this clearly, as a teacher in the church, has been the particular role of Joseph Sittler.

THE VITAL CENTER:
TOWARD A CHALCEDONIAN
SOCIAL ETHIC

Franklin Sherman

THE VITAL CENTER:
TOWARD A CHALCEDONIAN
SOCIAL ETHIC

In the realm of Christian social ethics, the question of nature and grace has frequently presented itself as a question of nature *or* grace. So at least it has seemed in the debate between the two great rival types of social ethics (in terms of methodology) that have been set forth by recent Protestant theologians: the one type based on the doctrine of creation, and employing such categories as "orders of creation," the "natural order," and natural law; and the other founded on Christology. If one may distinguish with the older theologians between the kingdoms of nature, grace, and glory, one may say that the former of the two contemporary schools of thought assigns social ethics to the first kingdom, the latter to the second; while both are realistic enough to acknowledge that a perfectionist "ethics of glory" is hardly appropriate to an age that appears to be still rather remote from the eschaton.

The greatest proponent of christological ethics has, of course, been Karl Barth. But Barth's detailed teaching in the *Church Dogmatics* is as yet little known in the English-speaking world, despite the heroic efforts of his Scottish translators. Of greater influence has been the *Ethics* of Bonhoeffer, who is equally christological in his approach. Visser 't Hooft's *The Kingship of Christ* served at an earlier point to acquaint American readers with the continental developments, especially as rooted in Cullmann's exegesis. From the American scene itself, at least two eloquent voices have recently been heard expositing a similar point of view. Joseph Sittler in *The Structure of Christian Ethics* speaks of an ethic determined by the "morphology of

grace": Christian ethics is to be understood as "a reenactment
from below on the part of men of the shape of the revelatory
drama of God's holy will in Jesus Christ." Likewise Paul Lehmann in his new volume *Ethics in a Christian Context*, deploring
the preoccupation of modern Protestant ethicists with anthropology, calls for an ethic founded on a "theology of Messianism,"
i.e., Christology. Lehmann's "koinonia ethics" is really a variant
of christological ethics.

If the European experience is any guide, one can predict that
these efforts will meet with a good bit of resistance, and not a
little misunderstanding. The present essay is intended as a contribution to the prevention or alleviation of some of this misunderstanding. Its thesis is that it would be well for all concerned if it were recognized that the term "christological ethics"
is equivocal; that Christology has been employed as an apologia
for very different types of ethics, some characterized by a continuity between nature and grace, some by a discontinuity; but
that what is valuable in each of these types can be embodied
in an ethic that cleaves to the "vital center" of Chalcedonian
Christology.

I

The program of christological ethics was first propounded at
a moment of emphasis on discontinuity, or as it has also been
called, "diastasis," between church and culture. And it is well
that it was so, for the moment in question was one of an
insidious threat, from the side of culture, to the integrity of
the church and its faith. The "Barmen Declaration" of the
Confessing Church in Germany, issued in June, 1934, took as
its task both to assert the christological basis that would support
the church in the ensuing years, and to anathematize the Nazi
or German-Christian attempts to compromise that basis:

> Jesus Christ as he is testified to us in Holy Scripture, is the
> one Word of God, which we are to hear, which we are to trust
> and obey in life and death.
> We repudiate the false teaching that the Church can and must
> recognize yet other happenings and powers, personalities and

truths as divine revelation alongside this one Word of God, as
a source of her preaching. . . .

We repudiate the false teaching that there are areas of our
life in which we belong not to Jesus Christ but another Lord,
areas in which we do not need justification and sanctification
through him.[1]

This also was the period of Barth's famous "No!" to Brunner's
proposal for a revival of natural theology, a *Nein* motivated
largely by the fear that any such effort to establish a "point
of contact" with the natural man would in fact result in the
establishing of an avenue for the ideological infiltration of the
church. Dietrich Bonhoeffer's position at the time was similar.
Typical was his reaction, as expressed in a letter to the Bishop
of Chichester, upon learning that the swastika had now made
its appearance within the official German church seal. "It is
always the same error," he wrote. "Many sources of revelation
besides and except Christ. Other constitutive norms for the
church than Christ himself."[2]

The danger of this emphasis, necessary as it was then or would
be at any time when the church's kerygma itself is threatened,
was that of encouraging an absolute dualism between church
and world, nature and grace. Withdrawn into its fortress, the
church might bravely defend the faith but default on its obligation to struggle also for justice, freedom, and proper order in
the civil community. Apparently Bonhoeffer in his later years
came to feel that some elements, at least, of the Confessing
Church had indeed fallen prey to this temptation.[3] At the same
time, he felt increasing sympathy with the secular humanists
among the opponents of Nazism, having learned to distinguish

[1]From Theses 1 and 2 of the Declaration, as in the translation
printed in E. H. Robertson's brief but valuable paperback, *Christians
against Hitler* (London: SCM Press, 1962).

[2]Letter of May 3, 1934. Bonhoeffer, *Gesammelte Schriften* (Munich:
Kaiser, 1958), I, 190.

[3]See for example his prison letter of June 8, 1944, as well as his
"Outline for a Book," sec. 1(c); *Prisoner for God,* trans. Reginald
H. Fuller (New York: Macmillan Co., 1953), pp. 148, 178f.

sharply between the alternatives to Christianity offered by such humanism (which he considered implicitly Christian) and Nazi neo-paganism. The result was his famous emphasis on the "worldliness" of Christianity, his redefinition of the life of the church as an existence "wholly for the sake of the world," his stress on the continuity between Christian ethics and ordinary human goodness.

The severity of the teaching, "He that is not with me is against me" is balanced by the saying, "He that is not against us is for us"; and the two are seen as complementary, not contradictory. The inclusiveness of the claim of Christ is implied in its very exclusiveness: "The more exclusively we acknowledge and confess Christ as our Lord, the more fully the wide range of his dominion will be disclosed to us."[4]

The same turn has been discernible in the thinking of Karl Barth, and is most strikingly documented in his own lecture of 1956, "The Humanity of God." In his early period, he acknowledged, he and his fellow "crisis-theologians" worked almost entirely with the concept of diastasis, with the notion of God as "wholly other." "We viewed this 'wholly other' in isolation, abstracted and absolutized, and set it over against man, this miserable wretch—not to say boxed his ears with it," Barth admits. The error, he now asserts, was the stressing of the *deity* of God apart from his *humanity*, an error which would not have been possible if they had had the good sense from the start to found all their theologizing on Christology (and, we may add, if their Christology had been adequate).

> Certainly in Jesus Christ, as he is attested in Holy Scripture, we are not dealing with man in the abstract; no with the man who is able with his modicum of religion and religious morality to be sufficient unto himself without God and thus himself to be God. But neither are we dealing with God in the abstract:

[4]Bonhoeffer, *Ethics,* ed. Eberhard Bethge, trans. Neville Horton Smith (New York: Macmillan Co., 1955), p. 180. Cf. the whole sections, "The Total and Exclusive Claim of Christ," pp. 178ff., and "Christ and Good People," pp. 178ff.

not with one who in his deity exists only separated from man, distant and strange and thus a non-human if not indeed an inhuman God. In Jesus Christ there is no isolation of man from God or of God from man. Rather, in him we encounter the history, the dialogue, in which God and man meet together and are together, the reality of the covenant mutually contracted, preserved, and fulfilled by them. Jesus Christ in in his one person, as true God, man's loyal partner, and as true man, God's.[5]

From this new appreciation of the humanity of God (he can speak also of the "humanism" of God),[6] Barth derives important consequences for the relation of Christianity to human culture. The "sense and sound" of the Christian message, he asserts, "must be fundamentally positive." Certainly there is a divine "No" to man, but in Jesus Christ this No has been taken up into the Yes. The church therefore dare not take up an attitude of distance or hostility to man and his cultural achievements, but rather is called to foster and protect all that belongs to the *humanum*. "It would not do", says Barth, "even partially to cast suspicion upon, under-value, or speak ill of man's humanity."[7]

In another recent writing, Barth has set forth succinctly the exegetical-theological basis of his new position. In his study *Christ and Adam: Man and Humanity in Romans 5*, he maintains that Paul in this chapter is asserting not that our relationship to Christ is to be understood in terms of our relationship to Adam, but vice versa.

> The relationship between Adam and us reveals not the primary but the secondary anthropological truth and ordering principle. The primary anthropological truth and ordering principle, which only mirrors itself in that relationship, is made clear only through the relationship between Christ and us. . . . Man's

[5]Karl Barth, *The Humanity of God,* trans. John Newton Thomas and Thomas Wieser (Richmond: John Knox Press, 1960), p. 46.

[6]Cf. the essay "The Christian Message and the New Humanism," trans. Stanley Godman, in Barth, *Against the Stream: Shorter Post-War Writings 1946-52*, ed. Ronald Gregor Smith (New York: Philosophical Library, 1954).

[7]*The Humanity of God*, p. 53.

essential and original nature is to be found, therefore, not in Adam but in Christ.[8]

Notice that Barth predicates this determination of man's nature by the humanity of Christ not only of Christians, but of all men, including Christian believers before they become such. "While we were yet helpless," sinners, enemies of God (Rom. 5:6, 8, 10), Christ died for us—and reigned over us.

> We were not, even then, in an entirely different world. Even then, we existed in an order whose significance was of course just the opposite of that of the Kingdom of Christ, but which had the same structure. . . . Our former existence outside Christ is, rightly understood, already a still hidden but real existence in him.[9]

The significance of Jesus Christ thus extends far beyond the "religious" sphere. "What is Christian," Barth concludes, "is secretly but fundamentally identical with what is universally human."[10]

Thus Christology, as set forth by these major representatives of "Christological ethics," has moved full circle from being employed as a principle of disastasis, to serving as the rationale for a virtual identification of Christian and humanist. And just as the critics earlier had objected to the lack of a "point of contact," so now, conversely, they protest against this coalescence of what they would prefer to regard as two distinct realms. Terms such as "Christomonism" and "Christocracy" have

[8]*Christ and Adam,* trans. T. A. Smail, "Scottish Journal of Theology Occasional Papers," No. 5, p. 8. (Also published New York: Harper, 1957).

[9]*Ibid.,* p. 6.

[10]*Ibid.,* p. 43. It should be noted that we are not necessarily endorsing Barth's comments as an accurate exegesis of Romans 5, but are presenting them as evidence of the development of his own (systematic) position. For an alternative exegesis, and a critique of Barth's, see Rudolf Bultmann, "Adam and Christ according to Romans 5," in William Klassen and Graydon F. Snyder (eds.), *Current Issues in New Testament Interpretation: Essays in honor of Otto A. Piper* (New York: Harper, 1962).

been coined to describe (and to disparage) the new position. Motivations of the critics appear to vary. Some of them seem primarily concerned lest too much be attributed to Jesus Christ —a rather strange concern for Christian theologians! One might well ask whether, indeed, it is possible for a theology or ethics that wishes to be faithful to the New Testament to attribute too much to him whom the opening chapters of the Gospel according to St. John and the Epistle to the Colossians describe as he "through whom all things were made," as "the light that enlightens every man," and as he "in whom all things hold together"; who furthermore, in the closing chapters of Matthew and Revelation, proclaims as the Risen Lord, "All *exousia* in heaven and on earth has been given to me," and "I am the Alpha and the Omega, the first and the last, the *archē* and the *telos*."

Other critics, however, are prepared to acknowledge the universality of this rule or claim of Christ; but, they insist, he does not rule over men or all institutions in the same way. Thus Emil Brunner, even in the passage where he is most severely critical of the christological ethicists, proceeds from a recognition of the legitimacy of their basic assertion, but immediately adds his own qualifications:

> The Kingship of Christ—yes, in all things and first of all! But this slogan, which the Reformers used (rightly) with caution, will produce something very different from Utopia or "ecclesiocracy," if we add: the direct Kingship of Christ through the Gospel, in the Church, the indirect Kingship of Christ through the Law in the world.[11]

Whether in terms of a duality between church and world, law and gospel, natural law and biblical revelation, the orders of creation and the order of redemption, or some other variant of the traditional doctrine of the "two kingdoms," these critics insist—and quite rightly—on the distinction between different

[11]Emil Brunner, *The Christian Doctrine of Creation and Redemption*, trans. Olive Wyon (*Dogmatics*, Vol. II [London: Lutterworth Press, 1952]), p. 321 (conclusion of his appended note on "The Kingship of Christ and 'Christological Social Ethics'").

spheres of ethical action, and the different norms pertinent to each. What they have sometimes failed to notice is that the christological ethicists themselves (partly, no doubt, in reaction to this criticism) also make such a distinction. Thus Oscar Cullmann, for example, in his key essay "The Kingship of Christ in the New Testament," as well as in his book *Christ and Time*, distinguishes between the two concentric circles of Christ's Lordship, the inner circle of the church and the outer circle of the world.[12] Karl Barth already in his essay of 1938, "Church and State" (the actual title of which in the original is "Justification and Justice"), differentiated between two christological spheres, the primary and the secondary, within which, respectively, the two elements indicated in the title fall. And in his 1946 essay "The Christian Community and the Civil Community," in which he makes such extensive use of the notion of analogy, he appears to be well aware that this notion implies a factor of unlikeness as well as of likeness between the entities compared. He constantly stresses the merely "external, relative, and provisional" character of the civil order. Denying that there is any such thing as a uniquely "Christian" state, he reminds us that Christians must participate "in the human search for the best [political] form": the tasks and problems of the political order, he reiterates, are " 'natural,' secular, profane tasks and problems," not to be confused with those of the church itself, much less with the kingdom of God.

> It belongs to the very nature of the state that it is not and cannot become the Kingdom of God. It is based on an ordinance of God which is intended for the "world not yet redeemed" in

[12]Oscar Cullmann, "The Kingship of Christ and the Church in the New Testament" (1941), published in English translation by Stanley Godman in the collection of Cullmann's essays entitled *The Early Church*, ed. A. J. B. Higgins (London: SCM Press, 1956); *Christ and Time: The Primitive Christian Conception of Time and History*, trans. Floyd V. Filson (Philadelphia: Westminster, 1950), see especially Part III, "Redemptive History and the General Course of World Events."

which sin and the danger of chaos have to be taken into account with the utmost seriousness and in which the rule of Jesus Christ, though in fact already established, is still hidden.[13]

And so far as concrete norms are concerned, Barth has already acknowledged in "Church and State" that in the state, as contrasted to the church, the categories of legal right, retribution, and the use of force are appropriate. "The state as state," he wrote, "knows nothing of love, nothing of the spirit, nothing of forgiveness."[14]

The sum of the matter, then, seems to be that from both sides what is desired is a recognition of the duality between church and world, but without a dualism; and on the other hand, sympathetic identification of the church with the world, but not an identity between the two. It is this which leads us to propose that, if a christological social ethic is to be formulated, it is a Chalcedonian Christology that is required. For it is precisely these two kinds of error that the Chalcedonian definition of the faith was designed to guard against: on the one hand, the "Nestorian" dualism between the divine and human natures of Christ, and on the other hand, the Eutychian amalgamation of them. Our assumption in saying this, however, is that the Chalcedonian formula did not, as often alleged, perform only the negative function of excluding such aberrations, but is worthy of commendation in its own right as a positive statement of the faith. From this perspective, Chalcedon is seen as standing in the great tradition of the christological confessions of Irenaeus and Tertullian, of Athanasius and Augustine—as indeed it viewed itself:

> Following, then, the holy Fathers, we all unanimously teach that our Lord Jesus Christ is to us one and the same son, the

[13]Karl Barth, "The Christian Community and the Civil Community," trans. Stanley Godman, in *Against the Stream*, p. 31; reprinted in *Community, State and Church*, ed. Will Herberg (Garden City, N. Y.: Doubleday Anchor Books, 1960), p. 168.

[14]*Church and State*, trans. G. Ronald Howe, as reprinted in Herberg, (ed.) *op. cit.*, p. 132.

self-same perfect in Godhead, the self-same perfect in manhood; truly God and truly man; the self-same of a rational soul and body; consubstantial with the Father according to the Godhead, the self-same consubstantial with us according to the manhood; like us in all things; sin apart; before the ages begotten of the Father as to the Godhead, but in the last days, the self-same, for us and for our salvation [born] of Mary the Virgin Theotokos as to the manhood; one and the same Christ, son, Lord, Only-begotten; acknowledged in two natures unconfusedly, unchangeably, indivisibly, inseparably [*asunchutōs, atreptōs, adiaretōs, achōristōs*]; the difference of the natures being in no way removed because of the union, but rather the property of each nature being preserved, and [both] concurring into one prosopon and one hypostasis; not as though he were parted or divided into two prosopa, but one and the self-same son and only-begotten God, Word, Lord, Jesus Christ: even as from the beginning the prophets have taught us, and as the symbol of the Fathers hath handed down to us.[15]

The four famous adverbs, on this view, serve not merely to define the limits of speculation, but to describe a unique and dynamic form of relationship that transcends both monism and dualism, and that is applicable not only to the traditional problem of the two natures, but also to the whole problem of the relationship between God and the world, church and society, nature and grace—an applicability which indeed is to be expected, if it really be true that Christ is *the* clue to the relation of divinity and humanity. It is this middle Chalcedonian way, we believe, that Dietrich Bonhoeffer has in mind when he opposes both what he calls "radicalism," which posits an absolute dualism between the ultimate and the penultimate, and "compromise," which simply sanctions things as they are. Though protesting all "thinking in terms of two spheres," Bonhoeffer yet refuses simply to identify with one another the elements that have been traditionally referred to those two spheres.

[15]The Chalcedonian Definition of the Faith, par. 4, in the translation as printed in T. Herbert Bindley (ed.), *The Oecumenical Documents of the Faith* (4th ed., rev. F. W. Green, London: Methuen, 1950), pp. 234f.

Just as in Christ the reality of God entered into the reality of the world, so, too, is that which is Christian to be found only in that which is of the world, the "supernatural" only in the natural, the holy only in the profane, and the revelational only in the rational. The unity of the reality of God and of the world, which has been accomplished in Christ, is repeated, or, more exactly, is realized, ever afresh in the life of men. And yet what is Christian is not identical with the supernatural or the revelational with the rational. But between the two there is in each case a unity which derives solely from the reality of Christ, that is to say solely from faith in this ultimate reality.[16]

If statements such as the foregoing are implicitly Chalcedonian, Bonhoeffer's formulation in at least one highly significant passage is explicitly so. It is in his prison letter of May 20th, 1944, that he speaks of the "polyphony" of life—in our terms, of a Chalcedonian relationship between nature and grace. "What I mean," he writes, "is that God requires that we should love him eternally with our whole hearts, yet not so as to compromise or diminish our earthly affections, but as a kind of *cantus firmus* to which the other melodies of life provide the counterpoint." Referring to the presence of the Song of Songs in the Bible as an example, he then adds:

Where the ground bass is firm and clear, there is nothing to stop the counterpoint from being developed to the utmost of its limits. The two are "undivided and yet distinct," in the words of the Chalcedonian formula, like Christ in his divine and human natures. Perhaps the importance of polyphony in music lies in the fact that it is a musical reflection of this Christological truth, and thereby also of our Christian life.[17]

[16]Bonhoeffer, *Ethics*, p. 65.

[17]*Prisoner for God,* p. 131 (my own correction of the published translation). Note especially the erroneous rendering of the first term in Bonhoeffer's Chalcedonian citation as "without confusion" rather than "undivided," thus yielding a tautology rather than a contrast. What he wrote was *ungetrennt und doch geschieden;* cf. the original, *Wiederstand und Ergebung: Briefe und Aufzeichnungen aus der Haft* (6th ed., Munich: Kaiser, 1955), p. 193.

II

Our contention, then, is that if a christological social ethics is to be articulated, it is a Chalcedonian Christology that is required. Even if agreement were secured on this point, however, this would by no means mean the end of the argument, any more than the adoption of the Chalcedonian formula itself in the fifth century put an immediate end to the christological controversy! At least three further and weighty objections can be raised to the whole enterprise of "christological ethics." One is that the whole matter remains perforce at the level of generalities, which may be useful so far as they go in encouraging an appreciative or a critical approach, as the case may be, on the part of the Christian toward social and cultural affairs, but which leave him without concrete guidance for decision. A second objection is that if an effort is made to derive from Christology something like "middle axioms" of a lesser level of generality, the procedure immediately becomes arbitrary (this criticism has been levelled especially at Barth's analogical method in "The Christian Community and the Civil Community"). The third objection is that, whether general or specific, assertions based on Christology will have no convincing power when addressed to a society consisting only partly, or hardly at all, of professing Christians.

All of these objections may be reduced to the point that whereas "Christology," by definition, deals with the realm of redemption, questions of social ethics pertain to the realm of creation, to a civil and cultural order that forms part of what even Karl Barth referred to as "the world not yet redeemed."[18]

[18]Barth, "The Christian Community and the Civil Community," as quoted above, note 13. It should be observed, however, that Barth's use of the term "redemption" is rather idiosyncratic, being determined by the framework of his *Dogmatics* as a doctrine of "creation, reconciliation, and redemption"; the term "redemption" is, on the whole, reserved for the eschatological consummation rather than the present accomplishment of Christ. Barth maintains that this usage is faithful to the New Testament; cf. *Church Dogmatics*, Vol. I, *The*

Therefore deductions from Christology will of necessity be irrelevant to social ethics.

Now there is a great deal of legitimacy to this whole line of criticism, just as there was in the criticisms to which we referred earlier, criticisms of the extremes both of monism and of dualism which have served to call christological ethics back to the vital center. Yet we may ask whether the present set of objections is not based also, to some extent, on misunderstanding. The fact is that the defenders and the opponents of christo-logical ethics may not mean at all the same thing by "Chris-tology," or even by the apparently wholly-concrete term "Jesus Christ."

We may distinguish in recent theology between at least two major types of Christology, the proponents of which, although they all formally profess allegiance to the whole of the New Testament revelation, in practice tend to stress, respectively, different aspects of it (as do the several New Testament docu-ments themselves). We may characterize the first type by the slogan, "Jesus Christ is Lord"; and the second type, by the slogan "Jesus Christ is Logos." The first is strictly historical in character: Jesus Christ is the central figure in the *Heilsgeschichte*, the mightiest of God's "mighty acts." The second is ontological: Jesus is the embodiment of an aspect, an element, a constituent factor of being itself; he is the Logos (Word, self-manifestation, self-objectification) of God, and at the same time the Logos (principle, moving power) of the created world. The first type, which we shall denominate "dramatic-historical" Christology, may be identified, in brief, as the Christology of the Book of Acts, and the second type, which we shall call "ontological" Christology, as the Christology of Colossians; though it would be more accurate to say that the first is the Christology of the

Doctrine of the Word of God, Part I, trans. G. T. Thompson (Edin-burg: T. & T. Clark, 1936), the note on pp. 468f.

The phrase "the world not yet redeemed" is actually a quotation from the fifth thesis of the Barmen Declaration (see Robertson, *op. cit.*).

whole of Luke-Acts, as well as the Epistle to the Romans, while the second is the Christology of the Fourth Gospel and the Epistle to the Hebrews as well as of Colossians.[19] The first type corresponds to what has been called a "Christology from below," the second to a "Christology from above"[20]—but note well that according to the first type, it is precisely he who appeared in lowliness whom God has "highly exalted" (Phil. 2:9): "God has made him both Lord and Christ" (Acts 2:36); while according to the second type, it is precisely he "by whom all things exist" (Heb. 2:10) who was "made like his brethren in every respect" (Heb. 2:17). Thus both Christologies have the dimension of heaven as well as earth, and to this extent are interpenetrating rather than parallel. Nevertheless, there is still a discernible difference. If, from the standpoint of Christ's appearance in lowliness, the dramatic-historical type proclaims his subsequent glory (as Lord), the ontological type proclaims also his antecendent glory (as Logos). The former is primarily a doctrine of the work of Christ (and may therefore be called a "functional" Christology); the second is a doctrine, in the first instance, of the person of Christ—but also of the work of this person.

The full implications of this divergence in Christologies far

[19] It will be apparent that we find expressions of a Logos Christology not only in those passages, such as the Prologue to the Fourth Gospel, where the term Logos is expressly used: we are including also under this rubric what is generally termed Paul's "Wisdom Christology." Cf. C. F. D. Moule in *Peake's Commentary on the Bible*, ed. Matthew Black and H. H. Rowley (London and New York, Nelson, 1962), p. 991 (on Col. 1:15-23): "It is (in all but the actual term) a 'Logos' Christology."

For the "christological foundation of the state," cf. Proverbs 8: 15f. (concerning Wisdom): "By me kings reign, and rulers decree what is just; by me princes rule, and nobles govern the earth." Proverbs 8, Ecclesiasticus 24, and Wisdom of Solomon 7: 22-27 are generally considered the major sources for Paul's notion of Wisdom.

[20] Werner Elert," Methodologische Vorfragen der Christologie," *Der christliche Glaube: Gundlinien der lutherischen Dogmatik* (3rd ed., Hamburg: Furche-Verlag, 1956), sec. 51 pp. 291ff.

transcend the scope of the present essay. Our concern here is with *the confusion that arises when statements about Jesus Christ as Logos are interpreted in terms of the theology of Jesus Christ as Lord.* Or, from the perspective of the Logos Christology itself, we may speak of this as the confusion that arises from *failure to clarify whether one is speaking of the discarnate or the incarnate Logos*—or of both. We are referring to statements such as the following by Dietrich Bonhoeffer:

> If (for Christian ethics) the world remains the world, that must be because all reality is founded upon Jesus Christ himself.

> It is only in relation to Jesus Christ that created things have their being.

> The true basis of government is therefore Jesus Christ himself.[21]

If by "Jesus Christ" here is meant that one whom, to be sure, we know as the Logos Incarnate, but who is here being spoken of in his role as Logos-in-general, i.e., as the "divine creative principle"[22] or the "cosmic reason which gives order and intelligibility to the world"[23] or "the side of God turned toward the world,"[24] then Bonhoeffer's statements are comprehensible, as is his further assertion that "we know of no relation of God to the world other than through Jesus Christ."[25] But if these statements refer only to Jesus Christ as the "Christ-event" in the sense of dramatic-historical Christology, i.e., to a figure in history in the years A.D. 1-30 (or whatever they may have been), then the statements in question are enigmatic, not to say obscurantist.

What Bonhoeffer would say to this, however, is that inasmuch as we *do* know the Logos Incarnate in the person of

[21]Bonhoeffer, *Ethics,* pp. 202, 288, 301.

[22]W. F. Howard, in *The Interpreter's Bible,* Vol. VIII, p. 442.

[23]Glen R. Morrow, "Logos," in *The Dictionary of Philosophy,* ed. Dagobert D. Runes (New York: Philosophical Library, n.d.).

[24]Oscar Cullman, *The Christology of the New Testament,* trans. Shirley C. Guthrie and Charles A. M. Hall (Philadelphia: Westminster, 1959), p. 255.

[25]*Ethics,* p. 321.

Jesus Christ, we can no longer think of the Logos in abstraction from the incarnation; we may, and indeed we must, call the Logos in any of his operations by the concrete name "Jesus Christ." And Karl Barth would, of course, say the same. At the least, this amounts to an insistence on the traditional doctrine of the *communicatio idiomatum:* what may be predicated of Christ in his divine nature may be predicated of him as a total person. But more than this, there is a concern here, so far as social ethics is involved, that norms or principles which present themselves as derivable from the deliverances of the Logos-in-general (usually known as "general revelation," or the "lessons of history," or "natural law") be held subject to the specific criteria of the teaching, work, and person of the Logos Incarnate. Even if it is the discarnate Logos that is of constitutive significance for social ethics, the Incarnate Logos has a finally regulative significance.

We see, then, that both schools of thought are agreed that questions of social ethics pertain primarily to the realm of creation; but for the one school (that of ontological Christology), "Christology" includes assertions about creation as well as redemption, while for the other (dramatic-historical Christology) it deals only with the realm of redemption. This latter observation, however, would not be wholly accurate if interpreted as implying a restriction of scope, for we must note that recent years have seen a major development of Lordship-Christology itself in a direction that tends toward the inclusion of the whole of the creation in its purview. We are referring to the growing emphasis on the "cosmic" dimensions of Christ's Lordship.[26] Not being able to make much sense, within a purely historical framework, of the affirmation that the principalities and powers were "created in" Christ (Col. 1:16), this theology has focused instead on the conviction that the powers have been overcome

[26]Allan D. Galloway's book *The Cosmic Christ* (London: Nisbet, 1951) is a major document of this development, as is Visser 't Hooft's *The Kingship of Christ,* referred to above (New York: Harper, 1948).

by him (Col. 2:15). By means of the affirmation of cosmic redemption, a universality is posited for the significance of Jesus Christ that brings this viewpoint very close, on this score, to ontological Christology. This being the case, it may be hoped that theologians of this persuasion may be led to reconsider their opposition to the use of ontological categories; surely the very term "cosmos" implies not only "the whole of reality," but also "reality *as* a whole," and an ordered whole. But it is precisely with this latter that ontology deals.[27]

As to the ontological Christology, or rather ontological-cum-historical Christology (for it never deals *merely* with the Logos-in-general), of which we have taken Dietrich Bonhoeffer to be representative,[28] what we might hope from it is that it become much

[27]And as Paul Tillich insists—and has demonstrated in his own thought—ontology need not exclude historical categories. See especially, on this point, the debate between Tillich and Reinhold Niebuhr in the two volumes of the "Library of Living Theology" devoted, respectivly, to their theologies (Charles W. Kegley and Robert W. Bretall [eds.], *The Theology of Paul Tillich* [New York: Macmillan Co., 1952] and *Reinhold Niebuhr: His Religious, Social, and Political Thought* [Macmillan Co., 1956]). It is from Niebuhr's essay in the former volume that we have derived the identifying terms for our two types of Christology: Niebuhr pits his own "dramatic and historical" interpretation of the faith against Tillich's "ontological" theology. William J. Wolf, in his essay in the volume on Niebuhr, implies a similar typology when he comments, "Niebuhr's primary categories for his Christology are obviously Messianic-functional ones rather than Logos-incarnational ones" (p. 237).

[28]Cf., in addition to Bonhoeffer's works in translation as cited above, his lectures on Christology from the year 1933, as found in the *Gesammelte Schriften* (Munich: Kaiser, 1960), III, 166-242. The subject matter, he remarks, might better be termed "Logology"; and he adds, "The christological question is in essence an ontological question" *(Die christologische Frage ist in ihrem Wesen eine ontologische Frage)*. A summary and interpretation of the lectures is available in Jaroslav Pelikan's contribution to Martin E. Marty (ed.) *The Place of Bonhoeffer: Problems and Possibilities in His Thought* (New York: Association Press, 1962).

more explicit about the transition that is made, in speech about
Jesus Christ, from the more specific to the more general aspects
of his nature and functions, i.e., from the Christ of the *Heilsgeschichte* to the Christ of creation. What actually happens when
a christological ethicist does attempt to become specific about
social ethics (or at least what ought to happen) is that he
develops, under the rubric of Christ as the mediator of creation,
or of cosmic Christology, a full-blown equivalent of the sort
of scheme of orders of creation or natural law developed by an
ethicist of the other type under the rubric of God-the-Father.
This is what Bonhoeffer has done in unfolding his doctrine of
the "mandates" and "the natural" (*Ethics*, Chaps. ii, iii, vii).
It is the possibility of this kind of transition from the realm
of redemption to the realm of creation (or from grace to nature)
that underlies also Bonhoeffer's notion of "Christian worldliness."
The Christian man, in being a Christian, is at the same time a
worldly man, because the Christ whom he worships as Lord is
at the same time the Logos of the world. It is this double
function of Christ, furthermore, which prevents the claims of
his Lordship from being heteronomous:

> The lordship of Jesus Christ is not the rule of a foreign power;
> it is the lordship of the Creator, Reconciler, and Redeemer, the
> lordship of him through whom and for whom all created beings
> exist, of him in whom indeed all created beings alone find their
> origin, their goal and their essence. . . . Jesus Christ's claim to
> Lordship, which is proclaimed by the church, means at the same
> time the emancipation of family, culture and government for the
> realization of their own essential character, which has its foun-
> dation in Christ.[29]

We see, then, that each of the two types of Christology needs
the other for its correction and completion. The Christology
of Lordship serves to prevent the Logos-Christology from
becoming unhistorical, while the Logos-Christology serves to
prevent the Lordship-Christology from becoming heteronomous.
How remarkable it is to find that the Chalcedonian formula,

[29] *Ethics,* p. 264.

which we cited in the first part of this essay as showing the middle way between nature-grace discontinuity and identity, also combines, in its penultimate clause, both of the christological predicates that we have dwelt upon in the immediately foregoing pages:

> . . . not as though he were parted or divided into two prosopa, but one and the self-same Son and only-begotten God, *Logos, Lord,* Jesus Christ.[30]

This is perhaps not so surprising, however, when one recalls that one of the principal aims, and achievements,[31] of the Council of Chalcedon was to reconcile the contrasting Christologies propounded by the schools of Antioch and Alexandria, which will be found to correspond remarkably closely to our "dramatic-historical" and "ontological" types, respectively.[32]

If one considers the Barth of the *Church Dogmatics,* one must acknowledge that his intention also, despite the earlier predominance of a language purely of "act" or event," has been to combine the two types. This may be seen already in the proposition summing up the christological section in Volume I, Part 1:

[30]Cf. citation above at note 15. Admittedly, the precise correspondence of the Formula to the terms of our discussion depends on how the concluding words of the clause quoted above are punctuated; in Bettenson, *Documents of the Christian Church* (New York: Oxford University Press, 1947), p. 73, for example, it is made to read rather differently: "one and the same Son and only-begotten God the Word, Lord Jesus Christ." But our quotation above reproduces exactly the translation and punctuation found in the standard work by Bindley and Green (*op. cit.,* see note 15), except that we give the original *Logos* instead of "Word."

[31]At least according to the positive evaluation of Chalcedon that underlies the present essay. Cf. R. V. Sellers, *The Council of Chalcedon: A Historical and Doctrinal Survey* (London: SPCK, 1953), on whom I am chiefly dependent for this orientation.

[32]Cf. the earlier works by Sellers, *Two Ancient Christologies: A study in the Christological Thought of the Schools of Alexandria and Antioch* (New York: Macmillan Co., 1940).

> The one God reveals himself according to Scripture as the Reconciler, i.e. as the Lord, amidst our enmity towards him. As such he is the Son come to us, or the Word spoken to us, because he is so antecedently in himself, as the Son or the Word of God the Father.[33]

"The Son come to us" is a category of Christology "from below"; "the Son antecedently in himself," a category "from above." In his detailed discussion of the Incarnation in the following part-volume, he acknowledges clearly the twofoldedness of the New Testament witness: it may appear either as the proclamation "that God's Son is called Jesus of Nazareth," or "that Jesus of Nazareth is God's Son"; more simply, either that "the Christ is Jesus" or that "Jesus is the Christ."[34] And he has carried through this double scheme consistently, so that his doctrine of reconciliation in Volume IV (with which, as in all the volumes, a discussion of ethics is interwoven) is developed in two great sections, entitled respectively "Jesus Christ, the Lord as Servant," and "Jesus Christ, the Servant as Lord."[35]

As to Barth's method in essays like "The Christian Community and the Civil Community," it must be admitted that it does appear arbitrary, if for no other reason than that it is so highly compressed. In particular, Barth has failed to make explicit what we have called the transition from the functions of the incarnate to those of the discarnate Logos. But if by Barth's "arbitrariness" is meant the fact that he derives from his theological premises particular concrete social-ethical norms rather than others (namely those of liberal democracy), then it must be said that those making this criticism have overlooked the element of arbitrariness—we may even say, of theological rationalization of ethical judgments reached on other grounds—involved in *any* Christian social ethics.[36] Here is a fruitful field for further study

[33]Barth, *Church Dogmatics,* I, 1, 457.

[34]*Ibid.,* I, 2, 14ff.

[35]*Ibid.,* IV, 1, Chap. xiv; IV, 2, Chap. xv.

[36]Stated with classic succinctness by Bonhoeffer with reference to ethics based on "natural law": "Natural law can furnish equally cogent arguments in favor of the state which is founded on force and

or investigation of "non-theological factors" in theological social ethics. Perhaps this is only an aspect of the "situational" element in ethics that has recently been so much emphasized: a man makes his judgments, not only as a theologian, but as a concrete person in a concrete historical and cultural situation.

Finally, as to the question of rhetorical effectiveness, the critics of christological ethics are no doubt quite right in pointing out that no christological assertions—whether based on Lordship or Logos—will have any special weight in a secular era, i.e., to the typical representatives of that era. It must be admitted that much Christian social ethics, especially of the Barthian school, has been sectarian in character: it has been addressed to the Christian community, concerning the fulfillment of *its* political tasks, rather than to the political community as such. The greatness of social ethics of the type of Reinhold Niebuhr, in contrast, has been its ready assimilability by the civil community. But on the other hand, perhaps the latter type has less motivational appeal to Christians as such. Here is another relatively unexplored field: the rhetoric of ethics.[37] Progress in resolving

the state which is founded on justice, for the nation-state and for imperialism, for democracy and for dictatorship" (*Ethics,* p. 303). Cf. further on the same point, James Luther Adams, "Natural Law: Some General Considerations," *Journal of Religion,* XXV (1945), 88-96.

[37]The only recent work that I know that deals explicitly and adequately with this question, apart from the work of ethicists of the linguistic-analysis school (the scope of whose inquiries has been rather limited) is the valuable but little-known volume by John Ladd, entitled *The Structure of a Moral Code: A Philosophical Analysis of Ethical Discourse, Applied to the Ethics of the Navaho Indians* (Cambridge, Mass.: Harvard University Press, 1957). Cf. Chap. ix, "The Rhetoric of Ethical Discourse: Justification."

"Of any particular ethical argument," Professor Ladd points out, "two questions can be asked: does the conclusion follow from the reasons given? and will the reasons persuade the listener? (or ought they to persuade him?)" (p. 146). The first he terms the question of the "logic" of ethical discourse, the second the question of its "rhetoric."

the problems involved would require first of all a clarification of what we really mean by "Christian social ethics." Do we mean primarily "social ethics for Christians," articulated primarily for *their* guidance; or do we mean a "Christian ethic for society," reasoned out by Christians, but stated in such a way as to be both relevant to and intelligible by secular men in a pluralist society? If the latter, then christological ethics in its pure state is hardly appropriate; it must, even if only for rhetorical purposes, undergo a transmutation into the language of the "discarnate Logos."[38] Perhaps this would be a social-ethical equivalent for what Dietrich Bonhoeffer—who remained a christological theologian to the last—meant by a "non-religious" interpretation of theological concepts.

III

There is one further objection to christological ethics that it has not proved possible to consider within the scope of the present essay, but which must at least be mentioned. This is the charge, which has been levelled by as formidable a critic as Reinhold Niebuhr, that christological ethics, on account of its including social questions within the realm of redemption,

[38]If this term does not meet with favor, perhaps those suggested by Prof. O. A. Dilschneider of Berlin would better commend themselves. In his discussion of the question of christological interpretation of the Old Testament, he affirms that Christ does indeed "meet us" in the Old Testament. But, he adds, these Old Testament witnesses to Christ "are not witnesses of a personal presence of Christ, but witnesses of a really-present Christ" (*nicht Zeugnisse einer personellen Gegenwart Christi, sondern Zeugnisse eines realpräsenten Christus*). Otto A. Dilschneider, *Gegenwart Christi (Christus praesens): Grundriss einer Dogmatik der Offenbarung* (Gütersloh: Bertelsmann, 1948), I, 214.
Dilschneider critizes the explicitly christological interpretation of the Old Testament (as practiced by Wilhelm Vischer) for engaging in an illegitimate change of genera from the presence *realiter* to the presence *personaliter* (ibid., p. 241). Our criticism of christological social ethics could be put in terms of its *failure* to make such a change of genera, in the reverse direction.

tends toward social indifference and/or utopianism. It tends to encourage the conception either that social problems are already solved, or that they can be solved easily.[39] To this, one could only reply, if one wished to defend "christological ethics," that it can indeed have such consequences, and no doubt has had although the likelihood of this will depend largely on the extent to which "redemption" is considered as already realized rather than yet-to-be-realized. But one would have to add that ethics based on natural law or on anthropology can also lead to ideological defense of the established order, or to utopian expectations about a new order, depending on how the natural law, or the nature of man, is in each case understood;[40] depending especially on what relative stress is placed upon the essential goodness of man or upon his existential distortion (to use Tillich's categories). Presumably if these two elements are held in balance, and combined with an informed calculation of the "more or less" of historical possibilities, an adequate social ethic will result. But the same can be done within the framework of christological ethics, and will be done if attention is paid not only to the incarnation, but also to the crucifixion—surely here it is impossible to overlook the virulence of the demonic powers —and to the resurrection (it is these three elements that correspond, in a christological ethic, to creation—fall—redemption in the other scheme). And if with this is combined a balanced view

[39]This was the burden of Niebuhr's exchange with Karl Barth in 1948-49 following the Amsterdam Assembly of the World Council of Churches. Niebuhr's part of the exchange is reprinted in his *Essays in Applied Christianity*, ed. D. B. Robertson (New York: Meridian Books, 1959) pp. 168-82.

This is also the implication of G. C. Berkouwer's line of criticism in *The Triumph of Grace in the Theology of Karl Barth* (Grand Rapids: Eerdman's, 1956), as well as of Gustaf Wingren in *Theology in Conflict* (Philadelphia: Muhlenberg, 1958). A major defect of Barth's theology, according to Wingren, is that there is in it "no active power of sin, no tyrannical, demonic power" (p. 25).

[40]Cf. our comment and the quotation from Bonhoeffer at note 36, above.

on the question of continuity or discontinuity between church and culture, nature and grace, together with an avoidance both of heteronomy and of mere generality—in short, if one cleaves to the Chalcedonian "vital center"[41]—then, presumably, in this way also, an adequate social ethic can result.

[41]Mention should be made of a work which came to the writer's attention only as the present essay was being completed, in which the Chalcedonian formula is employed as a theological criterion in a way very similar to that proposed here, at least, in the first part of our argument. This is the valuable study by Prof. Jacques de Senarclens of Geneva, entitled *Heirs of the Reformation,* trans. from the French by G. W. Bromiley (London: SCM Press, 1963, and Philadelphia: Westminster Press, 1964). "Since relations between God and man are not merely the prototype but already the realization of all other relations attested by the Holy Spirit," de Senarclens comments, "the way in which the divine and the human are rejoined in [Jesus Christ] is the norm of all other encounters" (p. 271). He speaks therefore of the "disciplinary significance of Christology for all aspects of faith and life" *(ibid.),* and in exploring this significance, especially for the doctrine of revelation, the church, and the Christian life, he makes specific use of the Chalcedonian definition.

It must be observed, however, that Prof. de Senarclens' strictures against the aberrancies in the direction of synthesis, or "confusion and change" between the divine and the human (with which he charges both Roman Catholicism and modern Protestantism), seem more heartfelt, and more cogent, than his critique of the errors of "division and separation," or diastasis. Indeed, his own position approximates to the latter tendency at more than one point. In this respect de Senarclens seems to be strongly influenced by the classical Calvinistic principle of *finitum non capax infiniti,* in contrast to the acceptance by Dietrich Bonhoeffer, for example, of the Lutheran *finitum capax infiniti.*

HIS CHURCH AND HIS WORLD

JERALD C. BRAUER

HIS CHURCH AND HIS WORLD*

The problem of Christ, his church, and his world is of such magnitude and complexity that no single analysis can exhaust it. This problem could be analyzed from many perspectives. This paper confines itself to the problem as it is related to the question of the church's social responsibility, particularly the Lutheran church's understanding of that responsibility. Our analysis does not grow out of a concern for Christology nor does it view the problem primarily from the perspective of the Lutheran confessions.

The issue is the relation of Christ's church to the world as that church seeks to carry through its social responsibility. Theologically, the problem could be stated as the relation of the community rooted in God's redemptive activity—the church —to the total sphere of God's creative activity—the world. Thus the question of God's church and his world, even from the perspective of social responsibility, involves the question of nature and grace, of creation and redemption.

It is clear that one's vision of the church determines, in part, one's understanding of, and activity with regard to, social responsibility. Lutherans have been accused of taking, at times, an irresponsible attitude toward the social order. This charge arose at times when Lutherans were so concerned with doctrinal purity and conceptual clarity of word and confessions that they ignored or undercut Christian ethics, both personal and social. This is not to say that doctrinal clarity is unimportant; it is to say that confessional and doctrinal purity never exist for themselves. They exist in order to set the church free

*This essay was originally delivered at The Fourth International Lutheran Conference on Social Responsibility, Stockholm, Sweden, July, 1963.

to risk its life in service and to correct its inadequacies so that it may love more fully and serve more widely.

If one's vision of the church determines, in part, one's view of and involvement in social responsibility, then we must pose the question of the nature of the church. A simple definition states that the church is the communion of all believers where the gospel is preached in its purity and where the holy sacraments are adminstered correctly (Augsburg Confession, Art. VII). It goes on to state that the church, called into being by God from eternity, is one, holy, apostolic, and catholic. Content, both theological and historical, is given to each of these adjectives.

The church is holy. It is like no other assembly on earth. Its holiness does not consist in its goodness but in its constant state of forgiveness through the continuing presence of the Holy Spirit. The church is the community of the forgiven, as the gospel proclaims. Herein resides its holiness. The church is apostolic in that it constantly stands under the message that the apostles were commissioned to proclaim. It shares this gospel with the first and with the last, with all ages. Christians also confess that the church is both one and catholic, a unity and yet a universality. The oneness centers in the "one Lord, one faith, one baptism." Whatever else it may be, however it appears to interpret this, the fact remains that the church has but one Lord. Under this one Lord, the church presses outward toward universality. Unity seeks breadth and diversity, for only in that can there be catholicity or universality.

We also confess that the very center of the life of the church is the Christ. We speak of the church as the body of Christ. This language points to the reality that in him believers "live, move, and have their being." They have risen with him. Thus, we confess that the church is the body of Christ and that all through him are members one of another.

There is a certain objectivity, a givenness, to such a definition that is both pleasing and necessary; but as we look at life as it actually is, we note something vastly different. The church does not appear to be what we believe it to be. Frequently the church turns out to be a captive of a given historical form or cultural conditioning. It is defined primarily in terms of our definitions and our confessions, and is made to meet our measurements. In this way we can claim the church and control it. All this is carried through ostensibly to protect the church, its purity, and its life. What is a necessary task for the good of the church, the constant attempt at doctrinal clarification, easily becomes an end in itself. That which poses as the defender of the church can often be that which restricts the loving service and self-giving of the church.

In much the same way, his church becomes the church of my nation, or my class, or my race, or my kind of people. This is what we witness all about us today. The phenomenon is not confined to any one nation. It is universal in the sense in which we profess in faith that the church is universal. The church in the modern epoch has proved to be not only the bearer of good tidings but frequently the bulwark of everything reactionary and conservative. In America the churches prove to be the last refuge of segregation. In Europe the churches have been long alienated from the working class. Indeed, it is difficult to picture the church we live in, know, and love, as the body of Christ, the communion of saints, the one, holy, catholic, and apostolic church. Apparently, correct doctrine in itself does not prevent us from distorting the faith.

There is a doctrine that is supposed to cover the discrepancy between the church as we experience it and the church we profess in faith, and that is the distinction between the church visible and the church invisible. It is obvious that the church we experience is all too human, too sinful, too limited, even too arrogant. Yet we also know that the church is more than it appears to be. Over against appearance, we proclaim our faith in the true nature of the church as it is known only to God and as it exists in, with, and under the visible appearance. Unfortunately, this doctrine, which is most necessary, frequently becomes the occasion to misunderstand the church. More than once in Christian history it has been argued that the external ordering of the church is of little consequence because that is not the true church. It does not matter if the state orders the externals of the church so long as the pure gospel can be preached and the sacraments administered properly. But the Nazi experience remains a lesson for us all. The doctrine of the distinction between the church visible and the church invisible dare not become an excuse to avoid a necessary judgment on the faithfulness of the church visible. To do this is to deny the reason why the doctrine is necessary in the first place.

The purpose of the distinction is to enable the church constantly to bring itself under the judgment of its Lord. The doctrine of the church invisible exists as a reminder that no particular historical manifestation and embodiment of the church ever fully or perfectly realizes the reality which the church bears and to which it points. This should not lead to an indifference towards the particular forms of the church nor to their deification. One takes the empirical church with the utmost seriousness, for in that church we live and die. We have no other church in history, and our life is in history here and now. Therefore this doctrine compels us to a constant reconsideration of the form and faithfulness of the church visible. It is the reminder that the church is his church, not our possession.

Precisely because the church is God's, it has by its very nature a social responsibility—that is, the church is responsible for all the aspects of life, the personal and the social, the individual and the collective. Any illusions former generations held concerning the possibility of radically separating these dimensions of life have been dispelled both by our knowledge of depth psychology and by recent historical experience. God's church is as widely and deeply responsible as was he who gave himself for the entire universe. His church continues his ministry for it represents his body still at work in the world.

The church bears the message of the good news of God's love for the world. In Christ, he has redeemed the world and reconciled the world to himself. This is the good news for the whole of life. Life is broken, it is frustrating, it appears and is frequently experienced as meaningless and even mean; but that is not the last word. The church bears the Word—God is faithful. His mercy endures forever. Before man has done anything, while he is yet in sin, estranged, God in Christ has sought him out and accepted him, forgiven him.

How easily these words flow from our lips. How many times we have uttered them from pulpits, formed them with pens, or tried to share them with friends. Unfortunately, we usually place them in a tight framework of our own. Speaking for the church or through the church, we subtly transform his church into *our* church, the good news into *our* good news. Often, in bearing witness to this message, we add to or subtract from it so that it becomes the good news if the hearer first does this or does that. It is difficult to allow the church to be his church; it is so much safer if it is our church. Then we can determine who deserves, who observes, and who preserves the truth; then we can decide exactly how far the responsibility of the church really goes, and frequently this is determined by our judgment of what is expedient at the moment. That which jeopardizes our church in its growth, its stance in society, its hold on doctrine, or its practices of worship is to be avoided. Thus, his church which lives to serve can easily become subservient in order to live.

However, the church cannot avoid social responsibility, because his church is at one with the scope of his redemptive action. The New Testament makes absolutely clear that the mission and ministry of Jesus were not directed at the subjective response of a handful of individuals. To be sure, his life sought to catch up into his own the full lives of human beings. The purpose of his life is made clear and precise to all who will read—"God was in Christ reconciling the world to himself." This was an integral part of God's making himself a people, the chosen people of Israel. This was not a strange God who dropped out of a mysterious "nowhere" to snatch a handful of repentant people from an evil and wicked universe. This was the Lord of the whole cosmos redeeming his world and his people. God had never forsaken his creation or creatures though they had constantly forsaken him. This great redemptive act is but the culmination of God's dealings with his world and his people.

How can such an act, a new creation, be confined to personal subjective reactions or to a church that narrows its ministry into a repudiation of his total ministry? The question is not whether Jesus dealt with problems of politics or economics. The question is whether the scope of his ministry involves the relations of the whole cosmos to its source and Creator, or whether that ministry is confined to personal piety. The Scriptures confront us with a ministry that involves the very center of life, of all life! The concern is with the rain on the just and unjust, with the laborer who works from the first hour and with him who works from the last hour, with principalities and powers, with life, death, things present and things to come, with Abraham, Isaac, and Jacob, and with the Gentiles. Paul could not find language adequate to convey his insights into the significance and consequence of the ministry, death, and resurrection of Jesus the Christ. To the extent that the church lives out of this reality, to the extent that the church is the Body of Christ, its ministry must be as broad and as deep as the good news he was and is.

Unfortunately, two major errors have plagued the church throughout history, and Lutheranism has not been exempt from these errors. There are some historians of dogma who argue that Lutheranism, among Protestant churches, has been particularly prone to these distortions. The first distortion views the world as so evil that the world almost appears to be essentially evil. Though it is contrary to the biblical doctrine of creation, it has been and it is possible to stress the broken and sinful character of the world so strongly that the goodness of creation is effectually lost. The world appears as the incarnation of the evil one—the center of lust, power, pride, and destruction. It is cut off totally from God, a vale of tears through which we must pass with as little contact and contamination as is possible. The world is hated and distrusted, and it is to be assaulted and captured by the storm troops of the Lord. We must redeem it!

The strange thing is that where Lutheranism reflected this attitude, it has not been consistent. Anabaptism saw the consequence of such a view and withdrew from the world, repudiating participation at all possible points and attempting to create a pure community of faithful redeemed living apart from the world. Like other Protestants, Lutherans refused to do this. Though the world was repudiated as evil, believers participated fully in its social structures—its politics, its economics, and its culture. A personal piety of the redeemed was fostered over against the evil, wicked world, but nothing was done about politics or economics for they were thought to be in no sense related to God.

This particular Lutheran distortion arose from a perversion of Luther's doctrine of the two kingdoms or two realms. That doctrine, not original with Luther, asserted a distinction in the way God was related to man and to the universe. Though a clear distinction was maintained between creation and redemption, an equally clear affirmation contended that the same God was at work in two different ways to maintain his will for all of life. There was no aspect of life divorced from God, though different segments of life, such as politics and the life of the communion of saints, were related to God in different ways.

The distinction between the realms was soon made absolute and the interrelatedness was denied. God was not believed or understood to be the one in whom all was rooted and through whom all was created and sustained. Thus it was possible for piety and for theology to deny that the world was God's and at base was good. There was no difficulty in asserting the centrality of God in preaching, in the life of the church, or in the forgiveness of sin. But it was virtually impossible to see God at work, in any way, in the world with its politics, economics, or public morality. These were all of the world, of nature—unredeemed nature. But the church was of God's mercy and forgiveness and so was of grace. Thus an absolute cleavage was affirmed between creation and redemption or between nature and grace.

The other distortion was a modification of the above. It could not bring itself to say that the world was essentially evil or virtually so; rather, it argued that the whole universe was essentially neutral and not really of consequence insofar as the gospel was concerned. In this view, the world was to be endured and tolerated, but one should not expect any positive good from it. This was often stated in the belief that the best one could expect from the world was to hold overt evil in check so as to maintain a minimum amount of peace and suppress the overly active evildoer. In this context, the church could at least preach the pure gospel to the external salvation of certain souls.

In both of these views of God's church and his world, the world is repudiated either through hostility or through indifference. The consequences are the same. The world is identified as nature either at enmity with God or totally indifferent toward him. Thus the world is not really God's world. The similarity is self-evident between this view and early Manichaeism or early Gnosticism, which asserted that an evil being had created the world. In the name of conceptual clarity, orthodoxy drove a wedge between God and his world; and in the name of the pious Christian life, pietism repudiated his world as totally corrupt and evil.

This confronted Christianity with a massive distortion of one of its deepest insights. The world and God were fundamentally unrelated except at a few points where grace broke through to reveal salvation from the hostile or indifferent world. Creation and redemption, nature and grace, were effectively isolated both in doctrine and in piety. History was actually divorced from God. It was to be escaped or ignored. Nothing else could be done with history because it was the continuing process of an evil world going nowhere but to a cataclysmic judgment. Certainly history was not the arena in which God meets man and through which redemption both was and is wrought. There could be no thought that the processes of nature, the various forms of culture, or the structures of society could be masks through which God the Creator and Redeemer works his will.

Thus one never spoke of his church and his world but only of his church and *the* world. The difference between the personal pronoun and the indefinite article marks the difference between two totally different theological orientations.

Only if we see his church in relation to his world and responsible for it, will we find it possible to envision a social responsibility of the church. If the world is essentially evil or if, at best, it is passively neutral, then there can be no genuine social concern, for such concern would either be wrong or it would be a waste of time. But Christian faith affirms that this is his world. Scripture is replete with such affirmations—in and through him the world was created; he suffered and died for it. God loved the world so greatly that he gave his only begotten son to redeem the world. It is difficult to see how we can miss the major motif of Scripture. The world is his; he has redeemed it. That is the steady chant of the Bible. In Christ something new happened to the world. The new Adam entered history and the church is the first fruits of the reconciliation. Thus it is his world, his cosmos, his creation. We are strangers in it no longer.

The world, then, is neither evil nor neutral; it is good, though stained with sin. It is only when one begins with this perspective that one can look honestly and fearlessly at the world and at man. One does not have to despise the world nor does one have to divinize it. Neither does one have to undervalue or overvalue man in the cosmos. Both are seen in their true grandeur, yet in their distortion. To be sure, the world is fallen and the old creation remains. Nature is still a fearful and terrible force constantly trying to convince us that the final victory over man —death—is hers. The world, including nature and all the physical and social forces that surround us, is still at enmity with us.

If this is all we see when we look at the cosmos, then certainly we are at enmity with it. We rightly fear and distrust nature and history. Confronted by vast meaningless forces that pull us we know not whence, and push us we know not whither; we shudder in uncertainty and anxiety. We feel cut off from and at odds with the powers of nature, the forces of history, and our neighbors who press around us unrecognized and ignored. Paul is correct; the whole creation groans together and is subjected to futility. We cannot play down the reality and depth of sin in the world. It is on every hand—in the fearful destruction of two recent wars, in the possibility of atomic annihilation, in man's hatred of man, and in man's fearful exploitation of man and nature.

We are not asked to ignore this or to soften the impact of these brute facts. We are asked to face them boldly. Man and the world are marked by brokenness, guilt, and anxiety. Man seems cut off from God and man—a stranger to both as both are strangers to him. In this world the forces of culture appear determined as much by man's concupiscence, limitless pride, and lust for power as they are by aesthetic creativity. Man knows this and deeply feels his guilt. Consciously or unconsciously, he knows himself cut off from healing resources, driven by urges, restless in his confusion and lack of wholeness. This feeling of guilt can lead only to self-hate and distrust of self, and so to distrust of all others. Unfortunately, this is the condition of man in this world, and the world seems only to sustain him in this reality and in this mood.

How then can we speak of Christ's world? In such a situation, how can we even raise the question of social responsibility? This is precisely the point where the church affirms its faith— this is his world. This broken, tortured, distrusting, hateful, spiteful world is his. The brokenness, distortion, and estrangement are not denied; it is precisely to that point that the healing power is applied. They were in Christ and they are in Christ. That is his word to his world. This word is not thrown at the world where the world cannot be grasped by its power. This creative word is brought to bear precisely at that point where the world most needs it—at the very center of its guilt and insecurity.

There is a new reality in life, a new creation born out of God's forgiveness in Christ Jesus. The church testifies to this and embodies this reality. In Christ, man is a new creation; the old has passed away; behold, the new has come. Paul is emphatic in pointing out that the new has come. The new reality is not to be won by our piety, our intellectual power, or by our aesthetic gifts—it has been given freely. We are accepted by the very Creator of the universe, the Source and Sustainer of our life. We dare to look upon our guilt, our brokenness, our estrangement, for we are strangers no longer. In him we are reconciled, and in reconciliation we are reunited. We are reunited to him and through him to our brethren. We dare now to be at home in this strange, powerful, mysterious universe.

To be sure, the reality of sin continues in the world and in us, but its power has been broken. The struggle goes on, but it is not a despairing or hopeless struggle. He has triumphed; the powers of evil have been broken. We do not deny the continuation of evil and sin; we affirm that in Christ the victory has been won. God has reconciled the cosmos to himself. It is his, and we have passed from death to life. This is not some vain hope or figment of the human imagination. It is grounded in the reality of the church; we participate in it at the very center of our lives. We participate in it through the reception of the Word in spoken power and in sacrament. It is partial but nonetheless real. It is this which is the power and life of the church, Christ, the living Word. This the church proclaims in word, deed, sacrament, and ritual. The church is his and the world is his, and his redemptive presence is at work in it.

From this perspective, the question is not, How does a holy Church redeem a sinful, evil, fallen world? Rather, the question is, Where in the midst of the sin which marks the world does one point to the redemptive reality which God has already wrought in his world? It is his world, but how can we bring the world to see and participate in this reality? Just as we cannot do it by denying the world, so we cannot do it by incorrectly affirming the world. The world in and of itself neither sees nor understands its new relationship with God. It is the special task of his church so to minister to his world that the reality of this reconciliation is made real. One sees this clearly in Luke's account of the disreputable woman who anointed Jesus' feet. Here the actuality of reconciliation was shown in a woman of the world, where it was least anticipated, over against the righteous ones where it would normally be expected.

The church's task is clear, though in no sense easy. It is to point to the redemptive work of God in his world. It is to help the world to see that the world is his and to participate in this new reality. This is a terribly difficult task in an age when the world is bent on a self-sustaining autonomy. But it is this very stance which creates so many of the deepest problems for our age. In spite of its claims for total autonomy, the world is constantly driven to a depth beyond autonomy, and it cannot bear what it senses in that depth. At the very moment it revels most in its autonomy, the world, of necessity, has created a new set of authorities by which to live. This represents both a condemnation of the church and a new opportunity.

It is a condemnation in that it reveals the inadequacy of the church to minister to the needs of what Bonhoeffer calls the "world come of age." The church proved incapable of demonstrating or witnessing to the world at those acute points where the world confronted ultimate questions and realities. The basic problem was that the world was not aware that it was confronting ultimate questions. It was understandable when men rebelled against a church which, in the name of the holy, had sought control over all social and institutional forms of Western culture. To be sure, the church affirmed that the state, family, education, science, and other such forms had an independence of their own. However, when these forms involved moral dimensions, the tutelage or control of the church was necessary. It was against this that modern man protested in the name of freedom from domination by the church.

As modern man built a new culture which repudiated the previous church-dominated culture, autonomy and freedom were the new direction in which culture moved. Politics, economics, or education were affirmed as totally autonomous realms of life in no way responsible to God, the church, or even to ultimate principles. However, man soon found himself in a most ambiguous position. He continued to assert the total freedom of man in these realms, but history kept confronting modern man with questions that went beyond simple autonomous formulations. In the name of freedom, modern man rejected the idea that the state or politics involved ethical or moral dimensions. Precedent, national destiny, or the inevitable forces of history became the new base for political life.

The church stood by and called a warning to the world and offered its time-honored solutions to the new problems arising out of the new-found autonomy. But the world rejected these answers as a new form of the old authoritarianism against which it had recently rebelled. The world was correct. By and large, the church really did not listen to the questions and issues actually posed by the world. The church appeared too eager to assume that it had a ready-made answer—a return to the tutelage of the church. In face of the Nazi horrors, the possibility of atomic annihilation, the restlessness of millions of underprivileged peoples, and the rising nationalism throughout the world, the situation was radically different from the age in which the church has formed, guided, and even dominated Western culture through particular institutional forms. Thus the world turned to a new set of authoritarian answers derived not from the church but from the state, from economics, or from one of the other realms through which man thought he could derive and sustain his freedom and make sense out of his life.

The church cannot now stand and say, "I told you so." Not without guilt can the church cast the first or the last stone. It failed to recognize the depth of the questions posed by the world and so failed to witness to those points which might have made apparent the reconciliation of the world in Christ. It is difficult to say whether the problem was in the failure of the church or in the failure to recognize the world as his world. In any case, the church was bent upon maintaining that the world was asking the wrong questions and providing the wrong answers. From the perspective of a church intent upon its own purity and position over against a world viewed as evil or neutral, this is a correct estimate; but it is a misreading of the actual situation.

Is not the task of his church in his world to understand why certain questions are asked by the world? Should not his church participate so fully in his world that it can at least have sufficient empathy to see both why the question is asked and why it might even be the wrong question? The church's problem is to get the world to see that the same motives might lead to a totally different question, which is the real question the world was seeking all along. Perhaps, then, the answer witnessed to by the church will bring a response to the question posed by the world.

Thus, his church cannot avoid a responsibility for his world. Unfortunately, we do not have at the present time an understanding of the gospel that appears to give us sufficient freedom of movement to the world. However, there is evidence that work is under way in many parts of the church—Catholic, Orthodox, and Protestant — to provide just such theological underpinning.

Lutheran theology has never been noted for a strong emphasis on social ethics or on action. To a certain extent, Lutheranism has been misunderstood and frequently caricatured at this point. However, the fact remains that the Lutheran confessions pay scant attention to social-ethical problems or issues, and the history of Lutheran theology has not made this a central concern. It was pointed out earlier that the doctrine of the two kingdoms has become the classic Lutheran formulation for this set of problems, and this was and is easily misunderstood by the Lutheran churches and by their brethren.

It is clear that in Luther, in Christian tradition, and above all in Scriptures, there is an unbroken concern to relate all aspects of God's world to his church. It is equally clear that the *way* in which the various dimensions of his world are related to him and to his church remains the key problem. Lutherans have insisted, correctly, that God's relationship with his world and with his church is a complex and multiform reality. However, in making this point, it has frequently been stressed so strongly that it is difficult to note how God is related to the world at all. That is the particular difficulty of the concept of the two kingdoms. It clearly distinguishes between law and gospel, between God's differing ways of relating to life, but it lends itself to the distortion of creating an absolute chasm between nature and grace or between creation and redemption. What is a necessary relative distinction easily becomes an absolute dichotomy. Even the extraordinary efforts of modern Lutheran theology to rehabilitate this doctrine have not succeeded in providing a basis for a new dynamic social ethics.

Such a dichotomy is unfaithful to the biblical view, to Luther, and to the careful distinctions of the confessions. But the dichotomy is real, nevertheless. This tendency, plus the urgency of the whole modern situation, has compelled a number of theologians emerging from Lutheran traditions to pose anew the question of God's relation to the world and to the church. Each, in his own way, is concerned to find a way of stating the problem of God's relation to the church and to the world in such a way that continuities between creation and redemption, nature and grace, are not destroyed. They all participate in the contemporary concern to maintain the distinctiveness of revelation over against a modern immanentism. On the other hand, they share a concern to understand the world as from God, dependent upon God, and redeemed by God. Only in this way do they believe justice can be done both to the comprehensiveness of God's action in the Christ and to the situation of the modern world.

The late Dietrich Bonhoeffer rejected the radical disjunction between church and world implied by the doctrine of the two kingdoms, and he questioned the continued usage of what he called "thinking in terms of two spheres." Bonhoeffer insisted that there are not two realities but only one, and that has become manifest in Christ. In America, Joseph Sittler came to a similar conclusion on different grounds. In his address to the World Council of Churches assembly in New Delhi, he called

for a fresh interpretation of redemption in its full cosmic implications—the total cosmos reconciled to God in Christ. Both his
openness to the depth dimensions of art, literature, music, and
nature and his apprehension of the biblical vision developed by
Paul and recapitulated by Irenaeus led Sittler to the rejection
of a dichotomy between God and world, between nature and
grace.

The fullest, most systematic and profound effort to restate
this problem has come from the pen of a Lutheran theologian,
Paul Tillich. Tillich rests his system on an interpretation of the
Christ as the new being, the new reality that has overcome the
estrangement between God and the cosmos, between God and
man. In this new reality the brokenness of human life is made
whole again. This clearly reestablishes the world as his world
reconciled to God in Christ. Furthermore, through the method
of correlation, Tillich contends that there is no dichotomy
between the new reality in Christ and the world as created and
redeemed through Christ. Though nature and grace are seen in
a dialectical continuum, that is not to be misconstrued as an
immanentism typical of recent idealism. The dialectic between
nature and grace, creation and redemption remains, but it is
taken up into the view of the new reality in Christ. Thus Tillich
shows his dissatisfaction both with the recent forms of idealism
and with the dualism that marked the doctrine of the two realms.

These three men are cited only as examples of theologians
who have emerged from a Lutheran context where they were
deeply imbued with the concept of the two realms. They were
raised in the midstream of the modern world but also within
the Lutheran cultus; they were formed by Luther's catechism,
and confronted the great theological and philosophical problems
of the modern epoch from this background. They are not cited
as the correct answer to long-standing problems, though they
might well be. Rather, they are cited as examples, from within
the Lutheran tradition, of attempts to break through the tendency toward dualism that has marked a good deal of Lutheran

theology and made very difficult a serious and continuous tradition of social-ethical concern.

Wherever else these theologians differ, they stand in agreement at four points that are basic. They may not agree as to their respective solutions at these points, but they converge in their agreement that these are the formative questions that must be confronted. First, they stand in agreement on a deep dissatisfaction with the individualistic ethic that marks so much of Protestantism today. This is good Reformation theology. We deal with principalities and powers, with vast forces that shape and misshape humanity. Decisions are made through a complex process of interchange that results in action and policies that affect the lives of masses of people. Our very psyches are informed by these huge pulsating mores and customs which we usually cannot understand but which are no less real. To speak of a personal ethic as the center of the Christian faith is to ignore life as it actually is and to invite futility or delusion. Not that the person and a personal ethic are denied or ignored; rather, these can be personal only when set in the context in which a person lives. A highly individualistic ethic is a retreat from reality, from his world, and thus from him.

Second, these theologians remind the church that a smug moralism is not a sufficient basis on which to deal with the world. Our basic problem in the church is that we seek to define too quickly and to locate prematurely what we consider to be the good. Usually, we find it exemplified in the good people, in the churches, or frequently it is the negative of some positive act enjoyed by the world. How difficult it is for the church, also for the Lutheran church, to transcend the judgmental moralistic attitude in its dealings with the world. Thus the church is fairly certain how souls are to be saved from the world but very dubious that God *has redeemed* the world. It is a difficult task for the church to be the guardian of morality in its members as well as one of the primary sources of morality for the world, and yet to avoid moralism. Only the constant reminder that the church is God's and that it deals with and is part of his world provides the resource to escape pharisaical moralism.

Third, these theologians reaffirm the centrality, supremacy, and ultimacy of grace. With the Reformation, they are deeply theocentric. Each in his own way sounds the heart of the good news as the proclamation that God is a merciful, forgiving God —that he accepts man and the world where they are, and that this reality stands at the very center of life. Man's broken relationship with God and with man is healed by God's action of reconciliation in Christ. Be reconciled, for you are reconciled, you are forgiven—this is the new reality into which man enters when he is grasped by the power of the unsearchable love of God. Only a reality this broad and this deep is adequate to the condition of man. Here there is no radical dualism and no moralism, and no truncated individualized ethic.

Fourth, the shared concern of these theologians is to widen the circle and deepen the participation of the reality of God's love so it will be commensurate with the totality of life and experience. They fear a restriction of the reality of God's reconciling action. Tillich includes the relation of creation and redemption even at ontic depth, as he refuses to ignore or deny the ontological implications of the Christian faith. To do so would be a denial of the fundamental insight that the cosmos was reconciled and that a new reality has entered the picture. It is this problem that Sittler attacks in his efforts to relate nature and grace. Out of this concern for the widest possible consequences of the cross and resurrection, there emerges a view of the faith that seeks to take into account every dimension of life. Thus it becomes possible to speak of God's world and to seek responsible relationships between it and God's church.

This is our situation today. We are confronted by a "world come of age," yet a world that repudiates its Creator and Redeemer. Our response to this must not be hostility but understanding and sorrow. We have to proclaim the reality that is already at work in the world; we are to embody this reality or rather this new life which has already grasped us. We deal with a world already reconciled, though it knows it not. But that fact is the secret weapon of the church, even though it is not a weapon at all. It is the basis for a new truth, a new healing of the nations. In this we participate daily in his church; and as the church is rooted and grounded in him, so are we. Thus his church is free to take up its service to his world, for through the church Christ serves his world today.

THE ETHICAL THOUGHT
OF EINAR BILLING

Conrad Bergendoff

THE ETHICAL THOUGHT
OF EINAR BILLING

In our day Swedish theology has come to have a prominent place in the thinking of the ecumenical church. Nathan Söderblom first caught the attention of leaders in many lands; Gustaf Aulén has become widely known through his work in dogmatics; Anders Nygren's *Agape and Eros* is acclaimed as a classic by readers in several languages. And today a set of younger scholars have found their place in the church at large. But the name of Einar Billing is hardly known outside of Scandinavia. Yet Aulén calls him a "church father" in Swedish theology, and says it was he "who transformed the whole theological situation" and "contributed in a decisive way to the emergence of an independent, characteristic, Swedish theology."[1] Folke Holmström[2] does not hesitate to say that Billing gave a more consistent analysis of the eschatological factor in the gospel than did Schweitzer, and that had his work been more complete, and available in some other language than Swedish, it would have had deep influence abroad. Anyone who has read Swedish theology in the last half century would find echoes of Billing in almost all of the later writers. Arvid Runestam refers to Billing as the "vicarious protagonist" who struggled with the problems of the age in a manner helpful to all his contemporaries,[3] and Gustaf Wingren[4] characterizes him as one of the "great theologians."

[1]In *Einar Billing In Memoriam* (Stockholm, 1940), p. 39.

[2]*Det Eskatologiska Motivet I Nutida Teologi* (Stockholm, 1933), pp. 103-130.

[3]"Einar Billing Som Teolog," *Svensk Teologisk Kvartalskrift*, I (1940), 82.

[4]"Om Einar Billing's Teologi," *Svensk Teologisk Kvartalskrift*, IV (1944), 271.

BILLING'S LIFE AND WORK

A brilliant scholar, Billing became a member of the faculty of theology at Uppsala in 1901. Nathan Söderblom was a colleague, and the two worked together intimately, the one in history of religion, the other in dogmatic theology. "Söderblom and Billing," a former student reminisced, "the two will always stand side by side in our history, a combination hard to match, aesthetically effective by their sharp contrast, but no less religiously and theologically remarkable."[5] After two decades Billing returned as bishop to Västerås where he had grown up in the espiscopal residence, his father Gottfrid Billing having served there as the bishop of Västerås diocese in the closing years of the former century. Until his death in 1939, Einar Billing was a recognized leader in the church and nation, but his scholarly work dates from the Uppsala years.

Billing's fundamental work was in the field of ethics. His lectures were never fully published, with the result that we have an unfinished collection of essays under the title *De Etiska Tankarna i Urkristendomen i Deras Samband Med Dess Religiösa Tro* (" The Ethical Thoughts of Early Christianity in the Context of Its Religious Faith"). Even these came out piecemeal, and it was thirty years after their first appearance that they were brought together and supplemented by other hitherto unpublished material under the above title (1936).[6] Billing's doctoral thesis had been on Luther's teaching concerning the state (1900), and his Luther research left a lasting mark on Swedish theology. Two other volumes complement *De Etiska Tankarna*, the one on *Försoningen* ("The Atonement"), 1908, the other on *Vår Kallelse* (Our Calling), 1909. An illuminating account of Billings' thought on the role of theology in the church is found in his pastoral letter on the occasion of his election as bishop.[7]

[5]Oscar Krook, "Einar Billing som religiös personlighet," in *Einar Billing In Memoriam*, p. 190.

[6]Andra Utridgade Upplagan (Second Enlarged Edition; Stockholm and Uppsala, 1936).

[7]*Herdabrev till Prästerskapet i Västenås Stift* (Stockholm, 1920).

It might seem anachronistic to review at this late date an unknown work of a Swedish theologian. But two good reasons justify this attempt. First, the influence of Billing was so pervasive that his work casts an interesting light on the work of Swedish theologians who have since attained international prominence. Second, the passing years have revealed Billing's originality and depth of insight, and there is rich reward for the reader of today. In 1939 a Swedish exegete, Erik Beijer, subjected *De Etiska Tankarna* to a critical examination in the light of New Testament scholarship since Billing, and concluded, "In extensive sections we cannot follow him today, but on the other hand we discover how clear was his view, how he anticipated developments which have occurred. We read this work of a systematician with profound gratitude and we make no mistake if we read it as a work of exegesis which will continue to serve as an inspiration in exegetical research."[8]

We propose first to analyze briefly the contents of *De Etiska Tankarna*, to learn the basic propositions which reveal Billing's conception of the original ethical viewpoint of the Christian church. We will find that the second part of the title points meaningfully to the connection between the faith and the ethics of the Christian. We will then seek the relationship of the major work and the book on the atonement and the Christian calling. This will show us the practical application of Billing's ethical thought both to the life of the individual and to the character of the church.

Billing begins his treatise on *De Etiska Tankarna* by investigating the character of ethics developed in Greek philosophy, for he believes that there is a profound difference, with respect to man's conduct, between the thinking of the philosophers and the writers of the Old and New Testaments. In concise statements he summarizes what he thinks are the results of the major Greek teachers.

[8]*Svensk Exegetisk Arsbok* (Uppsala, 1939), IV, 136.

THE GREEKS

Protagoras can hardly be said to give clear definitions of a man's duties since his maxim that "man is the measure of all things" really makes it impossible to distinguish between right and wrong. What each individual is left to decide is between the advantageous and the disadvantageous. Self-interest is the final criterion.

Socrates drove men to think more deeply on what actually is to their interest. They may deceive themselves in judging what is most beneficial. Yet Socrates never doubted that if man knows rightly he will act rightly. But in the process of discovering truth two persons would find that above and beyond their particular experiences and the ideas in which they expressed these, there would appear a more comprehensive rule than either had followed and which would assume the character of a universal truth to which each would have to submit.

In Plato the result was a distinction between a realm of sense and a realm of ideas, the former existing through and for the latter. The idea of the good is sovereign in the realm of ideas, and it prompts man to reach beyond the shifting, shadowy world of becoming, to the eternal light of the tranquil state of being. The soul has a recollection of a former experience of the ideal world and seeks to return to it through an ascetic denial of the sensuous, though in the world of the senses it may have an experience of the ideal by perceiving beauty. The good, the ethical, is determined by the ideal. Hence in Plato, despite his interest in the mysticism of Dionysius, the ethical is not religiously oriented but a philosophical concept.

The same is true of Aristotle. While denying Plato's independent ideas, Aristotle considered the idea the formative principle, developing the material so that it corresponds to the type, or "telos," for which the material exists. The universal is not above but in the material, and the ethical consists in the organic development of man in accordance with his potentiality. The soul is the "form" of the body and seeks to bring it to its realization. There is a First Cause which might be termed God, who is itself unchanged; but this cause has no relation, beyond the initial one, to the individual. The reasonable individual follows the direction of those who have insight into the ideal and strives to will what is its real nature. The state, if reasonably constituted, affords a means of discipline of the individual. The highest attainment is the state of contemplation in which the soul participates in the realm of the ideal, and thus becomes godlike. For such an activity the manual work of the less intelligent is a handicap, and the ideal is necessarily reserved for an aristocracy.

All of these—Socrates, Plato, Aristotle—were in reality seeking to rationalize and perpetuate the venerable forms of life in the small city-state. When this was lost in the universalism of the Alexandrian empire, each school of thought had to find its own concept of the good in a rootless cosmopolitanism.

Epicurus found his solace in individual happiness, and wanted only freedom to imitate the happy individual. But he defined happiness in terms of the intellectual, not only the senuous.

Stoicism came to be widely diffused and highly influential—even affecting early Christian thinkers. It spoke of a universal logos which created each individual reason and fulfilled itself in the individual. The mind, or *nous*, controls the sensations of the body so that they do not mislead or disturb the soul. The wise man is the good man, whose will and mind are continually involved in a struggle with fortune or fate, but who knows how to meet with equanimity the forces he cannot control. The Stoic is mainly concerned with the self and its conquest of misfortune.

The Stoics were the first to introduce into ethics the concept of duty. Duty is to live according to one's nature, which is one of reason. The idea of a common humanity derives from the Stoic teaching of a logos in each individual, and thus the possibility of compassion is introduced. Here too was the basis for service to each other and the quality of the humane. As over against Epicureanism, Stoicism preserved the duty of serving the state and the common good.

In reviewing the Greek and Hellenistic systems of thought and action Billing came to this conclusion: "No matter whether the dominion of reason over the senses be developed in the direction of the harmonious or the ascetic, the intellect or reason is considered essentially sound. It is to be evoked and developed, it is to be strengthened and purified, but always over against or away from the sensuous. Within itself there is no contradiction to be resolved, no struggle to be won, no impurity to be cleansed. Herein lies the most serious limitation of Hellenistic ethics" (p. 74).

ETHICS OF THE HEBREW PROPHETS

In turning from the Greek thinkers to the Hebrew prophets one goes from the realm of philosophy to that of history. Billing characterizes the difference graphically. The philosophers are "wisdom's owls," the prophets are "history's storm-birds." "What the discovery of the intellectual value of concepts meant for Greek ethical thought, that the passage through the waves of the Red Sea meant for the Israelites' ethical thinking" (p. 83). "It is in Israel's pondering God's deeds in history that its ethical achievements appear" *(ibid.)*. The prophet found more in history than universal truths or timeless ideas which might serve as examples for action; he found a "history within history, the history of God's dealings with his people" (p. 84). "But unlike the philosopher of history, the prophet does not interpret what happens; he himself helps to shape history by his witness to the God who acts, and by the ethical authority he possesses as His messenger. For this God who acts in history and who made Israel a people of his own, is the source of law and ethics, the incorruptible guardian of the good, the true, and the right" (p. 88). In comparison with its neighbors, insofar as we know their history, the people of Israel has always been characterized, more than any other, by its ethical seriousness. God shows no favors to his chosen people, but holds them strictly to his law. The prophets' vision of God sharpened their discernment of the transgressions of the people. When Isaiah beheld the holiness of

God he understood his own and his contemporaries' uncleanness.

The burden of much of the prophets' preaching was the treatment accorded the widow, the poor, the helpless. These, whom the religious courts neglected, were the concern of God; and their mistreatment revealed the ethical decline of Israel. The righteous God is a God of mercy.

GREEK AND PROPHETIC ETHICS COMPARED

In a striking passage Billing contrasts the ideal state of the Greek philosophers with that of the prophets. For the Greeks the ideal society is one of order and harmony, each person finding his place and fulfilling his role. The prophet (Isa. 32) also speaks of justice and righteousness, where the fool will not be called noble, but the noble will devise noble things. But the Greek has no place for "error concerning the Lord," "the craving of the hungry," "the poor"—these are the marks of the fool. The glory of the king and the princes that God will give his people is that they are like "a hiding place from the wind, like streams of water in a dry place, like the shade of a great rock in a weary land," "a father" (Isa. 22:21). If we seek the reason for this astonishing difference between two ideas of justice, we shall find it, not in individual teachers, but in the very

origin and source of ethical understanding on either side. On the Hellenistic side reason itself is source and norm. It was a remarkable work which this reason achieved. When the old order collapsed it found itself in a chaos of conflict and strife, with each one claiming to be right. Gradually, in both the individual and the social ideal, reason succeeded in separating the lower and the lowest from the higher and the highest and brought harmony out of chaos. But with this ordering of the elements reason has completed its task; now it remains only to contemplate its work. The prophets, on the other hand, gave little attention to this task which caused Hellenistic philosophy such difficulty. For them order is already given. Man does not have to create it, but only to submit to it. It rests always on the ancient, religious, foundation, which has not and cannot be moved. Its certainty depends on the way Israel in its history has met, face to face, the sov-

ereign guardian of justice and order. Theirs is the history that
has bound together in such a peculiarly inner way the two
demands which otherwise so easily become opposed to each
other—justice and grace (pp. 104-105).

To obey these demands brings with it a humility the Greeks
never knew or could understand, and for this obedience no
cultic offerings can be substituted. When man does obey he
but imitates what God has done for him, as a member of his
people, and each act of mercy and righteousness "is a part of
the great deed which God seeks to accomplish in history, a
contribution to the new world God there wants to create" (p.
106). The law in this period of the prophets was thought of as
a defense of the weak. In contrast to the code of Hammurabi,
which stresses private property, the law given Israel emphasized
the care of the poor. Hammurabi thinks of the law as given by
the king, Israel's king is bound by the law of God. Israel's
institution of the Sabbath provided rest for servants, strangers,
cattle. The motive for Israel's showing mercy is the prior grace
that God showed Israel. God will bring in the new era when
his people serve him gratefully, from the heart.

Deuteronomy summarized the teaching of the early prophets
and attempted to create a people living in conformity with the
will of God. Billing interprets Deuteronomy from the dual
standpoint of a chosen people and a covenant. No merit on
Israel's part determines its election by God, but rather this people
is elected to witness to other nations of God's holiness, power,
and mercy. The covenant spells out the obligation of the people
to whom the promises are given. Israel is to keep the law, and
is in no way excused because of its election for God's purpose.
Transgression will separate the people from God. Yet the election is irrevocable and God's promise will stand until in peni-
tence the sinful nation returns.

Hosea finds the guarantee of God's faithfulness in his character; his love for Israel cannot fail. But neither can his righteousness fail. The covenant is the people's promise to obey.
Deuteronomy as a written law is "near," to aid in their following

the law. Nevertheless, Billing believes that in defining the word of God the written law tends to reduce the infinite character of the word as proclaimed by the prophets.

THE RISE OF LEGALISM IN ISRAEL

The temptation now arose for Israel to think of the law rather than God and to expect his blessing in return for obedience to the statutes. The prophets had stood in awe before the acts of God; they demanded obedience as response to his deeds. In contrast, the legal aspects of the covenant were now stressed until even the election was thought of as a part of the law. Sinai rather than the miracle of the Red Sea became the source of ethical knowledge. Keeping the law became primary, awareness of God secondary. In contrast to faith in God's election, obedience to the letter of the law cannot muster the power needed to inspire an inner and joyful doing of the divine will. For faith "leads each Israelite who lives [on the promise] constantly and anew into history. Faith casts him trembling and humiliated to the earth before the God who works wonders in history—the sea recedes and mountains tremble where he passes by, peoples are consumed by the fire of his countenance—but it also lifts him up and makes him strong and confident, in that he sees that all this is ultimately God's wondrous deed of mercy and love to his people. And if a person asks what then he shall do, faith may not give him any detailed reply, but all the more clearly he learns from it 'with all thy heart and all thy soul and all thy strength'" (p. 151).

Ezekiel, a writing prophet, stressed the ceremonial and purificatory regulations along with the ethical, but seems to have given impetus to the former more than the latter. His book is characterized by reflection on the law, with the result that "the law not only came between the people and the God who had chosen it, but also between the God of revelation and his prophet" (p. 171).

The exile prepared Israel for a new revelation of God, and this is the word we have in Second Isaiah. There is here no compromise with trespasses, but there is an affirmation of God's purpose to fulfill his promise. Law is not abrogated in any item, but grace works a redemption that raises the promises of God to a *chosen* people far above the calculations of a *covenant* people. In the later chapters an individualism is present which carries further Ezekiel's application of the law to individuals when the people is dispersed.

Post-exilic literature does not follow Second Isaiah. A tone of pessimism grows louder, and doubt is expressed as to the meaning of Israel's history. Or does it have any meaning? As hope grew dim the law became the sole or supreme factor in holding the people together, and the law was thought of as compensatory. Billing characterizes a passage from Baruch as a "classic" in describing the common conception of the law. "Now we have nothing left except the Almighty and his law. If thus we set our hearts aright we will win back in rich measure all that we have lost and much more than we lost" (p. 202, quoting Baruch 85:3f.). In the latest Old Testament writings the tendency is to call on God to make good his side of the covenant, since the law is being respected by his people. The election idea lives on in prayers and psalms, but generally there is a feeling that forgiveness is to those who keep the law. Yet the events of history seem to disprove that the law can be kept so as to bring the promised blessings.

Billing carries his study of the Old Testament into the opening chapters of Luke's Gospel. There we find a small group who in faith were waiting for the "consolation of Israel." They are described as "righteous before God, walking in all the commandments and ordinances of the Lord blameless." Their hymns give a clear statement of the "grace and righteousness" of the prophets, and they awaited the hour when "being delivered from the hand of our enemies" they "might serve him without fear, in holiness and righteousness before him all the days of our life." As we listen to these "quiet in the land" (Ps. 35:20) "we are amazed to find that, despite all, there were still groups in

Judaism who seriously lived in the ancient faith of the prophets" that the God of Israel would "perform the mercy promised to our fathers and to remember his holy covenant" (p. 222).

For the most part late Judaism put great emphasis on repentance. But the sins for which repentance was stressed were mostly cultic, which could be calculated and atoned for. And when the law of retribution did not effect the condemnation promised Israel's enemies, Israel lifted its gaze into another world. Here the godless would receive their due while the people of Israel, after fitting repentance, would inherit a kingdom.

JESUS' ETHICS

For Billing, there is no great gulf between the Old and New Testaments, so that Christianity cannot be considered apart from the history of Israel. Indeed the connection is so close that there is no possibility of understanding Christian ethics apart from the prophets and the law, which Christ comes to fulfill, not to destroy. While Billing's treatment of the New Testament was never finished, the published fragments amply demonstrate the source and character of ethics in the primitive period.

To his contemporaries and disciples Jesus was known as a prophet, and he is the culmination of the series that began with Moses. He does not come primarily as a teacher, not even a teacher of the history of Israel. He comes with an announcement which changes that history: "The kingdom of God is at hand." When he speaks it is with an unprecedented authority, and the power of his words is the same power by which he acts and does wondrous deeds. By the Spirit of God "he makes known the gospel of the kingdom, and by that Spirit he drove out evil spirits" (cf. Matt. 12:28). The miracles are not signs confirming his claims, but the acts he can do by the power given him by the Father. When men question his power to forgive sins they fail to understand that this is the very purpose for which he came and that the kingdom of God is the forgiveness of sin. He is sent to herald the day of the Lord by dwelling among men and bringing forgiveness. "If the forgiveness of sins is to mean anything more than one paragraph among a thousand others in a system of dogmatics, if it is to be the heart of Christianity, religion in a kernel, then it can mean nothing less than this, that despite our sin we can have God near enough to help us and can be assured that we do so have him" (p. 313).

Jesus is conscious of having defeated the tempter and driven out the prince of demons from human hearts. He, the victorious one, can forgive sins. He plants the kingdom, like a seed, in the hearts of those who receive forgiveness, and, like a seed, this word of forgiveness grows and bears fruit. In Jesus the ethical follows the religious as sparks follow "the meeting of steel and flint" (p. 324). The grace of God calls forth the righteousness demanded by the law. The real question is not lack of knowledge of what is to be done, but the will to do it. The parables are not allegories, but stories with a single point. In these stories the characters are never at a loss to know what to do. Why in the circumstances of life do they not know the religious response? "Jesus, as all the prophets, is completely convinced that necessary knowledge of the will of God is not absent" (p. 339). His purpose is not to teach what to do but to give the power to do. He brought no new ethics. His command was "Do the will of God." "If we separate his 'ethical' teaching from his 'gospel' it becomes not only what it was in the medieval period but what it is turned into again every day in our evangelical church —a new law and a new source of ensnaring and confusing legal casuistry, which is what Jesus combated in all his ethical proclamation" (p. 338).

For all their avowed concern about the law the Scribes and Pharisees "neglected the weightier matters of the law, justice and mercy and faith" (cf. Matt. 23:23). They abrogated God's law by turning it into human statutes, "traditions of men." Jesus did not "abolish the law and the prophets but came to fulfill them." The kingdom is here. Christ calls men to enter by doing God's will. Righteousness and mercy meet in Jesus, and love becomes the sum of the law. This was the burden of the prophets too; but Jesus, more than they, applied love to the individual. In forgiving the sins of the individual he is conscious of calling forth a people of God.

JESUS' OWN MISSION

In a chapter on "The Son of Man and the Kingdom of God" Billing seeks to probe the thinking of Jesus about himself and his mission. He finds Jesus' word about the fig tree especially revealing. Israel is the tree which has ceased to bear fruit. The master of the vineyard orders it cut down. This was also the thought of John the Baptist who saw the axe already laid to the tree. But the vinedresser pleaded for another year, to see if perchance it might not year bear. Jesus is thus bringing a year of grace. In this period he wins no great crowds. But he does gather around him "babes, those who labor and are heavy laden," and to these he gives rest, and "an easy yoke and light burden" in place of the heavy load of human ordinances.

This passage in Matthew is a central one for Billing and recurs time and again in his various writings. He finds in it a close communion between the Son and the Father, and an expression of the Son's seeing what the Father wills in the kind of individuals who receive the kingdom. It is not the "wise and the understanding" but the lowly in spirit. To help these into the kingdom became his mission, though earlier it might have seemed that his main purpose should be to judge Israel. He has the power to judge. He can call for "legions of angels." But he is the vinedresser seeking to save the tree. He is the Servant who is willing to suffer death in his attempt to turn men toward the will of the Father. As Son of man, a title deriving from the book of Daniel, he is both servant and judge, exercising mercy and bringing out the true demand of the law.

The impatient want a quick revelation of the kingdom, even if it requires immediate judgment. Jesus knows that the kingdom consists of being born again, a second Genesis (Matt. 19:28), but in mercy the Father holds back the axe in order that none might be lost who could be won. There is no evolution of the kingdom; the change is too radical for that. But there is a growing of the seed; this takes time and cannot be forced.

Yet while the kingdom will come, it is already here. The kingdom of God is wherever the will of God is done. His kingdom and his righteousness always go together. "According to his promise we wait for new heavens and a new earth in which righteousness dwells" (II Peter 3:13). But as the Son is here the kingdom is already present. It has broken into the present world whenever men receive the grace of God's promise and do his will from the heart. The kingdom is present in Jesus' life, death, and resurrection, and they are members of the kingdom who find rest for their souls in him.

"THE LAW OF NATURE"

One section of *De Etiska Tankarna* seems on first glance strangely out of place. It bears the caption, "A contribution to the earliest history of the concept of the law of nature." But the reader soon understands why Billing introduces it here. The modern study of nature has led to the concept of order, of regular recurrence of phenomena, and "law of nature" has become synonymous with a kind of certainty— to some, the only certainty. Billing contends that something of its awesomeness is borrowed from earlier concepts of law. These were connected with the idea of the lawgiver, usually the king, and with his power. Today this has disappeared and the law of nature is given a sense of sovereignty inherent in itself. This becomes the basis of doubt as to miracles, which transgress the "laws of nature."

The history of Israel, and its faith, is quite different. It began with a miracle: the crossing of the Red Sea. Israel's "world view in a sense has its center in the miraculous" (p. 261). Yet the God who works wonders is the God of righteousness and rules by norms which are immutable. He establishes law and shows no partiality, even to Israel. Far from destroying the concept of law it is the God of Scripture who establishes order, and the religious concept of God in Israel has an ennobling effect on the concept of nature and its laws.

In the Old Testament nature is seen as a servant or instrument of God, not as an arena of demonic forces. Nature as it surrounds man may be mysterious, as it is in the book of Job. But it is subject to the control of God, who is a God of righteousness. Even in moments of violent manifestations in nature, faith in God inspires confidence. "Therefore we will not fear though the earth should change, though the mountains shake in the heart of the sea" (Psalm 46:2).

The will of God is as certain in human relations as in natural events. The dependence we have on nature is a symbol of the assurance we may have of God's promises in history. Second Isaiah, Job, and the psalms give evidence of the wisdom, the power, the glory of the Creator, but as signs of the wisdom, power, and glory of God in dealing with men and nations. The God who gave a law to created things also gave Israel a law to be obeyed, and in one place we find a natural phenomenon made a sign of the human relationship—the promise of the rainbow. The God of nature and the God of history is One. Indeed the law of nature is dependent on the idea of any one God whose will rules all creation. Genesis 1 establishes both creation and man as under one order or will. In its regularity nature teaches the reign of law, but back of it is the proclamation of a gospel: there is one God who rules all.

The prophets thought of the miraculous as natural to God's dealings. But as the covenant idea tended to codify the law and separate it from its giver, so the tendency grew to separate nature's working from God's deeds. The ordinary becomes subject to nature's law; God deals only in the extraordinary. This gave rise to such problems as the distinction between medical help and God's help, man's part in war and God's part. Should one in either case wait for God, or depend upon oneself? Billing quotes here a sentence of Schlatter: "A division in the soul (schizophrenia?) takes place when the divine begins only where the natural ends, and when the attitude of faith shows itself only as distinct from man's natural activity" (p. 282). How far this tendency could lead is apparent in the Book of Ecclesiastes where history, in following inexorable and impersonal law, becomes as cyclical and meaningless as in nature. Yet this example of skepticism is unique in the Old Testament (p. 283).

Still, later Judaism lost the sense of the meaning of history and of the present as well. God became so bound to his own law of retribution that he was practically excluded from history, which was determined from within itself. The law became absolute in nature, in history, and we are bound to it rather than to God (p. 286). Whatever be the fate of man, the sovereignty of the law must be upheld. In IV Esra we find the affirmation, "We who have received the law must be destroyed because of our sins, but the law does not perish—it remains in its glory."

Billing's concern is to distinguish between the study of nature and the study of history, both of which can be religious. He does not presume to unite the law of nature and God's law in Israel; he doubts that anyone can unite them. He believes, rather, that each must be respected for what it is. Conflict ensues when men presume to judge the one or the other without having qualifications for judgment. Research is necessary in the study of nature, spiritual struggle is necessary in the understanding of religion. We should protest against those who would make nature a religion, which results in mythology, as well as against those who would make religion an answer to nature's questions. We do well to remember that some of the veneration given to "laws of nature" comes from the original concept of all law as the will of the ruler.

Jesus never diminishes the inexorability of either the law of Moses or the law of nature, but he transcends both in revealing the Lawgiver's purpose. "The nature of righteousness, however strongly he may emphasize it, is not exhausted by the idea of retributive justice. Rather, even righteousness, in the final analysis, is subservient to grace. (Luke 18:7, 'And will not God vindicate his elect, who cry to him day and night?')" (p. 371). To those who lie under both the laws of nature and the law of Moses, Jesus can say "Take my yoke upon you, and learn of me." To do so was the "Father's gracious will," and the "wise and understanding" could find it in no other way except the Son reveal it (Matt. 11:25 ff.).

THE IMPACT OF MODERN BIBLICAL CRITICISM

When Aulén credits Billing with changing the theological situation in Sweden, he refers to the period when the new study of the Scriptures seemed to many to threaten the foundations of Christian faith. In the *Herdabrev* (Pastoral Letter) Billing tells us that "it was in my generation that the original shock came in the field of Old Testament exegesis. The book that for me as well as for many others confronted us with critical problems was Wellhausen's famous *Prolegomena to the History of Israel.* Never shall I forget the anguish the study of this book caused me. It was like an earthquake—everything seemed to give way under one's feet."[9] But the earthquake also showed what stood fast. "It was just the great biblical personalities." "Over the great prophetic figures there fell a new and unexpected illumination." They were not fortunetellers, not even solely concerned about the future. They "stand there, as they like to describe themselves, as guards on a watchtower, warning the sleeping nation against an impending peril or bringing the fearful a message of approaching salvation." They seek "God's meaningful history back of the seeming confusion. They want to perceive and to proclaim to their people what it is that is happening in historical events." It is not universal religions or ethical truths which the prophets declare, but the work of God in the present situation and what is therefore required of the people. "History is not a cycle, nor is it a gradual evolution, but a struggle between the wills of good and evil powers, a suspenseful drama, which yet in curious byways moves on toward the goal deter-

[9]*Herdabrev*, pp. 33-34.

mined by God, toward the kindgom of God."[10]

But above all, in this line of prophetic personalities, the figure of Jesus stood out the more distinctly after the earthquake. He is revealed as the real, unshakable foundation. Not for what he teaches, though he is a teacher, but for what he is and does, he becomes the creator of a succession of events no less real nor less important than the succession of phenomena that constitutes the realm of nature. "And when this succession of events of God's history seems at certain points to conflict with that of nature's systems, we do not of course understand how we shall reconcile them. But in the degree that miracles are integral links in the chain of actuality which we can discern, we are unwilling to let our difficulties of thought hinder us from looking on them as testimonies to the power of our God."[11]

THE MEANING OF THE ATONEMENT

This focus on Jesus as the real center and source of faith leads Billing to a searching inquiry, especially in the Synoptic Gospels, as to what is the meaning of the unique person, who is the greatest of the prophets and yet different from them. The result of the study is found in his book on the atonement, *Forsoningen* (1908).[12] He finds the key to the meaning of Jesus' person in the death and resurrection of Jesus, especially in the latter. "Jesus lives and continues his work of redemption; this is the all-dominant fact."[13] Jesus stands in the succession of prophets by proclaiming the same message as theirs: the righteousness and the mercy of the Father. He demanded an even more stringent observance of the law than did the Pharisees, but he pointed beyond the law to the mind and heart of the Lawgiver. And what the Father told him was the way in which man could experience a grace which did not transgress the

[10]*Ibid.*, pp. 35-37.

[11]*Ibid.*, p. 41.

[12]Alex Falk has included an English translation of this work in an unpublished dissertation "Einar Billing, The Theologian and His Theology." (Chicago Lutheran Theological Seminary, 1951).

[13]*Försoningen,* p. 23.

righteousness of the law. That way led to the cross, for it was of the forgiveness of sin, and the mission of Jesus was not to condemn but to forgive. "In order not to have to judge, Jesus went to his death."[14] "But in his death Jesus revealed both the love of God which transcends all the laws of righteousness and that righteousness which unyieldingly holds its own against unrighteousness."[15] Jesus can forgive sins and restore men to the relationship of children of the Father; but only he can do so, for even at the cost of his own life he came to offer men a grace of the Father that makes each believer a member of the people of God. "The teaching of Jesus concerning the kingdom of God is not a teaching concerning its nature, its 'mysteries' and its laws, but a concrete historical announcement, filled with dramatic suspense; the hour for the establishment of the long-awaited kingdom is finally, finally, here."[16] This is the kingdom of which the prophets spoke, but which only Christ can inaugurate. It is a kingdom where not one iota of the righteous will of God is discounted, but a kingdom where the giver of the law dwells in the heart of the individual, so that righteousness and grace meet in a new creation. The individual becomes a member of the chosen people whose particular history reveals the meaning of universal history.

ETERNAL TRUTH AND THE MEANING OF HISTORY

Billing meets head-on the celebrated demurrer of Lessing: "No eternal truth can be based on transient historical facts." Such an objection is based on Greek philosophical notions, and not on the biblical view of human life. The Lessing dictum is a part of the mechanistic natural system that cannot explain the valid facts of Old and New Testament history. The one presupposes beyond the phenomena of nature an immutable calm of being; the other relates the deeds whereby God participates in and guides the destiny of men.

[14]*Ibid.*, p. 87.
[15]*Ibid.*, p. 88.
[16]*Ibid.*, p. 66.

There is, says Billing, no one doctrine of the atonement. It is impossible fully to explain the meaning of the cross, and any one doctrine can stress only one or another side of a complex act. But, on the other hand, there can be no question as to the meaning of the resurrection. This is a historical fact that defies Lessing. 'He who believes in a living God can only base his faith on a historical fact."[17] The resurrection is as closely related to the history of the church—and of the world—as the passage of Israel through the Red Sea. "For us as for the first Christians the resurrection is the explanation of history, the history of a chosen people. It means the presence of the living Christ who is always near at hand with his blessing. Outside such a living Christ there is no living God whom we can approach."[18]

Here is the key to Christian ethics. The Christian lives through the power of the risen Christ. "He who sees that in the whole universe there is only one firm point on which he can ground his faith, the person of Jesus Christ, also recognizes the necessity of continually holding on to this foundation by a continuous, personal, ethical-religious struggle."[19] The God who chose Israel but did not on that account countenance any infringement of his will by this people, does not call the follower of Christ to anything less than a holy life. The possibility of living in a way that is acceptable to him lies in a daily forgiveness of sins which both respects the law as holy and enables the sinner to follow the image of God who created him.

This interpretation of history—of prophets, Christ, the Spirit

[17]*Ibid.*, p. 95.

[18]*Ibid.*, p. 117. Edv. Rodhe, "En blick på de trenne sista decenniernas svenska teologi," in *Svensk Teologisk Kvartalskrift*, 1927, 305-35, finds both Söderblom and Billing deeply influenced by the Swedish historian Harald Hjärne, who interpreted history as on-going. Over against those who spoke of progess in history, Hjärne saw only mystery. Söderblom distinguished between nature-mysticism and personality-mysticism, finding revelation in the sphere of the latter. Billing thought of God as still active in "election" or "calling" in lives of individuals.

[19]*Ibid.*, p. 107.

—is an order *(sammanhang)* of events, a succession of facts, "a context infinitely wider, richer, and firmer than all that the natural sciences can unfold before us." The Christian faith is based on historical fact, but not a transient fact. "The Risen One continues his work both of judgment on sin and grace for the sinner. Through Him the believer does the righteous will of God. Faith in the atonement is the kernel, indeed the summary, of faith in the living God."[20] By faith the believer becomes a part of God's history. "All of history is essentially a series of deeds in which God overcomes all opposition, an emerging realization of the will of God."[21]

CHRISTIAN VOCATION

The most widely read of the writings of Billing is his *Var Kallelse (Our Calling)*—like *Försoningen*, a tract written with young Christian students in mind. Toward the end of the first decade of the century a strong religious movement took hold of Swedish university youth, who went out in a sort of crusade to churches preaching a renewal of life. The leader in this endeavor was Manfred Bjorkquist, and a lasting monument was erected in Sigtuna Stiftelsen (an educational and religious foundation centered in Sigtuna). Bjorkquist (later Bishop of Stockholm) has testified to the great respect the youth had for Billing and to the influence of his writing on that generation.[22] Especially the book *Our Calling* had enduring results.

In this treatise Billing brings his doctrine of God's chosen people to bear on the individual, not least in our own day. The same God who has worked through prophets and Christ to bring grace to a people he has chosen to do his will, calls each individual to participate in his work and enables him to do so by the forgiveness of sins. This is a universal call. "We cannot receive forgiveness without the conviction that as it is offered to

[20]*Ibid.*, p. 134.
[21]*Herdabrev*, p. 41.
[22]*Einar Billing In Memoriam*, p. 86ff.

us, so it is offered to all."[23] The book is an interpretation of daily work in the light of the forgiveness of sins.

EVANGELICAL VERSUS ROMAN CONCEPTIONS OF VOCATION

Unlike the member of the Roman Catholic religious order, the evangelical Christian finds his vocation in ordinary daily tasks. "In these monotonous deeds of every day I am to put in from day to day not only my most eager interest, my strictest conscientiousness, but God's power and God's love. God is to continue to create, Christ to continue to redeem, through my daily work. *Finitum est capax infiniti!* (The finite can contain the infinite!)"[24]

Billing contrasts the attitudes toward work in Roman theology, in idealistic philosophy and in Reformed doctrine, with Luther's conception, and believes that only Luther has caught the New Testament meaning of daily work as "not a command, but a gift." He thinks monasticism gives a false view of calling. Idealistic programs are self-conscious and self-assertive. The Reformed are too concerned about a goal. "How our insignificant deeds can contribute to His purposes is something it is very seldom given to us to see beforehand. We have to begin in blind obedience. There lies the day's work ahead of us. It seems small and inconsequential. But God who gave it to us must also know its value, so go to it!"[25] These tasks are daily, but they come to us one at a time. "All of us have lost incredibly much energy, and caused incredibly much confusion by grieving over the past and worrying over the future instead of letting each day care for its own evil." Forgiveness alone can free us from a bitter past. Only the "assurance that the grace of God is new

[23]P. 18. References are to the English edition, *Our Calling,* trans. from the 4th Edition, 1920, by Conrad Bergendoff (Rock Island, Ill.: Augustana Book Concern, 1947). A new edition, to appear in the series "Facet Books," is scheduled for publication in 1965 (Fortress Press).

[24]*Ibid.,* p. 19.

[25]*Ibid.,* p. 26.

every morning" can free us from fear of the future. "I believe it to be a fact that we human beings are not able to take on more than just one day at a time."[26]

This concentration on the day that is comes from the faith that whatever our task is has a place in God's program, which should be our chief concern. "My Father is working still, and I am working" (John 5:17) is both an assertion of Jesus' consciousness of the meaning of his task and a directive for us to be content in doing faithfully what is before us. "Modern aestheticism with its complex 'art of living' is a direct heir of Catholicism with its multifarious ascetic practices. . . . Reflecting upon ourselves does not even give us an understanding of ourselves, rather it ends in snarling us up; and if we are constantly concerned about ourselves, we do not become strong but pitifully weak. It is only when we forget ourselves in great tasks which have been given us to wrestle with that we realize to our sorrow or to our happy surprise what we are able to do. . . . So we say that true growth comes when we forget to seek after growth, and not before."[27]

"In the forgiveness of sins we live through our own exodus from Egypt. Through it we become certain that God wants to lead us into His eternal kingdom. . . . Just as the prophets beat hidden gold out of their people's history, so each of us must do with our own little history." "Just as our calling confirms us in our faith in the forgiveness of sins, so the latter in turn gives us new strength and courage to take up in faith the new burdens which He places upon us, and clarifies our vision to read in them God's message to us."[28]

Billing is not unaware of the kind of labor which it seems impossible to term a task of God. A decade before the success of Communism he wrote, "I am convinced that if the church had not lost so much of the meaning of the gospel of the call, it would not have limited itself to a mere exhortation to workers

[26]*Ibid.*, p. 27.
[27]*Ibid.*, pp. 34-35.
[28]*Ibid.*, pp. 40-41.

to be content with their 'calling.' It would have been forced to
see that back of the struggle for the raising of the condition of
their class there was concealed a God-given call to the workers.
And if the church had been able to couple this idea of struggle
to the gospel of forgiveness of sins, how wholly different this
struggle might have become! To us now the idea seems fantas-
tically bold. But would it have seemed so, if, like Jesus, we
had always been filled with the assurance of a living God, who
ever creates anew, who 'worketh even now'? That the church
did not so succeed, depends, as in the case of the individual,
not primarily on a lack of understanding of the times, or the
like, but on a lack of faith in the forgiveness of sins."[29]

Gustaf Wingren[30] had criticized Billing's interpretation of
Luther in this book. But while expounding Luther extensively,
Billing gives his own, not Luther's, idea of the call, and we can
understand his feeling that modern life offers conditions that
Luther never foresaw. There may be reason, as Wingren suggests, to connect our calling more directly than Billing does
with the law. Yet the appeal of *Our Calling* is its completely
evangelical tone, and it is to be judged less by its consistency
with Luther than with the whole body of Billing's teaching. He
finds a place for the insignificant individual in the supremely
significant "mainline" of Scripture. Between Israel's call and
mine there is an unbroken connection, and the call to both is
to accept the grace of God so that we can do his work. The
Immanuel who would be with his people is the same Spirit of
God who is with us forever if we love him and keep his commandments, the ordinary simple duties.[31]

This view of the meaning of the gospel led Bishop Billing to
advocate for his own country a "Folk Church." In answer to
those who called for a "purer" church, and a separation of

[29]*Ibid.*, p. 42.

[30]*Luther's Lära Om Kallelsen* (Lund, 1942); English translation by
Carl C. Rasmussen, *Luther on Vocation* (Philadelphia: Muhlenberg
Press, 1957).

[31]*Our Calling,* pp. 43-44.

church and government, he stressed the "objective" nature of the proclamation, which did not depend on the "subjective" character of the members. We cannot here enter into this discussion, which occupied a considerable part of his *Herdabrev*. We only mention his application of the idea of a people of God to his own nation. He did not place it on the level of the Old Testament nation, but there is a sense in which the call came to his and every people to hear and heed the word which would set them apart to do his will. If some felt that this was not a sufficient response to the need of change in a "state church," it does nonetheless indicate the character of grace which Billing felt was the essential message of the church. Whatever the organization of the church it must be as wide as the mercy of God and bring the gospel to all, and not allow itself to be formed along human definitions of holiness. The grace of God is both universal and prevenient.

It is a stimulating experience to read Einar Billing even today. The earthquake which he experienced is not altogether over in the church. How to meet it we may still learn from him. He once compared theology to a house built too close to the ocean. The waves engulfed and undermined it, and men sought to support and repair it, when the wiser course was to build more wisely on better foundation. This was Billing's aim: to find a foundation that could withstand the waves of modernity, especially a naturalistic secularism. "The Bible," he said, "needed no external foundation for its authority. It is not a law before which we are to bow, but the book of the great gospel which constantly invites us to discoveries in a world whose dimensions surpass our understanding."[32] In the Bible he found a consistent work of God which goes right through Old and New Testament and the history of the church. Its center is Jesus Christ whose resurrection brings a power into the world which is as real as any power of nature. That power is a love, an *agape*, altogether different from the Greek *eros*,[33] and it creates in the

[32] *Herdabrev*, p. 41.
[33] Cf. Anders Nygren, *Agape and Eros* (London: SPCK, 1954).

hearts of believers a new power to do his will, which is not grievous or obscure. Since the forces which oppose God have already been dethroned the ethical life of the Christian may be described as a doing of God's will in the face of a persisting, yet vanquished evil will.[34] Christ is now at work and his kingdom will ultimately come, though in one sense it is already here, wherever his will is done, even by those who in their seemingly insignificant positions glorify their task by doing it in the power of the forgiveness of sins. We may not be able to reconcile the knowledge of God's will with the discoveries of nature; we accept both until we can understand more fully.

[34]Cf. Gustav Aulén, *Christus Victor* (London: SPCK, 1931; and New York: Macmillan Co., 1956).

BIBLIOGRAPHY
OF THE PUBLISHED WRITINGS
OF JOSEPH SITTLER

1941

"On the Literary Tradition in Preaching," *The Lutheran Church Quarterly*, XIV, No. 2 (1941), 164-73.

1948

The Doctrine of the Word in the Structure of Lutheran Theology, Philadelphia: Muhlenberg Press, 1948.

1953

"The Lund Conference of Faith and Order," *The Lutheran Quarterly*, V, No. 1 (1953), 49-55.

"God, Man and Nature," *The Pulpit*, XXIV, No. 8 (August, 1953), 16-17.

1954

"A Christology of Function," *The Lutheran Quarterly*, VI, No. 2 (1954), 122-31.

"A Theology for Earth," *The Christian Scholar*, XXXVII, No. 3 (1954), 367-74.

"Eschatology and the American Mind," in *Charisteria Iohanni Köpp . . . octogenario oblata*, Stockholm, 1954.

1955

"The Necessity of Faith," *The Christian Scholar*, XXXVIII, No. 3 (1955), 198-205.

"The Abiding Concern of the Church for the Jewish People," *The Ecumenical Review*, VII, No. 3 (1955), 221-24.

"Meant for Each Other," *Motive*, XVI, No. 3 (December, 1955), 6-9.

1957

"The Structure of Christian Ethics," in *Life in Community*. Edited by HAROLD LETTS. ("Christian Social Responsibility," Vol. III), Philadelphia: Muhlenberg Press, 1957.

"A Hammer, the Incarnation, and Architecture," *The Christian Century*, LXXIV, No. 13 (1957), 394-95.

1958

The Structure of Christian Ethics. Baton Rouge, La.: Louisiana State University Press, 1958.

"The Shape of the Church's Response in Worship," *The Ecumenical Review*, X, No. 2 (1958), 140-52. This article also appeared in *The Nature of the Unity We Seek*. Edited by PAUL MINEAR, St. Louis: The Bethany Press, 1958; in *Motive*, XVIII, No. 2 (November, 1957), 14-17; and in *The Ecology of Faith*. Philadelphia: Muhlenberg Press, 1961.

"The Treasure and the Vessel," *The Christian Scholar*, XLI (1958), 187-92.

"Strategy of Religion for Nurturing Sacred Images of Man," *Religious Education*, XIII (March-April, 1958), 138-43.

1959

"Theology and the Arts," *Response* (Lutheran Society for Worship, Music, and the Arts), I, No. 2 (Advent, 1959), 3-8.

"The Maceration of the Minister," *The Christian Century*, LXXVI, No. 23 (1959), 698-701. This article also appeared in *The Ecology of Faith*. Philadelphia: Muhlenberg Press, 1961.

"Festus," in *Preaching the Resurrection*. Edited by ALTON MOTTER. Philadelphia: Muhlenberg Press, 1959.

"The Faith Situation," *Motive*, XV, No. 2 (November, 1959), 2-7.

1960

"The Context of Confirmation," *The Christian Scholar*, XLIII, No. 4 (1960), 298-308.

1961

The Ecology of Faith. Philadelphia: Muhlenberg Press, 1961.

"The Interior Aspects of Change," in *Values and Ideals of American Youth*. Edited by ELI GINZBERG, New York: Columbia University Press, 1961.

"Lord, Have Mercy on Us—1961" (A Poem), *The Lutheran*, XLIII, No. 27 (April 5, 1961), 17.

1962

"Called to Unity," *The Ecumenical Review*, XIV, No. 2 (1962), 177-87. This article also appeared in *Vital Speeches*, XXVIII (February 15, 1962) 281-85; and in *Pulpit Digest*, XLII (July-August, 1962), 11-18.

"Faith and Form," *Theology Today*, XIV, No. 2 (1962), 207-11.

"Urban Fact and the Human Situation," in *Challenge and Response in the City*. Edited by WALTER KLOETZLI. Rock Island, Ill.: Augustana Book Concern, 1962.

"The Matrix of Form in Church Architecture," in *Christian Faith and the Contemporary Arts*. Edited by FINLEY EVERSOLE. New York: Abingdon Press, 1962.

1963

"The Care of the Earth," in *Sermons to Intellectuals from Three Continents*. Edited by FRANKLIN LITTELL. New York: The Macmillan Company, 1963.

"Introduction," in *Worship in Scripture and Tradition*. Edited by MASSEY H. SHEPHERD, JR., New York: Oxford University Press, 1963.

1964

The Care of the Earth and Other University Sermons. Philadelphia: Fortress Press, 1964.

This bibliography does not take into account the many unpublished papers and occasional pieces which comprise a good portion of the Sittleriana. The reader is referred, in particular, to the occasional pieces appearing with some regularity in *The*

Lutheran (a periodical of the United Lutheran Church in America and, after January, 1963, of the Lutheran Church in America) and *The Record* (the house organ of the Chicago Lutheran Theological Seminary, now the Lutheran School of Theology at Chicago), particularly during the years 1943 to 1955.